STAYING SOBER IN MEXICO CITY

STAYING SOBER IN MEXICO CITY

Stanley Brandes

 The University of Texas Press
Austin

Requests for permission to reproduce material from this work should
be sent to Permissions, University of Texas Press, Box 7819, Austin,
TX 78713-7819.

⊗ The paper used in this book meets the minimum requirements of
ANSI/NISO Z39.48-1992 (R1997) (Permanence of Paper).

Library of Congress Cataloging-in-Publication Data
Brandes, Stanley H.
    Staying sober in Mexico City / Stanley Brandes.—1st ed.
        p.   cm.
    Includes bibliographical references and index.
    ISBN 0-292-70905-6 (alk. paper)—
    ISBN 0-292-70908-0 (alk. paper)
    1. Alcoholics Anonymous—Case studies.   2. Twelve-step
programs—Mexico—Mexico City—Sociological aspects.
3. Alcoholics—Rehabilitation—Mexico—Mexico City.
4. Recovering alcoholics—Mexico—Mexico City.   I. Title.
HV5283.M62 M483   2002
362.292'86'092—dc21
[B]   2001048063

Para mis compañeros

CONTENTS

Acknowledgments   ix

Introduction   xi

1. **Moral Support in Mexico City**   1

2. **Religious Adaptations in Alcoholics Anonymous**   25

3. **Meeting and Moving**   53

4. **Storytelling**   78

5. **Gender and the Construction of Manhood**   99

6. **Blurred Boundaries and the Exercise of Social Control**   131

7. **Illness and Recovery**   157

8. **Sobriety and Survival**   179

Appendix A. The Twelve Steps of Alcoholics Anonymous/
   Los Doce Pasos de Alcohólicos Anónimos   201

Appendix B. The Twelve Traditions of Alcoholics Anonymous/
   Las Doce Tradiciones de Alcohólicos Anónimos   203

Notes   205

References Cited   211

Index   231

ACKNOWLEDGMENTS

In writing this book, I benefited from the assistance of many friends and colleagues. Elizabeth Colson, Christine Eber, Geoffrey Hunt, Roland Moore, Linda-Anne Rebhun, and Marcelo Suárez-Orozco all read the final draft in its entirety and offered excellent suggestions for improvement. Matthew Gutmann gave helpful advice for changes to Chapter Five. At various stages in the collection and analysis of research material, I profited from conversations with Liza Bakewell, Leticia Casanova, Carl Feinstein, Dwight Heath, David López Garza, Juan Luis Ramírez Torres, María Eugenia Módena, Sergio Villaseñor Bayardo, and Katharine Young. Adrienne Pine translated the Spanish language interviews into colloquial English for use in the present edition. Adrienne Pine translated the Spanish-language interviews into colloquial English and Peter Rawitscher produced the index.

To help fund this study, I owe thanks to the Center for Latin American Studies at the University of California, Berkeley, as well as to David Lewis and the Center for Alcohol and Addiction Studies at Brown University. I am also grateful for financial support from the Committee on Research at the University of California, Berkeley. The Center for Latin American Studies at Brown University provided me good office space to carry out my work. In seeking published source material, I got fine bibliographic advice from Andrea Mitchell and Suzanne Calpestri of the University of California, Berkeley. I also received valuable assistance from librarians at the Hay Library, Brown University.

To each and every one of these individuals, and others whom I might have overlooked, I offer my heartfelt gratitude for invaluable suggestions, encouragement, and support. My greatest debt of all goes to the men of Moral Support, who form the subject of this volume. Without their generous willingness to allow me into their lives and share their most intimate thoughts, this book could never have been produced.

INTRODUCTION

A California physician once cautioned me that there exist two drugs which are exceptionally powerful, but omnipresent and readily available: caffeine and aspirin. Both are ingested daily with very little caution or forethought. If they came on the market today, he claimed, they would require FDA approval. The problem is that they are socially acceptable, a fully integrated part of American and European lifestyle, and therefore far beyond the point of governmental control.

There is a third drug, alcohol, which is also ubiquitous, potentially dangerous, tightly woven into the social fabric, and only partly controlled. Unlike caffeine and aspirin, about which the public expresses little awareness and concern, alcohol has been the subject of intense public debate for over a century. Perhaps the difference lies in the fact that one consequence of imbibing—inebriation—becomes immediately apparent during the drinking episode. Another relevant factor is that alcohol, unlike other socially acceptable drugs, is layered with intensely religious and moralistic meaning. Wine is the subject of biblical commentary, a substance of sacred significance, the subject of countless proverbs and folk beliefs. To drink or not to drink always demonstrates one's social affiliation, whether based on gender, class, ethnicity, social rank, or age. For many people, alcoholic drink represents degrees of goodness or badness, illness or health. There is no place or time in which alcohol has been blessed with complete social and moral neutrality—except, of course, where it has been entirely absent. Moreover, as Dwight Heath points out (1988:397), drinking norms "are often endowed with a strong emotional charge"; they are "affectively loaded."

It is perhaps for this reason that alcohol use and abuse have spawned an abundant anthropological literature, largely grounded in understanding the drinking patterns of particular ethnic, linguistic, or national communities. A generation ago David Mandelbaum (1965:282), a pioneer in the anthropological study of alcoholic drink, asserted, "When a

man lifts a cup, it is not only the kind of drink that is in it, the amount
he is likely to take, and the circumstances under which he will do the
drinking that are specified in advance for him, but also whether the con-
tents of the cup will cheer or stupefy, whether they will induce affection
or aggression, guilt or unalloyed pleasure. These and many other cultural definitions attach to the drink even before it touches the lips." This
statement amounted to a blueprint for field research. It initially stimu-
lated a great number of ethnographic and cross-cultural studies, which,
together with their own intellectual offshoots, have developed into a
fairly sizable sub-field.

Considering the ubiquity of alcoholic beverages, and their intercon-
nectedness with the economy, society, and culture of the people among
whom they are found, it is surprising how little is known anthropolog-
ically about standard methods of treatment, especially in the Western
world. In a recent overview and assessment of the field, Geoffrey Hunt
and Judith Barker (1999:126) were moved to declare that "the available
literature on either the anthropology or the sociology of drug treatment is sadly sparse." This statement holds true as much for alcohol
studies as for social science research on less widely available drugs.
While there are a number of brief anthropological analyses of treatment
in cultures other than the U.S., book-length monographs based on fieldwork are scarce indeed. This situation is regrettable considering that,
as Dwight Heath (1991:98) says, "researchers and policymakers concerned with alcohol and other drugs—like many in education—have
become enthusiastic about the strength and potential of observational
ethnography. . . . "

There exist at least two full-length volumes on Alcoholics Anonymous
which are based on anthropological-style fieldwork and might therefore
be called ethnographic. The first, by Mary Catherine Taylor, is an unpublished Ph.D. dissertation completed in 1977. The author focuses on
what she calls the "recovery career" of alcoholics and bases her observations and conclusions on attendance at "a variety of meetings of different A.A. groups" (M. C. Taylor 1977:1). Although readers learn much
about A.A. ideology and the social conditions that improve a member's
chances for recovery, the study differs from the present one in that it remains general, rather than grounded in detailed investigation of a given
group of sufferers and their ongoing interactions. Although the dissertation defines and elaborates stages of individual recovery, it is unconcerned with an important dimension within this volume: the fate of the
group.

The best recent example of a book-length ethnography on Alcoholics Anonymous is *Alcoholic Thinking* by Danny Wilcox (1998). This volume, although lacking a cross-cultural dimension, represents a serious step in the right direction. As suggested by the title, the book focuses on general matters of ideology as well as on recovery procedures as advocated within the Alcoholics Anonymous fellowship as a whole. It is concerned much less with the functioning of particular A.A. groups as miniature societies and subcultures, which struggle on a daily basis with issues of leadership, interpersonal rivalries, the imposition of social control, and the sheer viability of the meeting. Wilcox tells us that his book is "based on the author's 13 years of experience as a practicing alcoholic, his training as an anthropologist, and observation and participation at over 600 AA meetings" (ibid.:xii). Wilcox's fundamentally non-critical perspective derives from his own recovery from alcohol dependency and therapeutic involvement in Alcoholics Anonymous. *Alcoholic Thinking* is rich with information about the organization that has obviously played a central role in the author's personal life. However, both methodologically and ethnographically the book diverges from my own, which is grounded in the long-term observation of a particular group of recovering alcoholic men in a major Latin American city.

The present book, which is the product of the serendipitous chain of events recounted in Chapter One, is at once narrower and broader than *Alcoholic Thinking*. It is narrower in that, unlike any other study that I know, it takes a single Alcoholics Anonymous group as its subject. It is broader in that it deals not only with the ideology of the men in this group, but also with their social relationships and group dynamics. I am interested less directly in therapeutic outcomes than in the fate of the group itself: in questions of leadership, social control, and the identity of individuals as members of the group. I initially followed this group by attending meetings two to three times a week for a period of eleven months, from August 1995 through June 1996. On at least three subsequent visits to Mexico City, most recently in March 2000, I revisited the group. On each such occasion, I reestablished contact with friends in the group and updated my observations. I therefore followed the group over a period of five years. This book largely concerns group transformations during the last half-decade of the twentieth century. As an in-depth, longitudinal study of a particular Alcoholics Anonymous group, it has possible implications for an understanding of twelve-step programs in general.

The research is based on field notes, recorded into my computer after each meeting, as well as interviews, which I taped in the homes of group members and later transcribed and translated. I also visited men with their families, sometimes as they celebrated baptisms and other special events, at other times in more everyday circumstances. In solid anthropological tradition, I carried out all the research myself, with assistance only for purposes of transcription and translation of the taped interviews. Although the men were fully aware of my presence as researcher, and freely offered information through the elaboration of life histories, I neither taped nor wrote during the meetings themselves. Given the emotional intensity and intended privacy of meetings, it would have been distracting and disrespectful to scribble in a notepad during the delivery of personal stories.

Any ethnography of Alcoholics Anonymous must deal explicitly with the issue of anonymity. On the one hand, as the reader will readily see, Alcoholics Anonymous in working class Mexico City is a lot less of an anonymous enterprise than one might imagine. At the very least, the identity of members is widely known to friends, relatives, neighbors, and, in fact, to anyone who might care to find out. For reasons considered at length throughout this volume, the content of intimate personal stories told during meetings is also a lot less private than most A.A. affiliates would consider ideal. The men of my study group are themselves concerned about the public revelation of intimate confessions, a situation which impels them to censor what they say during meetings. By contrast, in the privacy of their homes, I was able to elicit not only the range of personal thoughts that the men reveal in meetings, but also much more. I have full permission to use the interviews in publications. Much of the interview material itself replicates verbatim terminology which emerges in the formal presentation of personal stories, so that, by quoting from home interviews, I retain the flavor and authenticity of statements made during meetings. Wherever I cite individual statements, and, in fact, throughout the book, I employ pseudonyms. Moral Support, the name I have given to the group, is also a pseudonym, rather than a translation from the Spanish of the actual group name. Insofar as possible, I have also attempted to disguise the exact location of the group.

Like Danny Wilcox, I was a participant as well as observer in the group. On a regular basis I would be called to the podium to speak. Unlike Wilcox, I have never suffered alcohol problems and therefore felt no need for recovery. This situation might have proven awkward were it not for the declaration of one group leader, who encouraged me to stay with the group and make it a subject of study. While on the podium one evening, he addressed me directly: "Estalin," he said, "You are not a double A. You are a triple A!" To make me feel as welcome as possible, he explained that there have always been people who attend Alcoholics Anonymous meetings not because they are themselves alcoholic, but rather because they are Admiradores de Alcohólicos Anónimos—Admirers of Alcoholics Anonymous—that is, A.A.A., rather than A.A.

The men at first had difficulty pronouncing my name. The closest, easiest equivalent for them was "Estalin," or Stalin. "That's a Russian name, isn't it?" asked one of the men in the group shortly after I joined. In time, as I introduced myself dozens of times on the podium, the men each arrived at his own fair rendition of Stanley. At that point, I knew that I had become an integral part of their world. The research combined nicely with my daytime administrative work at the National Autonomous University of Mexico. Since I began my investigation near the beginning of my stay in Mexico City, when I still felt very much alone in the metropolis, the men were not only a source of information. They were companions, friends whom I would look forward to seeing as a way to fill long evenings. Over time I became a true Triple A, or Admirer of Alcoholics Anonymous, in that I held every one of the members of my group in high esteem and developed great affection for them. I am a less certain admirer of A.A. as an organization or therapy. The experiences of my group, when combined with a review of the available literature as analyzed in Chapters Seven and Eight, demonstrate that on this score the jury is still out. Alcoholics Anonymous in Mexico City is without doubt a source of intense emotional support for a great number of people with alcohol dependency. Whether it is the A.A. program, rather than some other combination of factors, which is responsible for their sustained sobriety, would be difficult to declare with assurance.

What is certain is that A.A. has achieved enormous success, in the sense of being a high-profile presence, not only in Mexico City but also throughout the entire Republic. In Mexico, some patients with serious alcohol problems are held in psychiatric wards or other mental health facilities. There also exist a number of private residential recovery centers for addicts, but these are high-income facilities (Rosovsky 1998:167). By far the most common institutional resource for the treatment of alcohol problems is Alcoholics Anonymous. In the words of Haydée Rosovsky (ibid.), who has devoted her career to studying Alcoholics Anonymous in Mexico, this organization "is, by far, the widest known resource of recovery reported by the general [Mexican] population, and it seems that an increasing number of professionals are promoting A.A." It is estimated that, in 1990, about five out of every thousand Mexicans above 15 years of age were members of Alcoholics Anonymous (Medina-Mora 1999:87). Informed observers believe that A.A. membership grows annually at approximately 10 percent per year (ibid.), an enormously high rate for a self-help recovery organization.

A central goal of this book is to explain the rapid proliferation of A.A. chapters throughout Mexico and, by extension, Latin America. As Mäkelä et al. (1996:27) state, although "AA is an American middle-class invention, . . . the AA program has been adapted to a cultural tradition different from the movement's origins. . . . " Hence, by the end of the twentieth century, "Latin America accounted for almost one-third of the world membership of AA. This shows that the movement has spread well beyond the range of traditional temperance countries" (ibid.:28). Chapter Two is explicitly designed to address the issue of how and why Alcoholics Anonymous has become so popular throughout Mexico. Although I make no claims for the representativeness of the single group that I studied, a detailed analysis of its organization and development can reveal a good deal about the impressive geographic diffusion of A.A. and other matters, which extend far beyond one A.A. unit alone.

In addition to explaining the striking proliferation of A.A. groups throughout Mexico, the book contributes to knowledge of masculinity in Mexico and Latin America generally. As explained in Chapter Five, the vast majority of A.A. affiliates in Mexico are male. Because alcoholic drink has been so critical to Mexican male identity, it is a challenge for the men of Moral Support, who abstain totally and absolutely from alcoholic drink, to retain their masculine self-image. A large portion of their meetings is devoted to redefining masculinity, in such a way that drinking becomes antithetical to rather than an intrinsic component of true manhood. In the current social climate, where gender identity is in rapid flux and subject to constant scrutiny and reevaluation, the men of Alcoholics Anonymous expend considerable creative energy searching for alternatives to the conventional meanings of masculinity in Mexico.

The men of Moral Support are also all members of the working class who migrated to Mexico City several decades ago from rural communities throughout central and southern Mexico in the pursuit of better living conditions and a higher standard of living. Although in most cases they managed to achieve this goal, their lives eventually disintegrated to the point where they placed jobs and family at risk. Heavy drinking had given them a sense of lost control over their destinies. A few of the men were able to reestablish the respect of relatives and recover from financial ruin. Many of them, however, continued to exist on the most meager earnings at the time of my study. Their economically precarious existence, as well as the inability to establish satisfying romantic partnerships, emerged continuously in personal stories. An analysis of these stories, especially as carried out in Chapters Four and Seven, contributes to an understanding of the social suffering of poor people in urban Latin America and stimulates a rethinking of the relationship between satisfying employment and alcoholic consumption.

The men's preoccupations with money and survival were evident throughout my association with Moral Support. As demonstrated in Chapter Three and the concluding chapters, members' repeated assertions of economic insecurity influenced both the conduct of meetings and the interpersonal relationships that prevailed within the group. In a voluntary association like Alcoholics Anonymous, where groups are financially autonomous, the very existence of the group depends on the solvency of its members. Scarcity not only creates personal hardship on a daily basis for recovering alcoholics, but also produces feelings of envy, inadequacy, and resentment whenever members find themselves unable to contribute on a regular basis to the common good. As a self-help group, dedicated to enhancing the health and well-being of its members, Moral Support experiences as precarious an existence as that of its individual members. Moral Support, like most Mexican A.A. groups, is indelibly affected by poverty.

By allowing the men to speak in their own words, this book is designed in part to show how economic marginality influences the struggle for health and survival among unemployed and underemployed workers in Mexico City. In this great metropolis, the destination of millions of poor migrants from the countryside, newcomers strive to recreate the texture of life in their small communities of origin. As shown in the final three chapters of the book, Moral Support, like many Alcoholics Anonymous groups in Mexico City, is intimately tied to the immediate neighborhood in which members meet. This circumstance helps affiliates to reestablish the bonds they lost before joining A.A. For these men, A.A. produces a sense of community involvement and semblance of control over their futures.

At the same time, it would be difficult to deny that the problems experienced by Moral Support are engendered at least in part by the presence of confrontational personalities, driven by unambiguous ideas of correct procedures. Further, Moral Support's goals are inherently contradictory, a circumstance that occasionally operates to the detriment of group survival. It is these micro-level social processes, placed in relief through detailed field investigation, which form the core of this book. At the same time, we must constantly bear in mind that Moral Support, like all self-help groups, functions within a wider socioeconomic context. To a significant extent it is the conditions imposed from above and beyond their small neighborhoods that determine the fate of groups and their members. Hence, especially in Chapters Two and Eight, we shall examine what Merrill Singer (1986:114) calls "the encompassing socioeconomic forces shaping contemporary drinking patterns."

STAYING SOBER IN MEXICO CITY

1. MORAL SUPPORT IN MEXICO CITY

Life in Mexico City can be daunting. Although estimates of the city's population vary, demographers invariably place the metropolitan area at more than twenty million inhabitants. That means that Mexico City shares with Saõ Paulo, Brazil, the dubious honor of being the largest city in the world. The city is located in a natural basin, the Valley of Mexico, which is ringed by a chain of lofty volcanoes that are often snow-capped. Throughout much of the year, automobiles and industry produce noxious gasses, which become trapped inside the basin and hover close to ground level, creating what some environmentalists consider the worst contaminated air anywhere on the globe. Daily newspapers display maps, charts and figures indicating air quality in each of four major quadrants of the metropolitan area. Only rarely does the atmosphere register "*satisfactorio,*" thereby bringing a sense of collective relief to the city's populace. About 10 percent of the city's residents live without proper sewage disposal, a situation that leads to the presence of dry fecal matter and other harmful substances—cited euphemistically in the press as "flying particles" [*partículas volantes*]—penetrating the atmosphere. It is not surprising, under these circumstances, that respiratory and other serious health problems abound (Castillejos and Serrano 1997; Rivera Márquez 1997).

And yet Mexico City throbs with contagious energy. People walk and drive faster in Mexico City than anywhere else in the country. Street life, except in the most exclusive sectors, is colorful and vibrant. Traffic is almost always heavy and yet for the most part flows smoothly, even though drivers obey a series of tacit rules rather than those indicated by lights and signs. This circumstance leads to a feeling that chaos is the only governing principle on city streets. However deceptive this impression, daily travel across crowded urban spaces exacts an inevitable emotional toll. *Chilangos,* as residents of Mexico City are known, probably complain more often about the difficulties of moving about the city than about anything else.

Partly because of sheer size, Mexico City is a place of startling contrasts. This megalopolis houses well over a quarter of the inhabitants of the entire country. (Under equivalent circumstances, New York City, the largest in the United States, would have a population of more than seventy-five million.) Mexico City is divided into sixteen boroughs called *delegaciones*. One of these alone, Ixtapalapa, contains more people than Madrid or Barcelona and nearly double the population of Mexico's second most populous city, Guadalajara. The striking enormity of Mexico City is one reason why scholars refer to it, as to most other Latin American capitals, as a primate city. Industry, services, commerce, jobs, and cultural resources are concentrated there to a degree unparalleled elsewhere in the country. Kemper and Royce (1979:278–279) summarize this situation with dramatic statistics: "Mexico City contains 45% of the nation's industry, 55% of the service sector business, and 45% of all commerce. With 42% of all jobs, it is the largest employment market in Mexico. Its workers are paid 53% of all salaries and wages and generate 46% of the Gross Domestic Product. The metropolis consumes about 45% of the federal government's total resources while contributing around 50% of total federal government tax income. . . . "

Prior to the Spanish conquest in 1519, Mexico City was of course the seat of Tenochtitlán, the Aztec capital, which was itself a large urban conglomerate. During the colonial era, for purposes of commerce, recordkeeping, and political control, Spaniards conveniently preserved this centralizing settlement pattern. (Elsewhere in Latin America, as in Argentina, Chile, and elsewhere, where major urban centers did not exist prior to the Conquest, Spaniards created them.) Subsequent circumstances, including the relentless late-twentieth-century flight from countryside to city, have reinforced the pattern to the point where it has become exaggerated beyond anyone's comprehension. Kemper and Royce (1979: 278) state that "perhaps 350,000 persons migrate yearly to the capital, while the natural demographic growth increases the population by a similar amount." The population explosion of the Mexican Republic as a whole and the search of a bulging labor force for jobs in the capital have been the most recent stimulants to the growth of Mexico City.

Mexico City is so huge that everything, even social contrasts, seems oversized. There is great poverty, but also enormous wealth. Portable food stands share city streets with restaurants of exquisite sophistication. The corruption of the police force in Mexico City is an open topic of discussion and yet the city has long provided a haven for political refugees from all over Latin America and Europe. In Mexico City, there are millions of people native to the city, millions of foreign residents, millions of indigenous peoples (representing every one of the more than fifty major language groups in the country), and millions of recently arrived migrants who arrive from every state in the Republic. Middle and upper class *chilangos* have access to art, cuisine, music, and literary life equal in quality to that which prevails anywhere else in the world. The working classes, many of whom earn a minimum wage of less than five dollars a day, barely survive in their crowded, inadequate houses, some made of corrugated tin and cardboard and lacking running water and sewage disposal. Elegant chauffeur-driven vehicles pause at stoplights to observe the churlish antics of the growing ranks of street children, who, at great personal risk and with the hope of earning a few pesos, perform in and among the traffic as acrobats, jugglers, and fire-eaters. Elsewhere in the city, armed guards protect splendid mansions hidden behind high protective walls, a symptom of the embattled mentality that prevails among the wealthy in most large Latin American cities today. Mexico City can only be understood as a highly differentiated urban conglomerate. People with vastly different living standards and ethnic backgrounds coexist in this megalopolis. At times they interact closely, at times they strive to avoid one another.

This is the city where I settled on New Year's Eve 1995. I first visited Mexico City in 1964, as a tourist. My mission now, thirty years later, was as different as was the city itself. I had come as an academic administrator to direct an education abroad program. Considering the duties of the job, research was a secondary and uncertain prospect. As a cultural anthropologist of Spain and Mexico, I had already acquired years of experience carrying out ethnological fieldwork in small, Spanish-speaking, rural communities. Amenities in these towns and villages were rudimentary. In Tzintzuntzan, Michoacán, for example, my family and I lived in a windowless adobe house, with a dirt floor, a roof with no ceiling, and no electricity or running water. And yet, thanks to social conditions in rural Mexico, I found it relatively easy to befriend townspeople, interview them, and participate in their daily lives. My work was motivated by the certainty that, given a patient dose of time and effort, I could acquire the knowledge and understanding that I sought.

In rural towns and villages, I had become accustomed to leaving my house with the assurance that only steps away I would find the welcoming reception of knowledgeable friends and informants. By comparison, fieldwork in Mexico City at first seemed impossible. Despite rich opportunities, I had dismissed the prospect as hopelessly intimidating and had planned to carry out documentary research of an ethnohistorical nature. I viewed fieldwork as incompatible with my administrative responsibilities. Above all, I was discouraged from fieldwork by the seemingly fragmented, atomistic, impersonal world around me.

On the face of it, there was little justification for these feelings. In the course of my studies, I had read a good deal of urban sociology, carried out through typical anthropological field techniques. William Whyte's *Streetcorner Society* (1955), a classic of the genre, had remained one of my favorite books and had influenced my selection of career. By the time I settled in Mexico City, urban anthropology, a relative latecomer to the field, was long an established sub-discipline (Foster and Kemper 1974; Hannerz 1980). And, as Carles Feixa's (1993) extensive survey demonstrates, Mexico is without doubt one of the countries with the heaviest concentration of urban anthropological research, from the groundbreaking studies of Oscar Lewis (1952, 1959, 1961, 1964, 1969) to the advanced, topically oriented publications of Feixa (1988), Gutmann (1996), Lomnitz and Pérez-Lizaur (1987), and numerous others. Moreover, most of this research has been explicitly qualitative in nature, carried out with intensive field techniques which differ very little, if at all, from those originally developed and elaborated in rural environments. That anthropologists have been able to apply traditional field techniques in the urban setting highlights an important finding of the research itself: urban Mexico is, in fact, far from the super individualistic, impersonal world that at first glance it appears to be.

Oscar Lewis was probably the first scholar to challenge these stereotypes of the city. In "Urbanization without Breakdown," published in 1952, he demonstrated that migrants from the peasant village of Tepoztlán to Mexico City were able to adapt to city life through reliance on an extensive network of supportive social bonds. His findings showed that family life in the city remained as stable as it was in the countryside, that kinship ties actually increased in strength over those that prevailed in the village, and that the *compadrazgo* system—commonly known in the social science literature as fictive or ritual kinship (see, e.g., Eisenstadt 1956, Foster 1953, Pitt-Rivers 1958, Mintz and Wolf 1967)—proved as extensive and vibrant among newcomers to the capital as within Tepoztlán itself. Lewis found that migrants from Tepoztlán retained their personal connections to the village, while establishing new bonds within the city. They therefore enjoyed an enriched social life. They did not suffer the anomie that might have been expected from the move to a metropolis such as Mexico City. Subsequent migration research has borne out Lewis's findings. Robert V. Kemper (1977) followed migrants from the village of Tzintzuntzan to Mexico City. Like the Tepoztecos, these former peasants were able to retain social bonds to their village of origin, while establishing numerous links within the urban context. Throughout his study, Kemper emphasizes "the great importance of personal networks in the urbanization process" (ibid.:111).

But it is not only among migrants from the same rural community that strong social bonds are formed in the city. In 1952, Lewis turned his attention to the *vecindad,* a type of working class residential building in which families, each in its own room, live around a central patio and share bath and kitchen facilities. Lewis studied two *vecindades,* which he called Casa Grande and Panaderos, located near Mexico City's downtown. The residents of these buildings came from twenty-four of Mexico's thirty-one states. Despite these disparate origins, they were able to establish a rich social network, which replicated in many respects the kind of life they had led in rural villages. Children played in the patio together under the watch of their mothers and grandmothers, who sewed and washed clothes in one another's company. Adolescents from the same *vecindad* banded together; the adult men went out together to the *pulquerías* to get drunk. Some *vecindad* residents lived out their entire lives in the context of their *barrio,* or neighborhood, where they formed lasting friendships. Many of the residents worked in their own neighborhoods as itinerant salespeople, shoemakers, and the like. They shared a similar culture, which they brought to the city from rural communities: this culture included a reliance on traditional medicine, the presence of religious images in their homes, and the celebration of family and communal fiestas. As Carles Feixa (1993:57) says, "The findings of Lewis were crucial for the development of urban anthropology. . . . Lewis demonstrates that the city is divided into little communities (*vecindades, barrios*) which operate as cohesive and personalizing factors."

Larissa Lomnitz's influential research on networks in Mexico City also relies in part on an analysis of a migrant neighborhood, which she calls Cerrada del Cóndor (Lomnitz 1977). Her detailed analysis of social networks among residents of Pericos Court, a building composed of fourteen apartments located around a patio, which appears very similar to the *vecindades* which Lewis studied, is paradigmatic of urban social ties. Links both within and outside of the residential complex are based on *confianza*, or trust, established over time through countless exchanges of goods, services, and mutual aid (ibid.:151–155). States Lomnitz, "The highest level of *confianza* is found in the extended family network, which is fully autonomous and maintains no relations with other people in the court. Networks based on joint families are less exclusive and do admit the incorporation of non-kin neighbors. The larger networks are more functional and more stable; they are based on kinship. In addition, there are dyadic relations that may produce multiple affiliation of a nuclear family to more than one network" (ibid.:154–155). The pervasiveness of networks among the migrants to Cerrada del Cóndor leads Lomnitz to conclude that "prevalent rural patterns of individualism and mistrust have become superceded by powerful tendencies toward integration, mutual assistance, and cooperation." This conclusion is echoed in the work of Kemper (1977:111), who demonstrates that, with increasing migration from Tzintzuntzan to Mexico City, "a pattern of enclaves—composed of kinsmen, compadres, and close friends from the village—has developed."

The portrait of urban life that emerges from this literature is radically different from that presented by a previous generation of anthropologists working in Mexico, particularly Robert Redfield. Redfield, influenced by Louis Wirth and the Chicago school of sociology, believed from his analysis of four communities in Yucatan (1941) that cities were highly impersonal, individualistic, and, as he puts it, disorganized, as compared with villages and towns. The research of Oscar Lewis, followed by Lomnitz, Kemper, and others, no doubt functioned as a corrective reaction to Redfield and the Chicago school. In large measure, this later research, based as it was on long-term, empirical fieldwork in Mexico City, conclusively refutes impressions of the city promoted by Redfield and his followers.

Mexico City is indeed intimidating to the newcomer. It is in many respects the insoluble ecological disaster that scientific observers sometimes make it out to be. At the same time, it is composed of numerous neighborhoods and small communities, which function socially in ways not so different from rural villages. The city also coheres, both within and among neighborhoods, through innumerable social networks, which link each individual to countless others in a complex web of egalitarian and hierarchical social bonds (Lomnitz 1982). This dual characteristic of Mexico City—on the one hand composed of countless interlocking urban villages, on the other pervaded by interlocking social networks—provides at least potentially favorable conditions for carrying out fieldwork. When I arrived in Mexico City to live and work, I was familiar with much of the relevant anthropological literature and could appreciate this message intellectually. I had to experience the city directly, however, before its compatibility with my own style of field research became evident.

I became aware of the possibilities of Mexico City as a field site in the same way that many anthropological research projects manifest themselves, through serendipity. I was fortunate enough to live within walking distance of my office. Twice each day I would take the twenty-minute stroll to and from work, only rarely departing from an established route. Occasionally, I would stop along the way to get my shoes shined by a middle-aged man whom I shall call Emilio. Now, getting a shoeshine is not something I normally do in the United States; convenience and cost dictate that I always shine my own shoes. But in Mexico City, where sparkling, clean shoes are a definitive sign of proper grooming and where professional bootblacks are inexpensive, I would indulge in this luxury several times a week. To attain the respectable appearance of a middle-class urbanite, the fifteen-minute delay that it took to get my shoes shined was well worth the price.

Emilio's shoeshine stand was not unlike the multitude of others that anyone living in urban Mexico encounters daily. In profile, it is formed of a basic L-shaped steel frame, consisting of a tall back panel and an elevated seat. An oilcloth awning serves as a roof to protect both the client and the entire workstation from rain and soot generated by the heavy traffic along the busy avenue where the stand is located. The stand is mounted on four wheels for easy transport to and from the street each day. To get a shoeshine, the client climbs high onto the seat and faces the bootblack—known in Mexican Spanish as a *bolero*—who sits on a low chair level with the client's feet. Emilio, like many bootblacks, keeps several squat stools alongside his stand for customers who have to wait for his services or friends who stop to pass the time of day.

Commonly, shoeshine stand awnings in Mexico bear advertisements for newspapers or soft drinks. Emilio's stand, by contrast, is painted a solid bright red, complemented by a striped red and white awning, which makes the stand distinctive and eye-catching. It is probably for this reason, more than any other, that I first stopped at this stand rather than any of the others along my way to the office. I continued to patronize Emilio exclusively because of the high quality of his work. Tucked away in the storage compartment below the client's seat was a greater variety of liquids, creams, and waxes than I would have ever thought possible for such an apparently simple operation as a shoeshine.

Emilio dressed neatly in a dark blue uniform with an embossed patch reading PRI, the acronym of the Institutional Revolutionary Party [Partido Revolucionario Institucional], which almost completely monopolized Mexican government for over seventy years, until the national elections of 2000. The uniform was a gift of the PRI to Emilio's union brothers, who could be expected in return to arrive in large numbers at PRI rallies and vote for party candidates. I found Emilio's shoeshine technique to be mesmerizing. In a non-stop series of brisk, short strokes, he wiped, scraped, washed, rubbed, and brushed, in an effort first to clean the shoe and then apply color and successive protective coats. Over the course of the shine, he alternated his attention back and forth from shoe to shoe. He also used the customary signal to indicate that the foot should be lifted onto or off of the narrow iron footrest—a sharp upward tap on the toe of the shoe. Emilio removed and replaced bottles and containers from the stand's storage compartment with astounding rapidity. The screwing and unscrewing of metal bottle caps, the popping and clanking of aluminum, glass, and plastic lids as they are put onto or removed from containers, produce an audible rhythm. Receiving a shoeshine was like hearing an improvised musical performance, Emilio the musician, customers the audience. At first, the dramatic quality of the shoeshine enabled me to block out the ceaseless flow of noisy traffic, rushing by only several meters away. After several months of shines, when Emilio's movements became more predictable, it was our conversation that I found most absorbing.

Anthropological fieldworkers train themselves to be conversationalists. It is above all through conversation, both casual and directed, that we obtain information. As the weeks turned into months, Emilio and I conversed at increasing length, a situation which I encouraged. I had few friends in my new neighborhood and found a measure of companionship in Emilio, who was unfailingly correct in his dealings with me. He knew instinctively when to chitchat, when to probe tentatively into details of my private life, and just how far he could go without causing offense. Over the course of time I pushed our conversation deeper and deeper. Small talk about the weather or air quality gradually turned into discussions of our ages and families. Emilio was forty-two, married with a teenaged son and daughter. Casual discussions were converted over time into tentative confessions of amorous relationships and problems on the job. The time I spent with Emilio was so engaging, in fact, that the lengthy discussions exacted a cost. I would plant myself in the chair for a shoeshine, expecting to be on my way after ten or fifteen minutes. Absorbed in conversation, Emilio would prolong the treatment he gave my shoes. Sometimes, if business was slow, I found myself on the shoeshine stand for three quarters of an hour or more, with Emilio applying creams, wax coatings, polish the entire time. For the rest of the day my shoes would exude such a strong chemical odor that I became hopelessly self-conscious. Nonetheless, I always went back for another shine. The lingering aroma seemed a small price to pay for such absorbing conversation.

One day, Emilio unexpectedly brought up the subject of alcohol. He was alcoholic, he said. He could never take another drink or he would inevitably resume life as a drunk. He had hurt his mother, he had hurt his wife and children, he continued. His great consolation was that he managed to sober up before his mother died, thereby giving her the peace of mind that comes from having a healthy child. As a topic of conversation, Emilio's alcohol abuse arose spontaneously, with no forewarning. I was determined to learn more. The next time I visited his stand, I probed a bit. Emilio gushed with emotion. He talked nonstop about his addiction, this time relating it to hurtful experiences he had suffered as a young migrant to Mexico City. As a Nahua Indian, wearing distinctive clothing, speaking very little Spanish, acting like the country bumpkin that he felt he was, he was constantly degraded by insults and dismissive remarks. "When I look at alcohol, I see poison!" he blurted out. Statements such as this aroused my curiosity even more.

When I visited Emilio's stand the following week, I decided to play it cool. I would not bring up the topic of alcohol. But it seems that Emilio had his own agenda. When I stepped down from the chair and was about to depart, Emilio looked me straight in the eye and asked, "Have you ever been to a group?" "To a group?" I replied. "What kind of group?" "Alcohólicos Anónimos," was the response. I explained that I had never visited an Alcoholics Anonymous meeting, but that I had long intended to do so. This response was in fact true. Food and drink are abiding intellectual interests of mine. Alcohol in particular is so integral to life in Mexico, particularly to male life, that it is virtually impossible for any anthropologist to avoid the topic.

Learning that I was interested in Alcoholics Anonymous, Emilio mustered his courage. In one nervous breath, he told me that he is a member of an Alcoholics Anonymous group and invited me to attend a meeting with him that evening. "Just come and observe," he said. "You like to read. You can look at the charts on the wall and read what they say, '*Vivir y deja vivir*' [Live and let live] and other things." He further explained that the group consisted entirely of men. When I asked why, he groped in vain for a coherent answer and became boldly insistent: "You just come and sit there and observe." Would it make a difference that I am the only *gringo*? "Not at all," he replied. "Everyone would be happy you are there." To reassure me further, he uttered a statement I would hear many times afterward: "There are no differences among us. Rich people, poor people, everyone is the same." So I gratefully accepted. We arranged to meet by his stand at 7:15, the end of his workday.

At the appointed hour, I returned to the spot where Emilio and I had agreed to meet. Although foot and automobile traffic were as heavy as ever, my companion and his shoeshine stand were gone. I waited patiently, wondering if I had been stood up. But, no, some ten or fifteen minutes later, Emilio emerged from a nearby portal and walked briskly in my direction. He had changed into a fresh white shirt and appeared immaculate, his hair neatly parted and swept back from his face, his nails scraped free of shoe polish, his brown skin glistening. In his hand he carried an umbrella and a small plastic bag filled with the day's dirty rags and work clothes. "I keep the *carrito* in that building over there," he explained. For a small monthly fee, he stores his *carrito*, or shoeshine stand, overnight in the house from which he had emerged. The landlord also provides him access to washing facilities. He apologized for being late; customers had arrived up until the last minute, he said.

What perhaps struck me most about Emilio at this point in our relationship was his extraordinary cleanliness. I had often caught him soaping and rinsing the shoeshine stand at the end of the day and I had never seen him disheveled even after twelve straight hours of grueling work. Cleanliness, I would later discover, was critical to Emilio's understanding of his alcoholism; it also seriously affected his relationship to his Alcoholics Anonymous group.

Punctuality turned out to be another of his repeated concerns. Emilio now seemed worried about getting to the meeting on time. We were running late, he said, and should hurry. We scampered several blocks to a bus stop. It was rush hour, the end of the work day for most of Mexico City, and there was even a bigger crowd than usual of passengers waiting for the bus. Busses and micros, small passenger vans, swept by the stop one after another, all going in the wrong direction. I offered to pay for a taxi, but Emilio refused. Given his evident anxiety about the hour, it seemed an eternity before the right bus finally arrived. We crowded inside. By the time we had pushed ourselves to the exit door at the back of the bus, we had reached our stop. We were at a metro station and again ran quickly, this time down a long flight of stairs, into the bowels of Mexico City's earthquake-prone subsoil. As a Californian, I shared with Emilio the experience of having lived in a land of "shaking earth," to use Eric Wolf's apt description of the Mesoamerican landscape (1959). I thought a lot about earthquakes during my residence in Mexico City, particularly after reading journalist Elena Poniatowska's vivid exposé (1995) of the horrifying destruction wrought by the city's earthquake of 1985. Earthquakes invariably came to mind when I was riding the metro. However risky this means of transport might seem, I drew some comfort from the fact that it at least provided refuge from smog and fumes. In Mexico City, transportation always presents a tradeoff.

After several stops, we ascended to the street, where we had to push our way through a large, bustling open-air market of the type found at many metro stations in Mexico City. The market was crowded with taco and tamale stands and rickety stalls where vendors sell candy, bread, clothing, tape recordings, wristwatches and electronic gadgets. We took the five-minute walk through an alley, down a wide commercial avenue, and along a residential side street. It took less than half an hour of travel to bring us to the Alcoholics Anonymous meeting room. I found myself in an unfamiliar world, a working class district where I was the only foreigner in sight. Over a year and a half of frequenting that district, the place became so familiar to me that I felt completely at ease among its streets, homes, and inhabitants. I came to experience the reality of Oscar Lewis's descriptions recorded at an earlier era and in a different sector of Mexico City. To use Ulf Hannerz's apt paraphrase (1980:70–71), "Lewis's urban acquaintances were the inhabitants not so much of the city in general as of particular neighborhoods of a village-like character. This was where they had most of their contacts, of considerable stability and intimacy." Certainly this statement proved to be true of the world I was about to encounter on that initial excursion with Emilio. It was Tuesday, September 19, 1995.

We arrived at the Alcoholics Anonymous meeting room at three minutes to eight, right on time. As we approached the door, Emilio pointed proudly to a sign attached to a fence and protruding high above the street. It displayed the A.A. logo, and announced meeting times and the name of this group: Moral Support. We entered through an iron gate and descended a long flight of stairs, still outdoors, to a patio located far below street level. A multi-storied concrete house lay to the back of the patio. Instead of heading toward the house, however, we veered right to enter a small one-room cottage constructed of cinder blocks and covered by a flat tar roof. Inside it measured about twenty feet long by a dozen feet wide. The cottage was cluttered with posters, drawings, charts, a blackboard, and other wall hangings, many of them textual. Emilio was right to have told me that I would have a lot to read. There was a slightly elevated podium and a desk at the front of the room and a sink and small lavatory at the back. Most of the room was occupied by rows of chairs with a center aisle, three chairs to one side of the aisle, two to the other. Three men were already present. Within twenty minutes, four others arrived. Counting Emilio and myself, we were nine.

Although I paid careful attention to the hour-and-a-half-long meeting, it was impossible for me to make sense of it. I had anticipated that the meeting would fill me with feelings of wonder and mystery—not uncommon emotions upon witnessing an unfamiliar ritual—and it did. Over the course of nearly three decades, I had entered new fieldwork settings countless times. Each encounter presented some formal ceremony, whether religious or secular, that was for me the most intriguing, but hardest, aspect of the culture to understand. Alcoholics Anonymous meetings in general possess definite ritualistic form and content and this first A.A. meeting predictably aroused my curiosity.

Almost as soon as we arrived at the meeting, Emilio sat himself down at the desk at the front of the room. He orchestrated the entire event, at times speaking himself, at times calling on others, who rose to the podium to present lengthy personal discourses. At least three aspects of the occasion struck me as remarkable. First, the speakers, all of whom clearly belonged to the working class, were extraordinarily poised and articulate. Their speech patterns varied quite a bit, shot through as they were by recognizable regional and status markers, most of which revealed little formal education. Despite the lack of schooling, they could all speak with apparent ease for fifteen uninterrupted minutes or more. Moreover, they expressed themselves with clarity, straightforwardness, and, in a few cases, oratorical verve. Although they relied on an abundance of fillers, mainly expletives and curses, to collect their thoughts, there were no awkward pauses. It seemed that, had they been allowed, they could have gone on talking forever. They appeared sublimely self-confident and in control.[1] This verbal facility is evidence, among other things, of the performatory aspect of A.A. meetings in Mexico City. A good performance does not usually come naturally. It is a talent acquired through hard work. Once mastered, it imparts the same sense of worth and satisfaction that comes from having learned any difficult task. In fact, the man whom I would consider the best orator in the group confessed in a personal story that he suffered from speech defects as a child. His playmates teased him mercilessly. Now, a veteran of seventeen years in A.A., he has long overcome both his speech problems and the emotional trauma they caused. Over the course of my study, I would have a chance to observe how a number of newcomers to A.A., initially nervous and ill at ease, effectively learned the art of public speaking.

A second striking aspect of the meeting was the content of the speeches. So many rich themes emerged that my ethnographic antenna became almost over-exercised. The men spoke movingly of religion, of the onset of their alcoholism, of their family backgrounds, of the history of Alcoholics Anonymous, of an anniversary in celebration of the group's founding to occur the following month. Among other topics, equality, which I had already detected from Emilio's street-side confessions, asserted itself as a theme: "Here [in A.A.] there are no differences. There are white people and black people and brown people." I looked around the room for confirmation. Everyone was decidedly brown, except for one solitary white—myself. "It is important [in A.A.] to believe in God, but which God doesn't matter; you can be a Buddhist or a Mormon or whatever." Again I glanced around. Although I was unsure who was what in terms of religious affiliation, I could be pretty certain that, among those present, I was the only Jew. I knew that these assertions of equality referred not to this group specifically, but to the Alcoholics Anonymous movement as a whole. And yet they seemed irrelevant to the social profile of the group: a clearly homogenous collection of brown-skinned, middle-aged, working class, Christian men.

Of course assertions of equality were not entirely irrelevant to the immediate context. Only after the meeting ended did I realize that speakers were above all directing their remarks to me, even though they rarely looked me in the eye as they spoke. The subtle proselytizing that occurred during the meeting was the third striking aspect of the event. Speakers were bent on reassuring me that, however distinctive I might seem, I would fit into the group. A few speakers directed themselves to me in an unambiguous way. They stated their pleasure at my presence. In simple terms, they tried to explain to me the principles of A.A. They tried to instruct me in its history. One speaker pointed to drawings of Bill and Dr. Bob hanging high on the front wall of the meeting room. "These are Bill and Bob. He was a doctor." While the gentleman spoke, he shook his finger rapidly back and forth, pointing indiscriminately to both pictures, as if he were unsure which person was which. "They founded A.A. They're from Brooklyn." The speaker was as uncertain as I was at that point of the founders' origins. Bill W. was a New Yorker, but Dr. Bob lived in Akron, Ohio, where the first A.A. meeting took place in June 1935.

Despite historical flubs, the speaker was trying to communicate an important message: if *gringos* such as Bill and Dr. Bob actually started Alcoholics Anonymous, I certainly could feel welcome to join. These founders were countrymen of mine; this fact should override obvious differences between myself and the others in the room. To erase any doubt I might have about his motives, Emilio closed the meeting with a few words thanking me for attending. Even though he is a "humble bootblack," he said, he "dared" to call me "*compañero.*" The assertion of egalitarianism manifested itself once again. Even if we were not social equals, Emilio's brief closing statement would act as a symbolic status leveler. This was my first indication that the term *compañero* bears a special meaning within Mexican A.A. circles. It is the word by which A.A. members address and refer to one another. The mere utterance of the word is powerful enough to forge a special social bond, in this case, a bond with me, an individual who had just barely stepped foot in A.A. for the first time.

At the mention of the word *compañero,* I was hit with an ambivalent feeling. I was proud to be accepted by these poor, marginal Mexicans. And yet, I felt that I had not yet earned that acceptance. It came a trifle too soon, too easily. It was also conferred without my explicit involvement or approval, as if I were extraneous to the process. In retrospect, I realize that Emilio's closing remarks provided my first exposure to the nearly relentless social control that is fundamental to the functioning of Alcoholics Anonymous in Mexico City.

Two days later, on Thursday evening of the same week, I attended a second meeting. This time Emilio sat along with ten other men in the rows of chairs, while an eleventh, planted at the desk at the front of the room, coordinated the event. Themes I had not yet heard began to emerge in the public testimonies, among them the addiction to tobacco. Amidst the plethora of wall hangings in the meeting room, I had noticed a No Smoking sign. Alcoholics Anonymous meetings are famous in Mexico

City for filling up with cigarette smoke. It is commonly said that recovering alcoholics substitute one addiction, smoking, for another, more immediately dangerous one, alcohol. In Mexico, the United States, and elsewhere in the world, A.A. members are occasionally given subtle encouragement, at the least outright permission, to smoke, in order to ameliorate the devastating impact of withdrawal from drink.[2]

Emilio's group, Moral Support, was different from all but a handful of A.A. groups in Mexico City. Smoking was prohibited and therefore became a legitimate issue for commentary within the meetings. In fact, investigators have commented upon an "apparent relationship between quitting smoking and stopping drinking," which coincides with an overall "commitment to a new life style" (Tuchfeld 1981:634). In the United States, successful control over one substance apparently encourages addicts to believe that they can abstain from the other as well (ibid.). In Moral Support members often used a term that I never heard outside the context of A.A. meetings: *tabaquismo,* tobaccoism, a word parallel both in grammatical construction and negative connotation to *alcoholismo,* alcoholism. Some of the men in the group do smoke, but always outside the context of meetings. Most of the men believe that if you can give up alcohol you can and should give up tobacco as well. In any event, no smoker would be allowed to indulge this habit while seated in the Moral Support meeting room. The prohibition on smoking was one reason why I, a health-conscious Californian, could eventually attend group meetings with regularity. Urban lore had it that merely living in Mexico City was equivalent to smoking two packs of cigarettes a day. I hoped to ameliorate the problem, whenever possible, by protecting myself from secondhand smoke.

At this second A.A. meeting, Emilio stepped up to the podium. He spoke, among other things, of how he and I met, referring to me throughout his talk as "*el señor* Estalin." It was not the pronunciation of my name that concerned Emilio, however. It was my title. After referring to me as "*el señor* Estalin" several times, Emilio changed his mode of reference: "I mean to say '*el compañero* Estalin,' if I may call him that." My status as a member of the group was being reaffirmed openly and it was only my second meeting. I was intrigued as much as flattered by the group's ready acceptance.

The group met the following Saturday, but I decided against attending. If I were to commit myself to fieldwork, I would have to consider a change of research strategy. I needed a few days to contemplate the matter. On Tuesday of the following week, I again attended a meeting. At this early stage in the study, each encounter was a unique experience and yet patterns were beginning to emerge. During an informal chat following the meeting, Jaime, a young man about thirty-five years old, wearing thick-rimmed glasses, asked me if I would speak to the group. David, who was with us, agreed that I should. "We want your impressions," he said. I answered that it would be an honor to address the group and that I would do so whenever called upon. "At the next meeting," stated David. "At the next meeting," echoed Jaime. I agreed. The script was set. I was committed to attending two days hence, even though at that point I had not yet decided definitively on a plan of research.

By this time, I had attended three meetings over a two-week period. I continued to frequent Emilio's shoeshine stand, located only minutes from my house by foot, and used these occasions to probe into matters that had piqued my curiosity. Finally, I admitted to him how much I enjoyed attending the meetings. His reply was simple: "We don't smoke. That's called *autonomía.*" *Autonomía*—autonomy—was a term he had used a number of times before. Clearly, it did not have the identical meaning as in English or he was using it in a way that deviated from standard Spanish. At this stage, however, I felt it appropriate to ask questions slowly, examining one matter at a time. I would leave this term for another occasion.

My public address would be a turning point and I was nervous about it. I would have to explain myself, articulate my intentions. My relationship to these men would be at least partly defined by this testimony, to take place the following day. My growing anxiety revealed my deep concern. I clearly wanted to study this group and had already formulated many unanswered questions. Listening to these men speak of their families and work and struggles with addiction, I had become fascinated by their lives and the role of Alcoholics Anonymous in it.

At the shoeshine stand, I confessed to Emilio that I wanted to carry out a study of the group. He said I would have to speak to the men first and wait for their reactions. He thought for a moment and then blurted out, "Speak to Pedro." "Pedro? Why Pedro?" I asked. "Is he the leader?" "No, but it's his house we meet in." (I learned only then that we were meeting in Pedro's house.) He and his family lived in the large building at the back of the courtyard. Emilio's advice that I should speak to Pedro was tentative evidence of a group hierarchy based on prestige, perhaps power. The research opportunity presenting itself to me now had become irresistible.

There were fourteen of us at the meeting the following evening, including a number of men I had not yet met. As expected, I was called to the podium and spoke about my interest in this group of men and their

struggle against alcoholism. I explained that I myself am not an alcoholic (perhaps a foolish, even futile disclaimer, given how readily alcoholics deny their condition) but that I had some experience fighting
addiction, the addiction to tobacco. Throughout a year of research on
this group, their prohibition on smoking would serve me well. (At subsequent meetings, I spoke often and in detail about the dangerous and
addictive qualities of tobacco and how difficult it had been to free myself of it.) Continuing the testimony, I described as simply as I could the
work of an anthropologist and told something of the research I had carried out over decades elsewhere in Mexico. I asked permission to study
the group and stated that I would try as hard as possible to maintain
their anonymity. David, a man in his mid-fifties who was leading the
group that night, commented on my talk prior to calling on the next
speaker. He said that I was welcome in the group; I would find in the
group "a family, because we are like a family." He stated, moreover, that
they would learn from me, not only I from them. "The process is mutual," he concluded. The final speaker of the evening was Pedro, who reiterated what seemed to be the general consensus: I was welcome.

To this point, Pedro had seemed to me the most worldly of the lot. He
is the only member of Moral Support who dons a suit jacket and tie for
meetings. And, though his social origins are no different from those of
the other men, his former employment as a police officer put him in
touch with facets of Mexican society far out of the reach of most of the
group. The impression of worldliness was confirmed by Pedro's testi-
monial that evening. "Sociologists, psychologists, others have come
here to study this marvelous phenomenon known as Alcoholics Anonymous," he declared. "Students have come here," he continued.

I knew he was right. I had already consulted the alcohol research unit
at the Mexican Institute of Psychiatry in Mexico City and discovered
that this group had been observed, as part of a citywide survey, about a
decade before by a student research assistant. The assistant had attended two meetings. The group was very young then. It was listed as
having three members, and in reports was singled out as the smallest in
the Institute's sample of hundreds of Alcoholics Anonymous groups in
the city. Whatever the impact of this prior research experience, the men
not only assented but actually seemed eager that I should study their
group. I had entered the field.

At an early stage of fieldwork, I made a strategic decision to focus on
one small group, rather than carry out a study of several groups or of
Alcoholics Anonymous in Mexico in general. To participate fully in an

A.A. group—the only way to obtain a trusting relationship with its members—above all means consistent attendance. Long lapses or sporadic visits to meetings evoke relentless questions and raise serious doubts about one's commitment. As indicated further on, these doubts even emerge in the public forum of the meeting. From the outset, I knew that, minimally, the men would ask of me neither more nor less than they required of one another: a good attendance record. Initially, I justified this implicit requirement in the familiar terms of public schools in the United States: I was a student and they were my teachers. Regular attendance would not necessarily result in a high grade, but I certainly could not obtain a high grade without attending regularly. In time, I became emotionally attached to the men in my group and for many of the same reasons that they had become attached to one another.

In satisfaction of a basic need, attendance at A.A. meetings provided me with evening company. At the same time, the research provided an ongoing feeling of accomplishment. After attending meetings, sometimes twice, sometimes three times per week, I would return home about ten o'clock. I would set out immediately to write field notes. Occasionally, I would become so drowsy that I would have to complete the notes the following morning. This was especially true after a meeting that provided rich ethnographic material as well as on days that I had visited the men in their homes. For the most part, however, I could finish writing by midnight.

Before I knew it, I was engaged in a pursuit that heretofore had seemed entirely alien and impossible: urban anthropology. Previous field stints in small villages and towns had always thrust me deep within a foreign setting, with little possibility for escape on a daily basis. In rural communities of Spain and Mexico, there were normally no English-speakers present other than my family. To enter the field in these settings required no more than a step outside the door. From that moment, everything I would experience and observe became relevant to whatever particular topic I happened to be investigating. In all these places, my family and I were continually affected by public opinion, by the need to conform. As one informant in southern Spain put it, "To live in a village is the best of worlds and the worst of worlds: the best because you always have company, the worst because everyone always knows what you're doing." Fieldwork, for me, represented this kind of total immersion. The suffering that the immersion sometimes caused was compensated by the friendships, knowledge, and ethnographic understanding constantly available to me.

Fieldwork with Alcoholics Anonymous in Mexico City was very different. It was structured around formal meetings, which occurred three times a week. The work was therefore routinized in the way that urban employment, based on a time clock, often is. To visit the men in their homes or elsewhere other than meetings required making an appointment. They were not likely to be home if I arrived spontaneously; even if they were, they were otherwise occupied and unable to attend to me. Fieldwork in Mexico City was thus compartmentalized temporally. It was also socially compartmentalized. In any given day, I might spend the morning with University of California students, lunch with an academic colleague, afternoon at the library of the Colegio de México, and evening at an A.A. meeting. This was a new kind of fieldwork for me, unfamiliar at first, but perfectly suited to my circumstances. I came to enjoy going to the opera at the Palacio de Bellas Artes one evening and to my A.A. meeting in an economically marginal part of the city the next. Although I was hardly immersed in the field, in the sense that community studies had provided, I nonetheless came to depend on those meetings for emotional sustenance. The men in the group became more than a source of information; throughout my residence in Mexico City, they were my most dependable companions.

I remained close friends with Emilio throughout the entire field stint, although, as I gained knowledge and self-confidence, I became increasingly independent of him. This development was intentional. Without such independence, I could not have established trustworthy relations with anyone else in the group. As will become evident, the group's cohesiveness is tenuous and ephemeral. In private, the men express harsh judgments of one another. To obtain the kind of deep understanding of the group that was my goal, and to forge a trusting bond with as many of the men as possible, I had to maintain an autonomous presence.

My initial strategy was to accompany Emilio to the meeting but depart on my own. Within a few months, I was going alone to the meeting, too, first by public transportation, but with increasing frequency by taxi. I got to know the winding streets of the neighborhood intimately. Whenever avenues leading directly to the meeting room were flooded by torrential summer rains or torn apart for sewage installation, I could direct cab drivers through alternate routes. They were invariably amazed by my navigational expertise. Some were also struck by a kind of panic or fear. "Are you sure you want to be dropped off here? *No hay nadie más que puros rateros* [There are only petty thieves around]. How do I get out of this place?" The increasingly violent atmosphere in Mexico

City, exacerbated by the drastic devaluation of the peso in December 1994 and consequent high unemployment, affected virtually every resident of the city. I relied on taxis for safety as much as convenience.

Taxi drivers became ever more wary of who they picked up as passengers and where they would travel, for drivers, too, became a prime target of urban violence. Taxis were very inexpensive by United States standards, but exorbitant in terms of the Mexican peso and the pitifully low cash resources of the men. After meetings, some of the men would walk me a block to the street where taxis were most plentiful. There they would wait until I was safely on my way. My constant reliance on taxis separated me from the men as much as anything else. I was, by their standards, rich; they were poor. At the same time it seemed to me that they came to enjoy protecting me from possible harm; waiting with me for the taxi provided for an expression of nurturance that drew us closer. It became a familiar routine, and an understandable one given my identity and vulnerability as a *gringo* alone at night in a marginal part of the city.

Alcoholics Anonymous is first and foremost an organization that concerns alcohol use and abuse. For the first time in my life, while living in Mexico City, my own drinking became subject to scrutiny. I was forced to ask myself: Am I or am I not an alcoholic? Since college days, with their weekend binges (in which I regularly participated), I had been thoroughly unconcerned about drinking. I never get drunk. I am accustomed to a single glass of beer or wine perhaps four or five times a week, with perhaps a second glass on weekends at parties. From the outset, during my testimonies, I confessed openly to continuing to drink alcohol. In fact, although I reduced my alcohol intake somewhat as a consequence of intimate contact with A.A., I never gave it up completely. I believe now that, out of solidarity with the men, I should have given up alcohol throughout the duration of the study. As it was, for the first time in my life, I suffered pangs of guilt whenever I took a drink, itself a demonstration of the subtle control that A.A. meetings exert on members.

A.A. meetings start out with the recitation of a sort of preamble, a general statement indicating that the only condition for joining Alcoholics Anonymous is the desire to give up alcohol. *"El único requisito para ser miembro de A.A. es el deseo de dejar de beber."* [The only requirement for becoming a member of A.A. is the desire to stop drinking.] Each time this statement was read, it crossed my mind that more than nationality, educational level, and social class separated me from the others in the room; I drank and they did not. Moreover, I did not even pretend to want to stop drinking. In this sense, I never actually became a full member of Alcoholics Anonymous. I was unable actually to calculate just how important my drinking was to the men. It might have been a gift to the men in my group to have joined their struggle for abstention; possibly, my efforts would have gone unnoticed. Although I occasionally felt guilty, I confess to harboring a mildly perverse sense of satisfaction from my stubborn refusal to abstain.

Most anthropological fieldworkers experience the need to vent their frustrations through some symbolic rebellion of a non-destructive sort. The oppressive social control to which they are sometimes subjected makes intentional non-conformity almost a pre-condition of research. It also reinforces one's identity as someone essentially different from the group under investigation. My occasional glass of beer or wine was an expression of this kind of rebelliousness. Fortunately, drinking did not disqualify me from carrying out my work. Referring specifically to the United States, Peterson and Brown (1987) believe that A.A. limitations on membership have discouraged social scientific researchers from choosing to study this organization: "while A.A. is not a secret organization," they say, "it is an anonymous group, which explicitly rejects as its own goal research on alcoholism or educational efforts about alcoholism. Further, most A.A. meetings are 'closed' in that attendance is limited to those who acknowledge a problem with the consumption of alcohol. This criteria [*sic*] alone would seem to many to make A.A. off limits to participant/observation by most social scientists, especially anthropologists" (Peterson and Brown 1987:5). At no time during my research on A.A. in Mexico City did anyone imply that I would have to stop drinking in order to attend meetings or carry out my stated research goals. Although I gathered interview material outside the context of group meetings, most of my information comes from participant observation in the traditional anthropological sense.

Throughout my fieldwork, I tried to keep a perspective on my major motivation for attending meetings: ethnography. Though I derived secondary personal benefits from meetings, my main goal was anthropological. I promised myself that I would not taunt or tempt the men with my drinking, but would retain alcohol as an integral part of the wider social world in which I moved. Hence, whenever I bought a bottle of wine at a nearby supermarket, I would go several blocks out of my way to avoid passing Emilio's shoeshine stand as I walked home. Though he knew full well that I took the occasional drink, it would have been insulting to carry liquor in his presence. On the other hand, another member of the group, Arturo, invited me to his nephew's first birthday party, where he himself served me several beers. I hesitated to accept at first, and yet he became so aggressively insistent that I decided to accede. This was the only time I drank in front of any of the men over the entire field-work period. Significantly, the party took place at a residence located over an hour and a half by public transport from the neighborhood where our group met.

I devoted one of my first public testimonies to an exploration of whether or not I could be considered an alcoholic. Pedro had provided me a pamphlet from Alcoholics Anonymous World Services entitled "Fifteen Questions That Only You Can Answer." The questions were designed as a self-diagnosis of alcoholism. On the podium, in front of the men, I reviewed the questions, one by one, and gave my answers to them. "Do you feel panic if you go several days without drinking?" "Do you suffer mental lapses, periods about which you remember nothing?" "Have you lost a job because of drinking?" Each question evoked from me a negative response. To be sure, definitions of alcoholism vary enormously from one organization to another. Perhaps to rationalize my own stubborn refusal to abstain, I was anxious to demonstrate to the men that, according to official criteria established by Alcoholics Anonymous, I could in no way be considered alcoholic. This discourse was only partly convincing to the men. Throughout my field stint, several *compañeros* persisted in occasionally taking me aside and whispering, "You know, *compañero*, you really should stop drinking." Others, however, would praise my ability to stop drinking after taking one or two glasses of beer or wine. In the end, I believe that my alcohol consumption did nothing seriously to impair my relations with the men or destroy our mutual trust.

The themes that I identified upon initial acquaintance with the group were the ones that continued to intrigue me: the tension between equality and hierarchy, the importance of ritual and religion, the assertions and redefinitions of masculinity, the role of humor and social control, among other topics. I tended to view the group as constituting a small society, embedded within and connected to a much larger one which provided the basic structure within which members of this small society could act effectively. This small society—the A.A. group—was itself guided by explicit rules and implicit assumptions, which expressed themselves in the imposition of a strict behavioral code. In other words, the group constituted a distinct, if not unique, subculture. My ethnographic focus throughout remained on group dynamics, on the inter-actions among the men and their impact on one another, rather than individual life development and engagement with alcohol. Alcoholics Anonymous, in Mexico as virtually everywhere, is designed first and foremost as a therapeutic resource. It seemed to me that its therapeutic success or failure could best be explained through a good understand-ing of the functioning of the group. We shall return at the book's con-clusion to the issue of therapeutic efficacy.

A question remains as to whether this study, centered as it is on the workings of one small group, might be considered in some way repre-sentative of Alcoholics Anonymous in Mexico or even throughout the world. Many studies of A.A. (e.g., Caetano 1993; Emrick, Tonigan, et al. 1993; Moos et al. 1993; Ólafsdóttir 1992) take a statistical ap-proach and compare group size, membership, beliefs and behavior on the basis of questionnaires or surveys. In Mexico City, the Mexican In-stitute of Psychiatry has sponsored a large-scale study, under the super-vision of Haydeé Rosovsky, of hundreds of A.A. units (e.g, Rosovsky, Casanova, y Pérez 1991; Rosovsky and Leyva 1990). Research assis-tants compiled a wealth of information on the basis of several visits to each group. Extensive data such as these provide an essential backdrop to my own research, which is not a study of A.A. in general, but rather an ethnography of a single group over time. Through an intensive focus on one A.A. unit, I could probe questions such as why A.A. has spread so rapidly throughout Mexico and why members remain within or stray from the group. Although A.A. groups throughout Mexico vary in for-mat and membership, published accounts indicate that affiliates every-where experience many of the same conditions and feelings that I was able to observe in Moral Support.

Research in Alcoholics Anonymous was complicated by the issue of anonymity, a precept so basic that it is built into the name of the organ-ization. I struggled with how I could possibly carry out a study of this kind if I had to keep everything and everyone anonymous. My immedi-ate solution was to tell the men, when I first asked public permission to carry out the study, that when writing or lecturing about them I would change their names and disguise the location of the meeting. I was mystified by the reaction; for reasons I could not yet understand, they seemed genuinely unconcerned about this matter. Only later did it be-come apparent that their identity is in fact known and that much of what they state in public can in no way remain a secret. Throughout this vol-ume, I discuss the conditions that lead to the breakdown of anonymity and the possible consequences of this breakdown for the therapeutic process.

Insofar as individual beliefs and confessions are concerned, I rely heavily on verbatim accounts from taped interviews taken outside the context of the meetings. I have full permission from the men to use the interviews in this way. In fact, a few of the men seemed annoyed that I would not reveal their true identity. Despite these sentiments, I resist doing so. It is mainly through these taped interviews that I am able to convey the flavor of meetings, the texture of the men's language in meetings, without reproducing the words actually uttered during the meetings.

I never taped a meeting; I never took notes during meetings. The men would remind one another constantly of the importance of paying careful attention to speakers, sitting and listening to what is being said without any distractions. I relied on my memory to reconstruct meetings after the fact, writing notes, as I have said, immediately upon returning home. These written accounts, plus notes taken during home visits and the taped interviews, provide the bases for this book.[3] My own feelings and interactions as a member of the group are an essential part of the study as well. Time after time, I heard my own reactions echoed in statements made by the others. I came to take my own experiences as possibly representative. Despite my intense contact over more than a year and a half, I remained in most respects an outsider, a condition that also furthered my ethnographic goals. Hence, wherever I speak of myself in these pages, I explicitly differentiate myself from or equate myself to the others.

2. RELIGIOUS ADAPTATIONS
IN ALCOHOLICS ANONYMOUS

Any scholar who begins to delve into a topic suddenly sees evidence of it everywhere. It is as if blinders had been removed; an automatic self-censoring mechanism inside the brain suddenly ceases to function. This was my experience with Alcoholics Anonymous. Wherever I traveled in Mexico, from the largest cities to small rural communities, I encountered the unmistakable logo with its double A encased within a triangle. In 1996, I had been carrying out research in the little town of Tzintzuntzan for nearly thirty years. And yet, until I began the study of Moral Support, I was unaware that the town, with a population of only three thousand inhabitants, houses two A.A. groups. Not long ago, there were three. However, two of the groups had trouble surviving because they met on the same evenings, thereby entering into an unfeasible competition for members. They fused, thus leaving two groups that meet on different days of the week. It is now possible for recovering alcoholics to attend meetings in Tzintzuntzan any evening that they wish.

Once I had discovered this surprising fact, I would attend A.A. meetings on my brief visits to Tzintzuntzan. After my first meeting, a member inquired of me, semi-rhetorically, "Have you noticed how many fewer drunks there are in Tzintzuntzan than there used to be?" I answered that honestly, yes, it did seem to me that there were many fewer drunks in town. I had made no scientific survey to back up my observation, nor was it possible for me to state whether there had been an actual decline in drunkenness or just in public displays of drunkenness. But there was no doubt that the town was visibly drier than before. "That's because of A.A.," the man explained.

Although the veracity of this man's explanation might be challenged, there is no doubt that in Tzintzuntzan, as throughout Mexico and Central America, Alcoholics Anonymous has experienced enormous growth. Vaillant (1995:268) reports that there are three times as many A.A. groups per capita in Costa Rica and El Salvador as in the United

States. A.A. groups in Mexico began in the 1940s with English-speaking residents of the country. Following translation of the Big Book into Spanish, Mexicans began to form their own groups. In 1956, the register at the New York office of Alcoholics Anonymous showed three Spanish-speaking groups in Mexico. By 1964, these had grown to 36. After the founding in 1969 of the Office of General Services of Mexico, A.A. began to flourish. In 1974 there were 928 officially registered groups. By 1988 there were more than 12,000 known groups, with the probability of numerous unofficial meetings as well (Rosovsky and Leyva 1990:7–8). In 1991, the Mexican Institute of Psychiatry reported the existence throughout Mexico of 14,000 groups with more than 300,000 members (Rosovsky 1991a:3). This record demonstrates an extraordinary growth rate.

On the face of it, this expansion should not be surprising. In Chapter Seven, we explore the abundant health problems engendered throughout Mexico by the problem drinking that characterizes broad segments of Mexican society. The presence of a range of therapeutic options in Mexico, including A.A., is therefore entirely understandable. And yet, this rapid growth might not have been predicted, given established notions about the kinds of people who are attracted to A.A. In theory, it is drinkers of middle-class, Protestant origin who should be most accepting of Alcoholics Anonymous. Consider the words of William Madsen (1974:156), who, as an anthropologist, pays particular note to cultural configurations: "A.A.'s philosophy and structure . . . are American and its foreign successes are most notable in related cultures such as Canada, Ireland, England, Scandinavia, New Zealand and Australia." Madsen attributes this distribution to "the core of Protestant middle-class values that unconsciously form the central philosophy of A.A." (ibid.).

As far as class affiliation is concerned, there is evidence from the United States that poor people find A.A. incompatible with their values and life-style. For example, the Skid Row alcoholics whom Jacqueline Wiseman studied felt nothing but disdain for Alcoholics Anonymous. States Wiseman (1979:233), "AA has never had much appeal for the lower class alcoholic. It is primarily a middle-class organization, focused on helping ex-alcoholics regain their lost status. Skid Row alcoholics dislike what they refer to as 'drunkalogs,' in which members tell with relish just how low they had sunk while drinking. They dislike what they call the 'snottiness' and 'holier-than-thou' attitude of the reformed alcoholic (or 'AA virgins' as they call them)." It is of course impossible to generalize about enormously diverse groups like members of the middle class and Protestants. However, from their portrayal in the literature, these two segments of society seem to have had one thing in common: advocacy of drinking patterns—including at times total abstention—which are in accord with the necessities of economic success.

The Mexican experience departs from the U.S. picture in that, in Mexico, A.A. has achieved enormous success particularly among working class Catholics. Madsen himself has remarked on the phenomenal growth of A.A. in predominantly Catholic, working class Mexico City (1974:157). What we need, he says, is "a study of A.A. in those Latin American cultures where modifications [from the American pattern] have made it compatible. The most significant of these is San Salvador, where A.A. has flourished for decades. Another is Mexico City, where after years of bare survival, A.A. is now growing rapidly"(ibid.).

An analysis of the values and structure represented in Moral Support responds to Madsen's call. It reveals points of cultural compatibility that go far toward understanding A.A.'s success throughout Mexico. An examination of Moral Support shows that it is above all in the religious realm that A.A. overlaps with the cultural expectations and social structure of Mexican urban workers. It is in the religious domain, too, that some of the most notable cultural modifications from North American patterns have taken place. The case of Moral Support helps explain through ethnographic detail why, in Raúl Caetano's words (1993:224), "Catholicism has not been an impediment to AA expansion in traditionally Catholic countries."

At the outset it is useful to evaluate whether and in what manner Alcoholics Anonymous as a whole may be considered a religious movement. There is no doubt of the organization's religious origins. It was the spiritual offshoot of a Christian fellowship and a direct byproduct of the conversion experience of one highly enterprising individual. The idea of Alcoholics Anonymous, if not the organization itself, dates from 1934, when Bill W., a New York stockbroker who had fallen on hard times, was hospitalized for a severe alcoholic episode. A former drinking partner and drunk who had achieved sobriety reached out to help Bill. He recommended that he visit the Oxford Group, a nondenominational, evangelical movement "that had no membership lists, rules, or hierarchy and whose members surrendered their fates to God as they conceived of some spiritual force" (Trice and Staudenmeier 1989:17). The Oxford Group attempted to embrace all religious denominations. It advocated making personal restitution for damage done to others, helping others in need, and refraining from the pursuit of personal prestige (ibid.). These principles would be immediately recognizable to anyone who has had even minimal contact with Alcoholics Anonymous.

Bill W.'s hospitalization culminated in what might be termed a religious conversion. Deeply affected by the experiences of his former drinking buddy, and longing to achieve sobriety, Bill W. suffered, in his words, from "a very deep depression, the blackest" he had ever known (W. W. 1945:464). He cried out in the darkness of his hospital room for divine help: "If there is a God, will He show Himself?" (ibid.). "The result was instant, electric, beyond description," he states in his autobiography (W. W. 1949). "The place lit up, blinding white. I knew only ecstasy. . . . A great wind blew, enveloping and permeating me. Blazing, came the tremendous thought, 'You are a free man'" (ibid.). Fortunately for Bill W.'s self-esteem, his physician reassured him that he was not hallucinating. In fact, the doctor reinforced the positive, spiritual dimensions of the experience by suggesting to Bill that he read William James's *Varieties of Religious Experience*.[1] He urged Bill W. to use his encounter with God as a pathway to sobriety. Bill W. had undergone a conversion. One scholar (Matthiasson 1987) has even interpreted Bill W.'s experience as shamanistic. However we interpret the event, Matthiasson (1987:19) is probably right in his estimation that "Bill's own recovery would not have been possible without his own religious experience."

The story of how Alcoholics Anonymous was founded is known mainly through the writings of Bill W. Starting in June 1935 with a meeting between himself and Dr. Bob, a surgeon from Akron, Ohio, the organization grew rapidly. Its principles and underlying philosophy were codified in a volume, written largely by Bill W. himself and published in 1936, formally titled *Alcoholics Anonymous,* but known colloquially as the Big Book. By 1936, A.A. meetings as they are known today were already underway in Akron, a city which, for hosting the first A.A. meeting, has acquired special spiritual significance for followers. Meetings began soon thereafter in New York City (Trice and Staudenmeier 1989:19). As outlined in the Big Book, the Alcoholics Anonymous program is built around two lists of principles known as the Twelve Steps and Twelve Traditions (see Appendices A and B). The Twelve Steps, to be followed by the recovering alcoholic sequentially, present the path to individual recovery; the Twelve Traditions represent the ideal functioning of A.A. groups and the larger A.A. fellowship. Significantly, the Twelve Steps are based on steps advocated by the Oxford Group as a means toward spiritual conversion and growth (Matthiasson 1987:18).

The number twelve, of course, is central to the Judeo-Christian tradition. Biblical citations of the words "twelve" and "twelfth" number more than 200, exceeded only by the numbers three and ten (Ellison 1957). We are familiar not only with the twelve tribes of Israel and the twelve apostles, but also by folk references like the twelve days of Christmas and cheaper by the dozen. Following British practice, in the U.S., we often count in terms of the dozen. We measure twelve inches to the foot and progress annually through twelve months a year (Brandes 1987:148–151). To have devised Twelve Steps and Twelve Traditions for its followers, Alcoholics Anonymous hit upon a particularly powerful number and symbol—a number and symbol of religious import—which must have produced an unconscious attraction to early followers of the movement.

In fact, at a Moral Support meeting, I drew upon numerology in my delivery of a personal history. It was the group's twelfth anniversary celebration. I mentioned that Alcoholics Anonymous honors the Twelve Steps and Twelve Traditions; that there are twelve months to a year; and that Moral Support was celebrating its twelfth birthday. "Twelve, to Moral Support, means life," I stated with all the dramatic flair I could muster, "A life without alcohol, in the company of family and friends who have a positive outlook." When I met Emilio at the shoeshine stand the next day, he complimented me on my "*discurso*," as he put it. He also said that Iván was impressed by the fact that I really know how to make connections. Of course, the connection is the one that most of these men probably had already made, however unconsciously. The number twelve, particularly in the domain of popular religion, pervades Mexican culture. The centrality of the Twelve Steps and Twelve Traditions in Alcoholics Anonymous has no doubt helped to promote its diffusion throughout Mexico and probably much of Latin America.

At the same time, as Matthiasson (1987:22) indicates, "There is an intentional effort made to disassociate A.A. from any conventional religious frame of reference." In order to attract individuals from a variety of religious backgrounds, says Matthiasson, "the emphasis is on 'spirituality,' with no religious over-tones" (ibid.). Members of Alcoholics Anonymous generally distinguish between religion, which implies affiliation with specific denominational organization, and spirituality, with reliance on what A.A. members refer to as a Higher Power. Kim Bloomfield (1990:1) points out that the medical and social scientific literature rarely differentiates between the terms spirituality and religion. She concludes that "It is yet to be empirically determined how separate and distinct spirituality and religion actually are" (ibid.). Her viewpoint is borne out by the Twelve Steps and Twelve Traditions, which refer repeatedly to "God." Although no A.A. member would insist on a rigid definition of God, it would be hard to deny that this is a central religious concept. Aside from the Twelve Steps and Twelve Traditions, one of the most famous references to God occurs in the Serenity Prayer, a regular feature of many A.A. meetings.[2]

There have been infinite attempts to interpret the notion of God in some unconventional light. Paul Antzé perceptively outlines the A.A. conception of a Higher Power as all-forgiving, a source of "strength and courage in hours of need" (Antzé 1987:163): "Nowhere in the A.A. literature or in any of the meetings I attended," he states, "was there any mention of a judging deity, a stern father or lawgiver. In fact the Higher Power as described by members seems almost infinitely ready to forgive mistakes. In these respects the Higher Power bears a strong resemblance to A.A. as a whole" (ibid.). For this reason, a number of observers have pointed to the fact that for many recovering alcoholics, the A.A. group functions as the Higher Power. Even Bill W. accepted a definition of the group itself as the Higher Power. States Bill (A.A. 1986:310), "If you arrive at AA with no religious convictions, you can, if you wish, make AA itself or even your group your 'Higher Power.' " Mainly for this reason, Trevino (1992) interprets Alcoholics Anonymous as a Durkheimian religion; in A.A. ideology and discourse, group conscience becomes a kind of Supreme Being.

A radically different interpretation of A.A. comes from A. Logan Slagle and Joan Weibel-Orlando (1986), who compare A.A. to the Indian Shaker Church. Both movements, they state, are in essence "revitalistic curing cults." Parallels between the two movements include "an antecedent period of social upheaval, the visionary impetus of the conversion of a focal charismatic leader, the primacy of the conversion experience, cult institutionalization through formulation of charter myths, codified doctrines, sacred texts, standardized rituals and paraphernalia, and ongoing membership in support networks" (ibid.:310). Arthur Cain (1964:61), a severe critic of A.A., has called Alcoholics Anonymous "a movement which is becoming one of America's most fanatical religious cults. . . . AA is now highly formalized," he continues (ibid.:62). "The meetings, believed to be absolutely necessary, are ritualistic. And any suggestion that The Program is less than divine revelation evokes an irrational outcry."

A.A. advocates object strongly to describing the organization as a cult. However, debates over terminology (Bufe 1991 carries out a systematic examination) may well obscure the major point: Alcoholics Anonymous is pervaded by religious imagery and rests on principles and rules of conduct that many scholars, if not all, would call religious. Charles Bufe, who weighs the evidence pro and con, asks (ibid.:92), "Is A.A. religiously oriented?" His answer: "Unequivocally, yes. While many A.A. members would argue that A.A. is a 'spiritual' organization rather than a religious one, there is little doubt that they are quibbling over semantics" (ibid.). George Vaillant (1995:244) underscores this opinion by declaring bluntly that A.A. is "a strictly moral and religious system." It is probable, as Linda-Anne Rebhun suggests (personal communication), that A.A. attempts to be nondenominational in the sense that it avoids affiliation with any established church; but that rather than presenting itself as nondenominational, it advertises itself as nonreligious. That many groups in Mexico—especially middle class Mexico—meet in Roman Catholic churches reinforces the symbolic and spatial connection between Alcoholics Anonymous and formal religion.

Alcoholics Anonymous not only embraces religious symbolism and terminology. It also has been associated, from its inception, with a particular religious tradition, Protestantism. For many years, A.A. was, with good reason, reputed to be "a self-help group serving middle-aged, middle-class, white, Protestant, English-speaking, extraverted males" (Vaillant 1995:267). States one researcher, "the overriding tone of the organization is religious and unmistakably fundamentalist and Protestant" (Rodin 1985:42). A few of the central philosophical underpinnings that link Alcoholics Anonymous to Protestantism include "the concept of surrender (akin to conversion), the confession and testimony of the saved, the personal relation to God, the individual's voluntary decision to seek help, the individual's responsibility for his or her own recovery, and AA's egalitarian structure that rejects authority" (Jarrad 1997:213). A.A. publications suggest, too, that the concept of a "Higher Power" was originally chosen "in order to refer to the Protestant God without offending non-Christians or agnostics" (Valverde 1998:133).

Mariana Valverde explores parallels between Protestant egalitarianism and A.A. ideology. She begins with the notion of self-diagnosis in A.A., that is, with the subjective criteria, self-administered, by which each person decides whether he or she is alcoholic.

One might conclude that AA's self-diagnosis abolishes medical expertise by universalizing it, in a move paralleling the Protestant Reformation's laicization of priestly authority. But AA goes further than simply rejecting the authority claims of physicians and priests: the organization has leveled a profound challenge not only to the qualification process but even to the techniques taken for granted by those professionals. The nineteenth-century clinical/disciplinary techniques described by Foucault—hierarchical observation, classification, and so forth—are overtly refused. In AA there is a positive refusal to collect information about anyone but oneself (Valverde 1998:124).

That is, ideologically, Alcoholics Anonymous is similar to the Protestant Church in that both entities undermine established hierarchies.

Robin Room (1993:181) has also noted this striking pattern:

Much of AA practice and organizational structure borrowed from or reinvented older forms in the culture. The Quaker meeting offered a model of a nonhierarchical meeting composed of personal testimonies and of a decision rule of substantial consensus rather than majority voting. Protestant denominations with "congregational polity"—the wing of Protestantism that applied the Reformation to church organizational structure—offered examples of acephalous organization, with anyone allowed to set up a new congregation. Fraternal organizations such as the Masons, the Oddfellows, and the temperance fraternities, all of which flourished greatly in late 19th-century America, offered models of mutual-interest groups with a strong emphasis on regular meetings and on fellowship, and in some cases on secretiveness with respect to the outside world (Room 1993:181).

There is no doubt that, organizationally and philosophically, A.A. has notable roots in Protestantism, especially American varieties of that religious tradition.

An even more direct connection is manifest in the Protestant advocacy of abstinence. Unlike Catholics, there exist Protestant denominations that have been rigorously opposed to liquor in any form. Protestant crusaders were the main promoters of Prohibition (1919–1932). In fact, it might be more than mere coincidence that Alcoholics Anonymous was founded just a few years following the repeal of Prohibition. A.A. substituted self-control for state control. Valverde (1998:125) notes that "In AA talk, the Protestant overtones of self-control tend to prevail over the scientific and psychiatric ones." Prohibition failed, most Americans believe, because it challenged the individual's right to control his or her life, including the right to control whether and how much to imbibe

(Marshall and Marshall 1990: 138–139). The repeal of Prohibition was therefore, as much as Prohibition itself, bound up with prevalent Protestant values. As Marshall and Marshall point out (ibid.:139), "Alcoholics Anonymous seems to work successfully for many problem drinkers in part because it helps them 'gain control' over their lives again." Self-control, a basic Protestant virtue, is promoted within A.A. and the term self-control is used in meetings frequently and with varied semantic overtones (Valverde 1998:125).

The literature on alcohol and religion in Latin America shows that a main reason why people convert from Catholicism to Protestantism is that Protestantism helps converts to stop drinking. In the Sierra Juárez of Oaxaca, Michael Kearney (1970:149) found that "although the usual objections to the *sabadistas* [Seventh Day Adventists] and Protestants in general are phrased in religious terms, the real motivation for wishing to suppress them is that, upon conversion, people stop drinking, and therefore stop participating in the various community and individually sponsored fiestas." Despite strong social sanctions against conversion, the number of Protestants continues to grow in the Sierra Juárez, mainly, says Kearney, because Protestantism helps converts to attain and retain sobriety. Concludes Kearney (ibid.:150), "drinking is the pivotal point in the Catholic-Protestant opposition."

In the town of Chenalhó, located south of Oaxaca in the state of Chiapas, members of Protestant denominations are rapidly increasing. Protestants in Chiapas "link rum drinking in fiestas with worshipping idols and wasteful, wanton behavior" (Eber 1995:11). According to converts, "Protestants who successfully give up drinking . . . do so through putting alcohol into God's hands. . . . If a person gives up rum in this way, it becomes God's burden, not his" (ibid.:220). Many Protestants in Chenalhó claim that they converted from Catholicism in order to become a part of an alcohol-free social world (ibid.:221). And far from the Americas, on the Micronesian island of Truk, women, who learned organizing skills in Protestant churches, have been mobilizing since the 1970s to control alcohol sales and use (Marshall and Marshall 1990). The connection between Protestantism and abstinence, then, extends to social worlds much beyond the United States. Although it certainly does not constitute a religious denomination per se, Alcoholics Anonymous parallels Protestantism, and has become associated with it, largely because of its advocacy of complete abstinence from alcohol consumption.

The undeniable historical and cross-cultural (Colson and Scudder 1988:60) association between Protestantism and abstinence promotes the popular assumption that the membership of Alcoholics Anonymous is largely Protestant. In fact, it seems that, in Mexico, Protestantism and membership in A.A. are alternative routes to achieving sobriety. An alcoholic who is truly motivated to stop drinking can take any of several courses of action, including conversion to Protestantism and joining A.A., a step which itself constitutes a kind of religious conversion. It would appear that becoming a Protestant provides sufficient support to the recovering alcoholic; membership in A.A. might well prove redundant. Likewise, it is probable that the recovering Catholic alcoholic who joins A.A. has no need of Protestantism, because regular attendance at group meetings gives the neophyte sufficient social and emotional support.

There are, of course, alternative spiritual avenues to recovery for Catholics as well. Andrew Gordon found that Dominicans in the U.S. Northeast rely upon a theological offshoot of the local Catholic Church known as El Movimiento de la Renovación Carismática (The Movement of Charismatic Renovation), whose "Saturday services dramatically depart from Catholic liturgy" (Gordon 1985:301). Participation in El Movimiento in fact represents a sort of religious conversion, designed mainly to help participants curb "drunkenness and the excesses of weekend drinking" (ibid.). Among the highland Maya, members of The Word of God (or Preferential Option for the Poor), who follow Liberation Theology, advocate strong controls on alcohol consumption. Says Christine Eber (1995:215–216), "In the struggle over alcohol control, Catechists [lay preachers in the Word of God movement] and Protestants have found common cause. Although Protestants say sobriety is not a prerequisite for membership, once a person has joined, fellow parishioners help him see that alcohol goes against God's word (if the person hasn't already accepted this)." Although Catechists are less absolute in their pronouncements against drink than are Protestants, joining Catholic Action is one avenue to increased, if not total, sobriety.

It is impossible to document with precision the number of Catholics and Protestants in Mexican A.A. groups. A.A. keeps no membership lists and records no relevant statistics. Moreover, questionnaires probing into members' religious affiliation would certainly be perceived as an intrusive penetration by an outside agency into private affairs. In any event, group memberships fluctuate radically from one moment to the next, rendering any possible calculation of religious association tenuous and transitory. A.A. ideology promotes a strict division between itself as an organization and any other organization, religious or otherwise.

Several of the Twelve Traditions bear on this matter, with Tradition Number Six being the most direct: "An A.A. group ought never endorse, finance, or lend the A.A. name to any related facility or outside enterprise, lest problems of money, property, and prestige divert us from our primary purpose." This political position automatically acts to suppress open discussion of religious affiliation among members. In fact, it was only by directly questioning the men in Moral Support that I could learn about their religious affiliation.

David is the only member of Moral Support who was raised Protestant. Coming from a small provincial town, David did not start drinking until he moved to Mexico City at the age of twenty. After sixteen years of heavy drinking, when he was thirty-six, David joined A.A. Like all new members, he was confronted by the need to distance himself from former drinking companions. "Of course, I had to discipline myself," he says. "I had to make the sacrifice not to hang out with people I used to hang out with. . . . I had to separate myself from them for a reasonable time, you know. I had to withstand humiliation from my own buddies, because they would see me and [say], 'Hey, come over here and have a drink.'" David's response on such occasions was a standard ploy available to all Mexican men who want to avoid drinking: "No, well, no, it's that I'm on medication."

Although formally Protestant, David's religion prevented neither him nor the other males in his natal family from becoming alcohol abusers. David's religious upbringing seemed irrelevant to his drinking habits. It certainly never became an issue in his or anyone else's *historiales*. During the period I attended Moral Support, David was entirely secular in outlook, except perhaps for his adoration of A.A. and adherence to a generalized, unspecified notion of a Higher Power.

Despite the undeniable connection between Protestantism and Alcoholics Anonymous, Mexico—a predominantly Roman Catholic country—seems to have embraced A.A. with enthusiasm. Conservatively, we could estimate that there are more than a quarter of a million Mexicans who attend A.A. meetings; Mexico City alone houses a minimum of 1500 registered A.A. groups. There are countless more which are unregistered and maintain no affiliation with a central organization. Without doubt, the vast majority of A.A. members in Mexico are at least formally Roman Catholic. It is, in fact, the close affinity between Alcoholics Anonymous and popular Catholicism in Mexico that in part explains the enormous success of that organization.

Consider, first, that Mexicans are on the whole a devout people who turn readily to religion for the solution to medical, financial, and other problems. One of the most popular avenues to alleviate any difficulty, alcoholic dependency included, is through making a vow to a saint. Vows, known as *mandas,* involve an exchange of favors between the saint and the supplicant. They constitute a form of what George Foster (1967) calls the "dyadic contract"—an implicit agreement between a pair of contractants who enter into the bond entirely of their own volition. According to Foster, *mandas* are a special class of what he calls the patron-client dyadic contract: they unite individuals of unequal power and status—in this case a human with a supernatural being. The sufferer pleads with the saint to cure an illness, help find employment, provide support for attaining good school grades, or whatever. Once the saint concedes his or her part of the bargain, the supplicant performs some promised deed in return, such as praying daily in the saint's honor, caring for the saint's image, or presenting candles and flowers to the saint.

In the case of alcohol dependency, Mexicans do not usually convert to Protestantism or join A.A. as a first step. Rather they have recourse to a particular kind of *manda* known as the *juramento*. To stop drinking, a person dependent on alcohol will usually seek help from the Virgin of Guadalupe, patron saint of the Americas, and the single most venerated saint in Mexico (Wolf 1959). The addict professes devotion to the Virgin and asks for her assistance in his attempt to stop drinking. A specific length of time for abstinence—a week, a month, a year or more —is usually specified. Formerly, to make a *juramento* it was necessary to make a pilgrimage to La Villa, site of the Basilica of the Virgin of Guadalupe, located on the northeastern outskirts of Mexico City. A spiritual advisor, in daily attendance at the Basilica (in previous years, only on Sundays), would be available to assist those who wished to *jurar,* that is, make a vow of abstinence.

Nowadays, any priest is empowered to provide this kind of help. The priest solicits information about the particular drinking problem of the supplicant and, together with him, decides upon a realistic period of withdrawal. The priest then presents the supplicant with a card, decorated with a printed saint's image (i.e., *una estampa*), upon which he writes the start and end dates for abstinence. From that moment, the sufferer is supposed to stop drinking. *Juramentos* differ from *mandas* in the way supplicants reciprocate. When an alcoholic makes a *juramento* and becomes sworn against liquor, no gift is presented to the saint other than faithfulness to the vow. The ability to control oneself, at the risk of divine retribution for failing, seems to provide reward enough for the Virgin.

Priests are apparently familiar with alcoholics who overestimate the amount of time they can go without a drink. Sufferers, buoyed by their newfound enthusiasm to get well, are inclined to swear that they will not drink for a period of years, even life. The priest, aware of the enormously seductive power of alcohol, attempts to keep the vow within reasonable bounds. After all, the alcoholic who breaks a vow to the Virgin of Guadalupe is in essence committing a sin. Alcohol might well produce serious problems for the addict in this life, but sinfulness can create worse ones in the next. Hence, spiritual advisors take a pragmatic approach, encouraging short-term vows of several months at a time, which can be repeated as frequently as the alcoholic reasonably believes he can stay sober. The *juramento* is a potential solution to drinking problems in the Mexican context.

Dwight Heath points out,

> Even after a Hispanic man has admitted to having alcohol-related problems, the same deeply cherished value of *machismo* may make it difficult for him to accept even the "first step" of Alcoholics Anonymous, to admit to being "powerless over alcohol." . . . Similarly, the kind of confrontations, public confessions, and humiliations that are integral to some group-therapy or halfway-house programs would be repugnant and counterproductive, whereas a vow to a saint or to the Virgin Mary might represent a strong and lasting commitment to abstain" (Heath 1988:399).

Traditional Mexican culture, at any rate, would seem to enhance the possibilities of the *juramento* as therapy for alcohol abuse.

Unfortunately, the success of *juramentos* is uneven at best. Tales abound in Mexico City of men who are officially *jurado*, but who ask permission of the Virgin (*piden permiso*) for one or two days of leave from their vow, usually to participate fully in a family celebration. To request a brief pardon of this sort does not require a trip to the Basilica. Men simply approach one of countless images of the Virgin of Guadalupe which are found in churches and street corners all over the city and ask for a day's reprieve (*permiso*) from their vow. I have never heard of a case in which the Virgin denied such a request.

In one instance, a lawyer, whose apartment overlooks the Cathedral in Mexico City, simply stepped onto his balcony and directed himself to the image of the Virgin of Guadalupe located inside the Cathedral. He wanted a one-day break from his *juramento* in order to be able fully to enjoy a friend's wedding. The Virgin apparently granted his appeal. He resumed his sworn period of abstinence as soon as his leave period ended. Stories like this one might or might not be true. I myself never met a man who asked for leave from his *juramento* and the tales do have the flavor of urban legends. Nonetheless, they indicate that, in the Mexican popular mind, there exists considerable skepticism about the recovering alcoholic's ability to carry out the terms of his vows.

Personal stories told at Alcoholics Anonymous meetings in Mexico City sometimes touch on the futility of making *juramentos*. Eduardo, a member of Moral Support in his mid-thirties, states that "You know, well, A.A. for me is everything because in the course of my life I made three *juramentos* out of which I kept none." Eduardo's first vow was for three months, the second for a year, and the third for half a year. And why did he break his vow, I ask. Replies Eduardo,

> I started drinking again because, well, my son was born, you know, my first son with a second wife. . . . Well, I had that wife and she suffered because of me through poverty, beatings, physical and moral. . . . And this is something I, well, regret, truth be told, because she was a good *compañera*. But my alcoholism, you know, it followed me and blinded me. . . . You know, I am very jealous, and really I believe that all men are, but only up to a certain point. But I cast judgment on that woman over time. I think I stressed myself out and then that child was born, and so to celebrate, to enjoy it and all that, I went and got them out of the hospital and I started to drink.

Eduardo explains his subsequent lapses in similar terms—frustration, impetuousness, the need to share in the fiesta fun. Family celebrations seem to be the main occasions upon which recovering alcoholics begin to relapse.

Nestor's problem, he confesses, is that he would always make the vow right after a drunk spell, when he was hung over. He would use the hangover as a excuse to postpone abstinence. The next day, when he was feeling well again, he would completely forget about the vow and start drinking. On one occasion, he made a vow to stay dry for a year and lasted ten months. On another, he swore off liquor for half a year and complied for a week. Pedro's experiences with *juramentos* are no more successful. He remembers taking a vow at 10:30 one morning; by 4 in the afternoon he was already drinking. Emilio completely disparages *juramentos* by saying that, when he made vows to the Virgin, all he did was "play around" rather than confront his obligations seriously. Carmelo has systematically avoided making a *juramento*. "The Virgin is too important to me," he says, "and you just don't make vows that you suspect you won't be able to keep. It's disrespectful; and I hold the Virgin in too much respect to do that."

Matthew Gutmann discovered that many of the working class men he knew in Mexico City used vows to the Virgin as an excuse not to drink. One of Gutmann's informants told him, "When people offer you a drink and you don't want one but they are really persistent, you can either say that you're taking antibiotics, or you can tell them, '*Estoy jurado*'" (Gutmann 1996:186), that is, "I'm pledged" or "I'm sworn" against alcoholic drink. Gutmann (ibid.) uncovered several instances in which men made vows to celestial beings other than the Virgin of Guadalupe — to the Virgen del Carmen in one instance, to God in another.

Gutmann's general conclusion about sacred pledges against drink confirm my own observations. Says Gutmann (ibid.:186–187),

> The state of being jurado is a clearly and widely recognized cultural category among men . . . that exempts them from drinking, and indeed often brings the respect of others. (I am unaware of the practice among women.) And although one might expect to encounter teasing with respect to a man's being jurado—such as what might go on among friends when one of them is trying to cut back on sweets, for instance—I never heard anyone try to tempt a man with a drink if it was known that he was jurado. The option of being jurado reflects a general concern over the perils of excessive drinking, and men's choices regarding estar jurado reflect the differentiated experiences and beliefs of adults . . . with regard to alcohol.

The custom of making vows to the saints in order to stop drinking also reflects the interconnection between religion and alcohol in Mexico.

The men of Moral Support, both in and outside of meetings, evince little interest in formal religion. One reason might be that their participation in the thrice-weekly meetings leaves them little time and spiritual energy for church services and activities. Another possible explanation is that Moral Support itself becomes a kind of religious community, the meeting room a surrogate church. These parallels by no means negate the essential compatibility between Mexican popular religion and the Alcoholics Anonymous program. To the contrary, much of what is said and practiced in Moral Support is fundamentally consonant with the culture of Roman Catholicism in Mexico.

My initial impressions of Alcoholics Anonymous were formed largely by the physical setting in which Moral Support meetings are carried out, although, in time, I visited a range of other groups both within and outside the city. The layout of Mexican A.A. meeting rooms varies considerably from group to group, according to the type of meeting. Jarrad's typology of meetings (1997:214–216), based on research in Boston and Brazil, applies to Mexico as well. Groups that hold what he terms "speaker-discussion meetings" and "discussion meetings" arrange chairs in a circle so that all participants face everyone else and can interact easily. The convener or moderator might occupy a desk or chair, but in any event is situated alongside the other members; in terms of spatial position, he occupies no higher rank than they. "Speaker meetings," by contrast, situate the moderator at a desk near the front of the room. In speaker meetings, speakers use a podium, located near the moderator's desk. Both moderator and speaker face the others in attendance, who are seated in chairs arranged in rows. The effect is that of a small auditorium.

In Mexico, as in Brazil (ibid.:219), speaker meetings are most common. Moral Support, a classic speaker-type meeting, convenes in a room with an arrangement that reflects its congregational style. The room I encountered when first attending Moral Support—the little stucco cottage in Pedro's patio (Chapter One)—has an entrance toward the back of the building, near which there is located a latrine in a closet-sized alcove, separated from the rest of the space by a thin cloth curtain. At the back, too, rests a small sink, a table for the coffee and tea, and an urn for heating water. Chairs are arranged in six rows of five seats each: three to the left side of a central aisle, two to the right. At the front of the room is the podium, called the *tribuna,* as well as a desk for the moderator, known in Mexico as the *coordinador.* (In Brazil [Jarrad 1997:218], the meeting organizer is also termed *coordinador.*) The room might be taken for a small classroom.

The most prominent piece of furniture at Moral Support is the podium, which is raised one step above floor level. It is covered by a fuchsia-colored velveteen cloth to which are affixed in dark colors the group name and the Alcoholics Anonymous logo: a triangle inside a circle, with the letters A.A. inside the triangle. Each side of the triangle bears a word indicating a core value: Unity (*Unidad*), Service (*Servicio*),

Recovery (*Recuperación*). A sign posted on the street level, outside the meeting room, also bears this logo, as well as the group name and meeting hours, 8 to 9:30, Tuesday, Thursday, and Saturday.

Almost every inch of wall space at Moral Support is filled with pictures and posters. Lining the front wall, behind the podium and the moderator's desk, are two framed black-and-white line drawings of A.A. founders Bill W. and Dr. Bob. In the context of Moral Support, both their faces stand out for their whiteness. The men, portrayed from the waist up, are shown wearing suit jackets and ties. Their hairstyle, with its glossy sheen, and the part positioned just slightly off center, clearly dates back to the 1930s. Bill W., the organizational genius behind A.A., looks out directly from right behind the podium over the rows of chairs. To the side, over the moderator's desk, Dr. Bob stares off into the distance through thin wire glasses. The two portraits—in effect American icons—appear as exotic, in this working class Mexican environment, as are ecclesiastical images of the saints, with their medieval and Renaissance garb. This is not to say that Bill W. and Dr. Bob are venerated, as saints are. But they represent the high moral standards and values of the international A.A. movement. They stand as a constant reminder that this one meeting is part of a universal whole.

Several members of Moral Support refer frequently in their personal stories to the portraits of Bill W. and Dr. Bob; they point to these figures as authorities, in support of their stance on weighty issues that sometimes emerge in the course of meetings. Although Bill W. and Dr. Bob are in no sense miraculous beings, worshipped for their supernatural qualities, there is evidence that, symbolically, they function as sacred symbols. For instance, during the delivery of a personal story, Renaldo explained that he would miss meetings during the following week. He would be returning to his far-off home town to visit his mother. "*Mi madre es muy religiosa, muy católica,*" he said—"My mother is very religious, very Catholic." At that moment he glanced behind the podium and extended his arm in the direction of the portraits, stating, "That is, she has a lot of images on her walls, just like these pictures."

Hung on the meeting room walls, too, are a number of boldly printed texts. Facing the audience from the front wall are two large posters listing the Twelve Steps (*Los Doce Pasos*) and Twelve Traditions (*Las Doce Tradiciones*). These receive little attention at Moral Support, but presumably operate to remind members of the official A.A. guidelines for personal behavior and collective responsibility leading to recovery. A prominent sign on the front wall reads, "GRACIAS POR NO FUMAR"

—Thanks for not smoking. On one of the side walls hangs a framed, Spanish language version of the Serenity Prayer: "God grant me the serenity to accept the things I cannot change, the courage to change the things I can, and the wisdom to know the difference."[3] The members of Moral Support, however, favor another poetic text, the "I Am Responsible" (*Yo Soy Responsable*), recited at the end of each meeting and also posted on the meeting room walls.

The Moral Support meeting room is certainly not a church. But in a number of ways it replicates the kind of sacred space that would be familiar to any Mexican Catholic. The chairs are arranged, as in any church, in congregational fashion. The podium functions as a kind of altar; there is even a small shelf above the *tribuna* upon which rests a candle. Although the candle is used during power outages alone, it is reminiscent of votive candles in church, especially as it sits just below the portrait of Bill W. As stated, the images of Bill W. and Dr. Bob function somewhat like Catholic saints' figures in a church. It is crucial to emphasize that the men in Moral Support do not think that their meeting room is a church; nor do they pray to Bill W. and Dr. Bob. It is simply that the furniture arrangement and wall hangings symbolically replicate what any Mexican Catholic might expect to find in a place of worship. Sacred texts hanging on the meeting room walls add to the overall religious imagery.

When Moral Support changed locales from Pedro's home to a storefront several blocks away (Chapter Three), the square shape of the new meeting room required a rearrangement of chairs, podium, desk, and wall hangings. But the basic pattern was retained: a tiny, congregational-style auditorium, with the podium front and center and walls filled with images and sacred texts, hanging where members could most easily view them. It is easy to understand why, in the middle of a personal story one balmy March evening, Emilio declared bluntly, *"Esto es como una iglesia para mí. Vengo aquí con toda tranquilidad"*—"This is like a church for me. I arrive here completely at peace."

Apart from the church-like setting in which Moral Support meets, the meetings themselves are, in anthropological terms, ritualistic or ceremonial. They are marked by a predictable order of activities and codified speech patterns. They conform in every respect to Kertzer's definition (1988:9) of ritual as "formal," "highly structured," following "standardized sequences," "enacted at certain places and times that are themselves endowed with special symbolic meaning." Continues Kertzer (ibid.), "Ritual action is repetitive and, therefore, often redundant, but these very factors serve as important means of channeling emotion, guiding cognition, and organizing social groups." Later chapters bear out the veracity of these words.

To most people, the word *ritual* conjures religious associations. However, as Kertzer points out (ibid.), scholars have distinguished sacred from secular ritual (e.g., Gluckman 1965, Moore and Myerhoff 1977). For some observers, A.A. meetings might be a perfect example of secular ritual. The meetings can be considered religious if one accepts a Durkheimian view of religious ritual as, in Kertzer's words, a celebration of "people's emotionally charged interdependence, their societal arrangements" (Kertzer 1988:9). "What is important about rituals," continues Kertzer (ibid.), "is not that they deal with supernatural beings, but rather that they provide a powerful way in which people's social dependence can be expressed." During Moral Support meetings, the mutual dependence of participants on the group is articulated repeatedly and at every opportunity.

As the following chapter demonstrates, Moral Support is replete with codified language and behavior, a good part of which is clearly religious in flavor, especially if we assume a Durkheimian perspective. Meetings follow a standardized, predictable sequence of activities: introductory remarks and readings by the moderator; fifteen-minute personal stories delivered in succession by six speakers; recitation in unison of the "I Am Responsible" poem; the collection of monetary donations; and the final handshaking, which the men would no doubt define as outside the bounds of the formal meeting but which nonetheless serves to frame it. However brief the parting handshakes and goodbyes, everyone is expected to participate.

Aside from the general ritual structure of Moral Support meetings, the content of the proceedings is overtly religious in at least one respect: the "I Am Responsible" prayer. I refer to this poem as a prayer not because it mentions God or the saints—which it does not—but because group members treat it as a sacred text. In fact, the men of Moral Support call this poem "*la oración*" ["the prayer"]. The poster hanging on the meeting room wall reads:

Yo Soy Responsable	I Am Responsible
Cuando cualquiera,	When whoever,
dondequiera	wherever
extienda sus manos	extends his hands

pidiendo ayuda,	asking for help
quiero que la mano	I want the hand
de AA esté siempre	of AA to be always
allí. Y por eso	there. And for this
Yo Soy Responsable.	I Am Responsible.

The opening phrase "I Am Responsible" is capitalized, indicating its status as a title.[4]

At the conclusion of the six personal stories that form the core of every meeting, the moderator calls out, "The meeting has ended. Now it's time to recite the 'I Am Responsible,'" or, "Now let's hear the 'I Am Responsible.'" Everyone rises and turns toward the framed text. Although they all know the words by heart, some read from the document, others simply face it blankly. The poem clearly holds sacred meaning as indicated in part by the fact that, after reciting the "I Am Responsible," everyone crosses himself, just as he would during Mass. Each man also shakes hands with every other person in attendance, reminiscent of the handshaking that accompanies the "giving peace" during Mass.

Making the sign of the cross is the most overtly Catholic part of Moral Support meetings. However, there is a second parallel to Catholicism: confession. In Roman Catholicism, confession takes place in a socially asymmetrical context: parishioners confess sinful behavior to a priest in the privacy of confessional booths. They achieve absolution through acts of repentance, as delegated by the confessor. Alcoholics Anonymous personal stories (see Chapter Four) are also autobiographical. Narrated under the assumption of confidentiality, these stories sometimes concern shameful, humiliating deeds, carried out while an active alcoholic. Although the deeds are not defined as sinful, the men of Moral Support consider them morally reprehensible. They require repentance and, wherever possible, should be corrected by restitution to the injured parties. Unlike in the Catholic Church, where absolution is achieved mainly through private acts of a devotional nature, in A.A. it is the act of confession itself—carried out not in private to a priest, but in public to the group—that is supposed to help the alcoholic earn forgiveness.

Valverde (1998:91) believes that A.A. narratives approximate gay and lesbian coming out stories, which constitute the building blocks of the gay and lesbian movement. A.A. stories, like coming out tales, express in direct, frank terms the individual's affiliation with a group that is generally misunderstood and unappreciated by society at large. Both types of stories are at least potentially cathartic in the telling. To that extent, they move the storyteller toward psychological recovery. There is a major difference between the two types of narratives, however. Gay and lesbian confessionals usually reveal the narrators' pride in their sexual orientation and willingness to announce their identity openly. The recovering alcoholics of Moral Support, by contrast, are ashamed of past behavior, troubled by guilty feelings, and, at least in theory, hopeful that their revelations can be kept within the walls of the meeting room. Perhaps, as Valverde also says (ibid.), A.A. stories bear likeness to "the narratives of violence and abuse that constitute various survivor groups." Most survivor tales, like A.A. narratives, resemble the archetypical Catholic cycle of transgression, guilt, and confession as means to moral cleansing and repentance.

Then, too, the social structure of Alcoholics Anonymous is consonant with a key element of Mexican popular Catholicism: the *compadrazgo,* a major variant of what anthropologists call ritual or fictive kinship (e.g., Foster 1953 and 1969, Paul 1942, Mintz and Wolf 1967). *Compadrazgo,* in George Foster's words (1969:262), "is the Spanish term denoting the reciprocal relationships resulting from the several ritual sponsorships required by the Catholic Church: baptism, confirmation, first communion, and marriage. In addition to these, numerous subsidiary sponsorships, sometimes of people and sometimes of inanimate objects, have developed in many places." Throughout Mexico, ritual sponsorships extend at the popular level far beyond those of any other Catholic country. Occasions for sponsorship include a boy's first haircut, a girl's ear piercing, graduation from primary and secondary school, the initial occupancy of a house, and the founding of a store, among numerous others. As Foster points out (ibid.), "Baptism produces the most important *compadrazgo* relationship. When a child is born, the parents seek godparents (*padrinos*), who hold the infant as the priest baptizes it and who are its spiritual sponsors before God. Lifelong ritual relationships between the child, its parents, and the godparents result. . . . "

For working class families in Mexico, the ties established by the *compadrazgo* are more important than any outside the immediate family. Moreover, as Manuel Carlos (1973) and Robert Van Kemper (1982) have shown, although *compadrazgo* ties in urban Mexico might lose some of their formality among middle and upper classes, the *compadrazgo* continues to thrive in the city context. Surveying the available literature, Kemper has shown that, within cities, "the formal aspects of the *compadrazgo* are preserved best among neighbors within the working class" (Kemper 1982:24), that is, among people exactly like those of Moral Support. Sponsorship among the Mexican working class automatically formalizes relations between godparent and godchild, as well as parents and godparents. These relations bear special rights and obligations; they also entail particular modes of address and behavior. As a folk elaboration of official Church principles, the *compadrazgo* establishes a particularly close relationship between the parents and godparents of a child. These relations at the popular level often rival and even exceed in closeness those between godparent and godchild.

Coincidentally, sponsorship is also an integral feature of the worldwide Alcoholics Anonymous movement. As with the majority of religious sponsorships in Mexico, A.A. sponsorship occupies an ambiguous, semi-formal status of uncertain origin. Consider the words of an official A.A. pamphlet (1989), explaining *apadrinamiento*, the Spanish word for both "sponsorship" and "godparenthood." The pamphlet opens with an account of the founding of Alcoholics Anonymous. Bill W.'s initial encounter with Dr. Bob in Akron is interpreted as the first A.A. sponsorship. The sponsor-sponsee relationship existed, claims the anonymous author of the pamphlet, even though the term sponsor (*padrino*) did not exist in the context of A.A. at the time. (Indeed, A.A. itself did not even exist.) The author then proceeds to disclaim sponsorship as a requirement of A.A.: "To whomever has the desire to stop drinking we extend a welcome if they unite with us!" (ibid.:3).

There are other stories about how the institution of sponsorship came into being. According to Mäkelä and associates (1996:166), "The designation comes from the early days of A.A., when members sponsored newcomers into a hospital for detoxification, vouching that the bill would be paid. The sponsor would visit the person during treatment and upon release take him or her to a meeting." I know of no documentation to support this account, which is reminiscent of an urban legend. Whatever the actual origin of the institution, Mäkelä and associates (ibid.:120) feel confident in stating, on the basis of data from eight different societies, that the sponsor-sponsee relationship is "a crucially important part of AA." They caution, however, that "the idea of sponsorship is not part of the official program" and that "the form and content of the relationship are communicated mainly in the oral tradition" (ibid.:121).

Table 1, based on membership surveys and reproduced from Mäkelä's study (ibid.:167), demonstrates cross-cultural differences in the pervasiveness of A.A. sponsorship.

TABLE ONE. Percentage of A.A. Members Experiencing Sponsorship

	Iceland	Mexico	Poland	Sweden	German-speaking Switzerland	California
			All members			
Has a sponsor now	57	78	25	35	31	72
Has ever had a sponsor	62	84	27	47	49	87
		All members with at least one year of sobriety				
Has a sponsor now	61	83	26	43	35	74
Has ever had a sponsor	69	90	39	57	63	92

Question wordings:
Have you ever had a sponsor?
1 No
2 Yes
Do you now have an AA sponsor or sponsors?
1 No
2 Yes

Source: Mäkelä et al. 1996: 167. Reproduced by permission.

Of the six societies represented, Mexico stands out overall as the country with the greatest predilection for sponsorship. In Mexico, 84 percent of the respondents have had a sponsor at one time or another; 90 percent of Mexicans surveyed with at least one year of sobriety have had a sponsor. Among the societies represented in the table, California's figures are almost as impressive, although they are probably affected by the high proportion of Hispanics in the state.

It seems likely that the prevalence of A.A. sponsorship in Mexico, and possibly in California as well, is a byproduct of religious sponsorship in this part of the world. At the very least, we can declare with confidence that A.A. sponsorship is fully consonant with Mexican social structural principles. The very term *padrino*, simultaneously meaning "godparent" and "sponsor," encapsulates the overlapping of popular religion and A.A. social organization in Mexico. It is safe to surmise that the institution of sponsorship in A.A. made acceptance of A.A. easier in Mexico than it otherwise might have been.

In Moral Support, sponsorship is an automatic byproduct of introducing someone new to the group. (I know of no instance in which a new member arrived on his own and subsequently sought a sponsor.) The newcomer, known in Spanish as the *ahijado*, or godchild, is the sponsee; the established group member becomes his *padrino*, or godfather. As in the case of religious godparenthood, to serve as *padrino* in A.A. is prestigious and honorable. And yet, as in the religious realm, there seems to be a wide degree of behavioral flexibility in playing the roles of A.A. godparent and godchild. In this respect, the situation in Mexico replicates that elsewhere. Based on extensive cross-cultural evidence, Mäkelä and associates (1996:166) observe that "The personal style of individual sponsors varies widely. In some cases sponsorship becomes intense, and the sponsor may spend hours and nights with his sponsee struggling with the problems of early sobriety or later crises." In Moral Support sponsor-sponsee relations display nothing like this degree of intensity. However, as with religious godparenthood, the men of Moral Support view A.A. sponsorship at the very least as a potentially valuable resource in their struggle to achieve and maintain sobriety.

A.A. sponsorship, like its religious counterpart, involves a number of formal obligations. The *padrino* should provide emotional assistance to the godchild and instruct and guide him in ideological and moral precepts of the organization. Although the men of Moral Support repeatedly articulate this obligation, they rarely put it into practice. Advice to newcomers, as we shall later discover, tends to be dispensed in public, through the delivery of personal stories, rather than in the form of private conversations. There are exceptions, however. Emilio speaks warmly of his *padrino*, a physician who introduced him to A.A., but whom he now rarely sees. After four years in A.A., Emilio received the *padrino*'s counsel that it was time for him to "take up service," that is, to spend a half year term of office preparing coffee and tea and cleaning up before and after meetings. Emilio proudly states that he followed the suggestion, even though the job was time-consuming and placed upon him a heavy burden of responsibility. As my own *padrino*, Emilio constantly offered advice and guidance. In fact, it was his performance of this official role that in part enabled me to learn about the group quickly and effortlessly.

Of course, Emilio's performance as *padrino* was more than purely altruistic. Sponsoring an apparently rich, powerful *gringo* like myself must have also accorded him prestige. There is evidence that in Latin America, where patron-client relations are salient (Roniger 1990), people choose A.A. sponsors to achieve goals other than staying sober. Jarrad (1997: 227) tells of a Canadian woman, living in Brazil for over two decades and attending A.A. meetings regularly. She states that "For some time it seemed to be rather fashionable to choose me as a sponsor. People I didn't even know in AA would come up and ask me. They're mostly men. Well, let's say I'm a little tough on my sponsees . . . like somebody comes to tell me something I know is an absolute lie. I say, 'Why come to tell me lies? I didn't ask you anything. If you're going to tell me something, tell me the truth: it really doesn't make any difference to me.' Most of them leave" (Quoted in ibid.).

In addition to dispensing advice and providing emotional support, there exist material obligations on the part of A.A. godparents and godchildren. As in the religious realm, the A.A. godparent must provide a gift to the godchild. With baptismal sponsorship, for example, the godparents usually pay for the baptism and buy the child a gift. Gifts to the godchild and/or financial backing for formal rites and celebratory meals are, in fact, usual for all sponsorships in Mexico. In Moral Support, the *padrino* is obligated to pay for a cake, which is shared among all group members on the occasion of the godchild's completion of one year of sobriety.[5] As in religious godparenthood, as well, A.A. godparents and godchildren employ special terms of reference and address. In Moral Support, A.A. sponsees tend to call their sponsors *padrino*, although it is less common for a sponsor to call his sponsee *ahijado*. I have often heard members of Moral Support bid goodbye to sponsors by saying, "*¡Muchas veinticuatro horas, padrino!*"—"[May you have] Many twenty-four hours, *padrino!*" Emilio claims that even though fifteen years have passed since his *padrino* introduced him to Alcoholics Anonymous, "Whenever I see him I say '*padrino,*' we say hello and we embrace. . . . "

To explain, Emilio tried to replicate a conversation that might occur when he encounters his *padrino* unexpectedly: "*Ahijado, ahijado,* how are you?" "*Padrino,* fine, thank God." "You're still going to your group?" "Well, of course. It's thanks to the group that I'm fine, and not just me, but those around me today, my family, my kids. . . . I am grateful to you." Emilio openly expressed the affection and esteem he holds for his sponsor. He referred specifically to the sponsor's success in fulfilling the twelfth Tradition, to *"llevar el mensaje"*—literally, 'to carry the message,' that is, to proselytize. "And of course he's a person who has passed the message on to many others," continued Emilio. "He's brought them to the A.A. group. And thanks to that man there are many homes in which there is happiness. There is happiness because he has known how to make it work." In recounting this imaginary scenario, Emilio probably portrayed a romanticized version of his relationship with the *padrino* whom he hardly sees, despite living nearby. As my sponsor, he is obliged to teach me how godchildren should feel about sponsors and act toward them. Mäkelä and associates state (1996:166) that "Sponsors serve as role models. . . . " Emilio in this encounter was doing just that: instructing me through narration and example.

In Moral Support, as in Alcoholics Anonymous generally, there exists no formal equivalent of the *compadrazgo*, a term which refers specifically to the special bond between a child's parent and godparent. And yet a terminological parallel exists. In the religious realm, when a child's parents and godparents become *compadres* to one another, they immediately begin addressing one another as *"compadre."* In speaking of this person to others, they also refer to him as *"Mi compadre Fulano,"* or simply, if context allows, as *"Mi compadre."* Often, in popular speech, the contraction *"compa"* is substituted, especially as a term of address.

By virtue of common membership is Alcoholics Anonymous, the men do not consider themselves to be *compadres.* However, they are *compañeros* and regularly address one another by this term. Coincidentally, the contraction for *compañero* is identical to that for *compadre*: *compa.* In fact, *compa* is employed much more frequently than *compañero,* as a term of reference and address. Indeed, the men of Moral Support maintain a relationship with one another not very different from that between *compadres.* The relationship is voluntary and contracted solely at the will of the participants. Similarly, the relationship automatically establishes between the contractants a set of rights and obligations. To be someone's *compa* within the context of A.A. is fundamentally equivalent to being his *compa* in the religious realm, and linguistic terminology reflects this similarity.

There is an additional way in which A.A. replicates popular Catholicism in Mexico: the occurrence of periodic fiestas. There are, in fact, two kinds of A.A. fiestas, which parallel Catholic celebrations. First is the life cycle rite, marking the individual's passage through critical developmental stages. Important life cycle rites in Catholicism include baptism, confirmation, first communion, marriage, and extreme unction. The

A.A. equivalent is the anniversary of a member's sobriety. In Moral Support, members refer to the first A.A. group they ever attended (for some men, Moral Support itself, for others, a different group) as "*El grupo en que nací*"—The group into which I was born. Recovering alcoholics look back on their first meeting as a kind of rebirth, as being born again. Each year thereafter, they celebrate the anniversary of their sobriety, calculating the precise date from the day that they first attended an A.A. meeting. An anniversary can only be celebrated legitimately if the individual has had no relapse. In case of relapse—which to any member of A.A. means imbibing even a single drop of alcohol—the date has to be recalculated according to the drinker's initial Alcoholics Anonymous meeting subsequent to the drink.

A second kind of fiesta, comparable to calendrical community celebrations in popular Catholicism, is the anniversary of the particular A.A. group's founding. The group anniversary is usually celebrated on a Sunday, when most people can attend, but on a date as close as possible to the actual group founding. Both types of fiestas—birthday celebrations and the group anniversary—follow the same sequence of activities. They begin with a formal A.A. meeting, open to attendance by the family and friends of Moral Support members. The meeting is followed by music, food, and dancing. The main difference between calendrical and life cycle celebrations is how they are financed. The individual birthday is the financial responsibility of the celebrant and his family, who are supposed to provide food and entertainment for all the members and their guests. In Moral Support, some eligible men go for years without celebrating their anniversary, for lack of money or a family support system to help with food preparations. By contrast, the group anniversary is financed through a general collection from all the men. Tasks related to putting on the party are assigned to volunteers, mostly including the wives, daughters, and other female relatives of members.

There is, then, a striking parallel between A.A. and popular Mexican Catholicism. In both domains, there exist life cycle and calendrical celebrations. At Moral Support, the men strive in these fiestas to replicate the usual merriment of Catholic celebrations. However, the complete absence of alcoholic beverages, among other things (see Chapter Five), alters the tone of the proceedings markedly. As anyone who has been to a Mexican fiesta can attest, alcoholic beverages are essential to the formal exchanges that occur during fiestas as well as to the partying that follows.[6] As early as the turn of the century in Mexico, pro-temperance scientists lamented the drunkenness that routinely accompanied "dances and gatherings," "banquets and cocktail parties," and "weddings" (Ponce 1911:202–203). And yet, even without alcohol, the fiestas I attended at Moral Support show off the courage and resilience of men who are determined to live normal lives while taking what, in the Mexican context, is the drastic step of abstaining.

Fiestas are not the only aspect of Moral Support that mimics popular Catholicism. The sponsorship system, Christian imagery in speech and text, and spatial arrangement of the meeting room all work jointly to produce a familiar cultural milieu. To join A.A. in working class Mexico City does not mean abandoning one's religious tradition. It means adapting it to the circumstances at hand. This is why we should not be surprised that, despite its Protestant origins, A.A. has been highly successful throughout Latin America.

Kenneth Davis points out (1994:23) that Spanish was the first non-English language into which Alcoholics Anonymous literature was translated.[7] The first Spanish speaker joined A.A. in 1940 and soon thereafter made a translation of the Big Book. And surveys show that an overwhelming majority of Mexicans and Mexican Americans place their trust in Alcoholics Anonymous as a solution to drinking problems (ibid.). The analysis of religious adaptation as it occurs in Moral Support goes a long way to explain why.

3. MEETING AND MOVING

Alcoholics Anonymous is an acephalous organization which reaches its maximum expression in the context of its meetings. According to one standard definition, A.A. meetings are "relatively formal, quasi-ritualized therapeutic sessions run by and for any alcoholics in the community who wish to attend them" (Leach et al., 1969:509). Whether in Mexico or elsewhere, the meeting is the social and restorative foundation of Alcoholics Anonymous. The meeting allows members to unite on a regular, predictable basis for the express purpose of achieving and maintaining sobriety. According to A.A. precepts, sobriety is impossible to attain without meetings. Ideally, they become a fully integrated feature of daily life for the recovering alcoholic.

Behavior during meetings is, at least in theory, paradigmatic of the members' approach toward life in general. According to A.A. ideology, the alcoholic is someone who has lost a sense of routine, failed in obligations to self and others, and been overwhelmed by a loss of control. Within the context of the meeting, the alcoholic substitutes predictability for chaos, duty for irresponsibility. Meetings occur at regular intervals. The attendance, punctuality, participation, and financial contribution of A.A. members are held as symptomatic of unwavering sobriety and a positive attitude toward life. Members who attend meetings sporadically, display chronic tardiness, become distracted while others speak, and donate money reluctantly are perceived to be at risk. Unreliable conduct is, by A.A. standards, characteristic not of the recuperating alcoholic, but rather of the active alcoholic, whose egotistical behavior and casualness in fulfilling obligations demonstrate their remoteness from recovery. In contrast, responsible conduct during meetings demonstrates control over one's life and offers a reasonably good prognosis for sustained sobriety.

Alcoholics Anonymous promotes strong bonds among group members. To anthropologist William Madsen, Alcoholics Anonymous is a familiar social institution, a voluntary association. "Birds of a feather do indeed flock together," says Madsen (1974:155). "A.A. represents a bonding of alcoholics for the same basic reason that stamp collectors enjoy other philatelists and that physicians belong to the A.M.A. The main difference is that the bonds of A.A., which are forged in a common history of suffering and alienation, are far stronger than those between Rotarians or labor union members." Joseph Kessel states that the A.A. members he came to know "all had one thing in common: a stronger link bound them than social environment, nationality, family or even love. . . . they were united by a bond of fellowship, they were brothers till death, just because they had all suffered from the same devouring disease" (Kessel 1961:4). These authors draw our attention to emotional ties among A.A. affiliates, which are based on a biomedical condition which they are presumed to share. (In Chapter Seven we consider the disease model of alcoholism.) Whether in the United States, Mexico, or elsewhere, the Alcoholics Anonymous meeting provides the spatial and behavioral context within which these feelings are established and perpetuated. Alcoholics Anonymous is greater in scope than the meeting; but without the meeting it fails to exist.

In Mexico City, the centrality of the Alcoholics Anonymous meeting is reflected in linguistic usage: colloquially, the meeting is virtually synonymous with the group. Members are as likely to ask, "Are you going to the group (el grupo) tonight?" as they are to say, "Are you going to the meeting (la junta)?" To be sure, the men in Moral Support express a keen sense of identification with Alcoholics Anonymous members everywhere. Whenever I would leave Mexico City temporarily, one or the other would remind me that I could find a group (that is, a meeting) wherever my travels might take me. But, despite this identification with a worldwide movement, the men's primary bond is with their own group, Moral Support. Meetings, as we see in the following chapter, provide the medium of socialization into Alcoholics Anonymous. Meetings are also, as Chapter Six demonstrates, the avenue through which social control is exercised. A.A. members are often unaware of their responsiveness to a variety of informal but extremely effective controlling mechanisms. Nonetheless, it is these mechanisms that hold the meeting together during inevitable times of crisis, just as they have the capacity to rip meetings apart.

William Madsen, referring specifically to the United States context, understands Alcoholics Anonymous in terms of two different but related social scientific concepts. The first is that of minority movement, a banding together of people who have suffered discrimination and abuse not unlike that experienced by ethnic minorities. "With a shared history of socially administered abuse," Madsen says (1974:158), "alcoholics in A.A. have banded together to seek to improve their condition and to educate the public. As a part of their group movement they produced the philosophy that no one can understand an alcoholic but another alcoholic." He states further that Alcoholics Anonymous, like all minority movements, "has created an integrated set of core values that all good members must accept without reservation. The shared deprivations of the past and the commonly held values of the group combine to give A.A.'s a sense of togetherness which is accentuated by their sense of apartness from the rest of society" (ibid.).

This sense of apartness leads Madsen to a second social scientific model, that of folk culture. He invokes Alfred Kroeber's famous definition of peasants as constituting "part-societies with part-cultures" (Kroeber 1948:284) to describe A.A.'s status as a subculture. Although Madsen's analogy between Alcoholics Anonymous and peasantry comes across today as antiquated and theoretically forced, the analysis points to an important conclusion: in A.A., as among peasants, there exists an intensity of social interaction over time which produces localized subcultural diversity. In fact, as more recent research has shown (e.g., McCrady and Miller 1993, Mäkelä et al. 1996), Alcoholics Anonymous is not one undifferentiated entity. It is rather a loose affiliation among groups of quite distinctive character. A pointed attempt to analyze group distinctiveness emerges in the work of Tonigan, Ashcroft, and Miller (1995), who measure A.A. group cohesiveness as a function of the degree to which meetings are structured around the famous Twelve Steps, which constitute one of the main ideological underpinnings of A.A. therapy (see Appendix A; Alcoholics Anonymous 1952). Groups that rely on the Twelve Steps, state the authors, tend to be more cohesive than those that do not. Their general conclusion is that "AA groups should not be regarded as homogeneous. . . . "; the authors "caution against 'omnibus' profiles of AA affiliation and outcomes" (Tonigan, Ashcroft, and Miller 1995:620).

A key to understanding intra-cultural variation within A.A. is Kurtz's (1979) distinction between the A.A. program, on the one hand, and the A.A. fellowship, on the other. The program, he says, constitutes the official ideology of the worldwide Alcoholics Anonymous movement. The program is codified in Alcoholics Anonymous literature, particularly the so-called "Big Book" (Alcoholics Anonymous 1976) and the *Twelve Steps and Twelve Traditions* (Alcoholics Anonymous 1952). The fellowship, by contrast, is the ideology put into action; it is the everyday elaboration within groups of A.A. precepts, as set out in the literature.[1] Without the Alcoholics Anonymous program, in Kurtz's sense, there would be no worldwide movement. The common ideology, as codified in key literature, is what gives Alcoholics Anonymous its distinctive identity and unified presence in the world. But the program might or might not have much to do with what occurs everyday, on the ground, in what he calls the fellowship. The fellowship is manifest above all in A.A. meetings. It is the fellowship, that is, the meeting, which produces and promotes variation among groups.

The A.A. program is played out exclusively in the context of local groups. This is why the group, and its periodic meetings, provides a valid social and cultural unit of analysis. The meeting is where face-to-face interaction occurs among A.A. members. This interaction over time produces feelings of mutual identification. The Big Book provides an apt, if romanticized, description of these feelings. In the words of one recuperating American alcoholic: "We [of my group] are people who normally would not mix. But there exists among us a fellowship, a friendliness, and an understanding which is indescribably wonderful. . . . The feeling of having shared in a common peril is one element in the powerful cement which binds us. But that in itself would never have held us together as we are now joined. The tremendous fact for every one of us is that we have discovered a common solution" (Alcoholics Anonymous 1976:17).

The existence of fellowship, in Kurtz's terms, means that each meeting develops a distinctive character, a procedural style which is a product of multitudinous collective and individual decisions. Each A.A. group is therefore a unique entity endowed with distinctive social and cultural attributes. Some of these attributes, however, derive from explicit imitation of a parent group. For example, members of Moral Support are aware that they are a carbon copy of Promise of Recovery. Promise of Recovery is the "mother group," as some of the members call it, in that it gave rise to Moral Support. Through a process that we examine in later chapters, groups in Mexico City undergo a process of fission and, less commonly, fusion. Promise of Recovery is known as particularly fertile in that it has spawned a variety of groups, including Moral Support. Although related groups vary in number from one historical moment to another, they all share a given *autonomía*. The social dynamics that prevail in each group, however, depend on individual members and the complex ways in which they relate to their *compañeros* [co-group members].

Group identity is codified in group names, which are selected by a vote of the membership whenever a new group is formed. Groups frequently name themselves after admired leaders in the A.A. units from which they derive. Grupo Jaime Víctor in Mexico City is one such case. When several men broke away from a home group, Promise of Recovery, they named the new group, not after one of their own, but for the founders of Promise of Recovery. The naming of other groups in Mexico City—Grupo Tío Dick [Group Uncle Dick], Grupo Sergio Berumen Torres, and Grupo Jack Alexander—follows a similar principle. Names are also given for the neighborhood in which the meeting takes place, as in Grupo Portales, Grupo Pedregal del Sur, Grupo San Pedrito, Grupo Candelaria, and Grupo Puerta del Rosal. One group in the small town of Tzintzuntzan, Michoacán, calls itself Grupo Colibrí, or Hummingbird Group. Since Tzintzuntzan, in Purépecha, means Place of the Hummingbirds, the name Grupo Colibrí in effect establishes a connection between this A.A. group and the village in which it meets. Group names sometimes reaffirm ideal values, aspirations, and personal qualities fostered by the Alcoholics Anonymous movement. Typical examples are Grupo Amor y Sabiduría [Love and Wisdom], Grupo Nueva Vida [New Life], Grupo Volver a Vivir [Return to Life], Grupo Realización [Fulfillment], Grupo Primero es lo Primero [First Things First], Grupo Nueva Ilusión [New Hope], and so on. The pseudonym Moral Support fits within this well-established category and would seem appropriate anywhere in Mexico, including Mexico City.

Ethnographic analysis, focused on a single group, can provide a vision of the A.A. meeting as a rich and complex universe, in which group members exert a profound influence upon one another. The meeting demonstrates its power over the members only when experienced over a reasonably long period of time. By carrying out fieldwork with members of a group for a year or more, the social impact, sub-cultural character, and therapeutic value of A.A. meetings can be appreciated and evaluated. Long-term fieldwork provides an opportunity, not for that elusive objectivity that many social scientists seek, but rather for anthropological observations free of romanticized images which pervade much of the available literature concerning A.A.

In Mexico, the Alcoholics Anonymous meeting is called a *junta,* from the Spanish verb *juntar,* "to assemble, to congregate." The *junta* is governed by a set of rules or guiding principles, which vary from group to group. It is these rules, both explicit and implicit, that are a major source of what we might call subcultural variation within the Alcoholics

Anonymous movement as a whole. Members of Moral Support—the name I give to the group I studied—refer to the totality of these rules as *autonomía,* literally autonomy. The derivation of this usage comes from a prevailing circumstance within Mexican A.A. groups: many of them are virtually autonomous of any central organization, even A.A. centers in Mexico City, not to mention those in other countries. *Autonomía*— which, in standard Spanish, is a semantically awkward term in this context—refers to the application of autonomous rules of governance within the A.A. meeting. Moral Support members cherish their autonomy in both senses of the word. That is, they value the particular ensemble of rules that gives their meeting a special character as well as the independent organizational status that allows them to apply these rules and change them should they so desire.

Whenever debates about rules arise, members of Moral Support state, in a tone of voice that simultaneously reveals matter-of-factness and defiance, that their group is *"fuera de serie"*—literally, "outside of series" —that is, non-mainstream. Moral Support is different from most groups in its prohibition of smoking. Members also believe that their minimal reliance on *"literatura,"* that is, on the Twelve Steps and Twelve Traditions, sets them apart. However, many groups in Mexico City are similar to Moral Support in this respect and Moral Support is therefore less unique, less *fuera de serie,* than its members believe it to be. In fact, as Tonigan, Ashcroft, and Miller (1995) demonstrate, muted emphasis on written doctrine is a major force within the Alcoholics Anonymous movement as a whole, a force that extends across international boundaries.

When I first visited Moral Support, I was struck most by formal rules and procedures, which amount to a blueprint for what Moore and Myerhoff (1977) would call "secular ritual." Moral Support holds three weekly meetings, on Tuesday, Thursday, and Saturday evenings. Meetings last an hour and a half, beginning at eight o'clock and ending at nine thirty. This schedule, implemented years ago on the basis of standard time, which had always prevailed in Mexico, was shaken in 1995 by an unanticipated innovation: the sudden introduction of daylight savings time. Possibly in response to emergence of the North American Free Trade Association (NAFTA, known in Mexico as the TLC, or Tratado de Libre Comercio), Mexico adopted daylight savings time. This measure proved disconcerting to many Mexicans, particularly working class Mexicans, who wondered how you could simply declare an hour of the day to be something that it obviously was not.

In Moral Support, where members are perpetually worried about attendance and fluctuating group size, there was concern about how daylight savings time would affect the very existence of the group. Like many working class people in Mexico City, a number of Moral Support group members remain on the job until nightfall. With daylight now lasting past eight o'clock, the hour that Moral Support meetings begin, there was fear that the men would fail to return from work in time for meetings. Members briefly considered the possibility of starting the meeting later than eight o'clock, a measure that was never adopted. My impression is that daylight savings time reduced punctuality, but probably did not affect overall attendance.

Although Moral Support meetings formally begin at eight o'clock, a few men are always there before that hour. Among these is the secretary (*secretario*), one of the two group officers. (The other is the treasurer [*tesorero*], briefly discussed later.) The secretary at least in theory serves a six-month term. He arrives earlier and leaves later than the rest of the men, because he is the bearer of the keys to the meeting room. He unlocks the door, straightens the chairs and cleans up at the meeting's end. His duties are essentially housekeeping activities: sweeping, dusting, mopping, replacing furniture, cleaning the toilet, preparing and serving coffee and tea, washing and drying mugs, and the like. Even before the men arrive the secretary fills the electric urn with water in preparation for coffee and tea.[2] Typically, while the water is heating, several additional men appear. They chat until eight, when the meeting begins, regardless of attendance.

One of the early arrivers volunteers as *coordinador*, that is, meeting moderator. The role of moderator rotates among the men on an informal basis, such that the same individual never serves during two consecutive meetings. A man who wishes to coordinate the meeting on any given day arrives before most of the others and seats himself at the desk in front of the room. This action constitutes tacit occupancy of the moderator role for the evening. Some men are reticent to take initiative and prefer to wait for encouragement before occupying the desk. One *compañero* will issue a cheerful invitation to another, "Go ahead, *compañero* Moisés, sit yourself down and moderate!" The men rarely reject a generous, open invitation of this kind.

The moderator's sturdy wooden desk is situated at the front of the meeting room. The desktop is protected by a slab of glass, under which sits a crowded display of saints' images and calling cards from Alcoholics Anonymous groups around the city. Pressed under the glass, too, is a yellowed sheet of onionskin bearing old-fashioned typewriter script of the standard A.A. preamble, which moderators must read at the start of every meeting. On top of the desk there sits a candlestick (for predictable blackouts during the summer rainy season), a small metal bell, and a miniature Mexican flag.

Meetings begin in a formulaic fashion. The moderator, who sits facing the rest of the group, starts by introducing himself (*Buenas noches, compañeros. Soy Fulano y soy un enfermo alcohólico*—"Good evening, compañeros. I'm Fulano [So-and-So] and I'm an alcoholic sick man"). He then asks for a moment of silence to "clear the mind." After a few seconds, the moderator rings the small bell to break the silence, at which point he reads the preamble, an official policy statement issued by Alcoholics Anonymous World Services.

> *Alcohólicos Anónimos es una comunidad de hombres y mujeres que comparten su mutua experiencia, fortaleza y esperanza para resolver su problema común y ayudar a otros recuperarse del alcoholismo. El único requisito para ser miembro de A.A. es el deseo de dejar la bebida. Para ser miembro de A.A. no se pagan honorarios ni cuotas; nos mantenemos con nuestras propias contribuciones. A.A. no está afiliada a ninguna secta, religión, partido político, organización o institución alguna; no desea intervenir en controversias; no respalda ni se opone a ninguna causa. Nuestro objetivo primordial es mantenernos sobrios y ayudar a otros alcohólicos a alcanzar el estado de sobriedad.*

> Alcoholics Anonymous is a community of men and women who share their mutual experience, strength and hope to resolve their common problem and help others to recover from alcoholism. The only requirement for being a member of A.A. is the desire to give up drink. To be a member of A.A. neither honorariums nor fees are paid; we maintain ourselves through our own donations. A.A. is not affiliated with any sect, religion, political party, organization or institution whatsoever; it does not wish to enter into controversies; it neither backs nor opposes any cause. Our primary objective is to stay sober and help other alcoholics achieve a state of sobriety. (author's translation)

This preamble provides an organizational and ethical framework for the men in Moral Support. The men often refer to it in their public addresses. This strategy emerges particularly when disagreements arise within the group. The men on these occasions appeal to doctrinal evidence—in effect, to *la literatura*—to support personal points of view.

After reciting the preamble, the moderator reads aloud from an Alcoholics Anonymous volume entitled *Pensamiento del Día* (Anonymous 1995), or *Thought of the Day*. The book is organized chronologically, one page and one thought for each day of the year. Moderators select the evening's reading according to the date of the meeting, rather than for the airing of any particular theme. Each page contains, first, the thought for the day, second, a "meditation" on that thought, and, finally, a prayer deriving from the thought. Thoughts vary considerably, although a spiritual tone pervades them all. There are repeated warnings about the dangers of taking even a single drink, declarations of the personal changes wrought through association with A.A., expressions of faith in God and Alcoholics Anonymous, rejections of egotistical attitudes, reminders of the importance of contributing one's service to A.A., recollections of the horrors of alcoholism, and related topics. At Moral Support meetings, moderators read the entire page twice. Theoretically, the thought of the day provides a possible theme to be developed throughout the meeting, although only rarely does anyone return to it. The entire presentation by the moderator lasts perhaps ten minutes. Occasionally, a moderator will start the reading slightly prior to eight o'clock to assure that as much time as possible is preserved for public addresses, which constitute the heart of the meeting.

These addresses in Mexican Spanish are called *historiales*, that is, personal stories. According to the prevailing ideology among members of Moral Support, *historiales* are the equivalent of therapy. Delivering and listening to personal stories are what gives each individual the strength to stop drinking and remain sober. Anyone familiar with Alcoholics Anonymous knows that the manner in which personal stories are incorporated into meetings varies enormously from group to group. In Moral Support, stories are supposed to last exactly fifteen minutes. A clock hanging on the wall of the meeting room chimes at the passing of each quarter hour, to indicate that it is time for one speaker to step down and another to begin. Perhaps the most important duty of the moderator is to call the men one by one to the *tribuna,* or podium, at the front of the room to deliver a personal story. "*Compañero* Marcos," he says, "Please step up to the *tribuna.*" Or, in the case of the first speaker of the evening, "*Compañero* Gilberto, would you do us the favor of opening the *junta?*"

To deliver a personal story is to *subir a tribuna,* "to step up to the podium." The podium, a central feature of the meeting room, is actually elevated a step above floor level; in the literal sense, therefore, a speaker rises to address the others present. But the expression *subir a tribuna* also has a metaphoric connotation, that of becoming elevated morally and spiritually. While standing at the podium, the speaker assumes an aura of importance, which automatically accords him certain courtesies. He is supposed to be the undisputed center of attention. All eyes are on him, everyone focused on his personal story. There should be no distractions from what he is saying. This is his therapy. Any disruption threatens his sobriety.

In return, the speaker must deliver to the group an *historial* with particular qualities, most importantly details of his daily life and thoughts, conveyed directly and honestly. Each *historial* is a public performance open to evaluation. In fact, both audience and speaker occupy performatory roles.[3] The personal story provides everyone present the opportunity to behave in an appropriate manner. The men constantly scrutinize one another for evidence of propriety. Conformity to certain standards defines whether one is an upstanding or imperfect member of Moral Support. This evaluative process weighs heavily on all the men. As becomes evident later in the book, it eventually drives some of them away.

The moderator is also on display and subject to a variety of implicit and explicit rules. Because each personal story lasts only fifteen minutes, there is only room in the hour and a half session for six speakers. With only six or seven men present, this limitation causes no problem. Everyone can have a turn. However, when eight or more members attend, as is usual, the moderator must make some hard choices. For this purpose he consults the group log, a sort of desk calendar, always stored in the moderator's desk and completed daily by the moderator during each meeting. The log, an A.A. publication, is printed with space to list the date of the meeting, name of the moderator, number of members present, theme of the meeting, and list of speakers. Only the theme of the meeting is left blank, since group procedures stipulate flexibility in this regard, rather than adherence to the "literature." Moderators who feel a need to fill in this item occasionally inscribe *"libre"* [free] as the theme, which is indeed the only accurate description.

As they select the evening's speakers, moderators strive within limits to provide equal opportunity. Speakers ideally should rotate in such a way that everyone rises to the podium with more or less the same frequency. The moderator consults the log to determine who has delivered *historiales* during recent meetings and who has not. His selection of speakers, however, is complicated by principles that compete with that of equal rotation. For example, of the six time slots, the first and last are considered key to the overall tone and success of the meeting. Hence, the few members who display consistently fine oratorical skills and deliver upbeat messages tend to be tapped repeatedly to start and end the sessions.

Moderators are evaluated as much for their selection of appropriate speakers in these important time slots as for their ability to provide fair rotation. Further, they should ideally avoid calling on members who arrive late or attend meetings sporadically. Punctuality and good attendance are correspondingly rewarded with increased opportunities to address the group. Chronic latecomers and those with an inconsistent attendance record should spend at least several sessions sitting quietly in their chairs, listening to others. The relative success or failure of meetings depends largely on wise speaker coordination. Moderators are thus under constant pressure to select speakers in conformity with tacit principles of rotation. If a coordinator seems to apply personal favoritism in the selection of an evening's speakers, he is subject to criticism. Since the principles of speaker selection sometimes conflict with one another, moderators seldom satisfy everyone in the group.

The group secretary, too, comes under collective scrutiny. He must serve coffee and tea in as unobtrusive a manner as possible. When the meeting is already underway, the secretary uses discrete eye and hand motions to catch the attention of each *compañero* and determine if he wants tea or coffee.[4] An A.A. meeting without the availability of coffee and tea is inconceivable and virtually every man who attends can be counted to partake of these beverages. The men respond to the secretary's inquiry, not verbally, but by sign language: the two index fingers crossed in the form of a "T" to indicate tea (*té*), or the index finger and thumb of one hand curved like a half moon "C" to signal coffee (*café*). The secretary should collect and wash the cups at the end of the meeting, after all the speakers have had their say. Much as everyone understands that secretaries are anxious to leave the meeting at the same time as their *compañeros,* those who clean while the meeting is still in progress are criticized for rudeness and disruptive behavior.

Just as meetings invariably start promptly at 8 P.M.—or occasionally even a little earlier—they end precisely at nine thirty, at which time the moderator declares the meeting over. In a procedure reminiscent of the collection of donations at church, he removes a small wooden tray from inside the desk and places it on the desktop for the deposit of donations, called *la séptima*. At the same time he usually issues a reminder, extracted from the A.A. preamble, which states, *"nos mantenemos con nuestras propias contribuciones"*—we maintain ourselves through our own donations. The moderator drops a coin or two in the tray and the rest of the members do the same. The group treasurer collects the money from the tray and uses it to pay for rent, electricity, and refreshments.

The *séptima* collected, a closing ceremony takes place. This involves the recitation of the *"Yo soy responsable"* [I am responsible], a declaration of the proselytizing mission of Alcoholics Anonymous (see Chapter Two). At the conclusion of this prayer, most of the men cross themselves, as they would at Mass. The men at this point become markedly more relaxed. Big smiles come across their faces as they shake hands. The meeting thus concludes, as they break into small groups for gossip, informal commentary, and advice based on the personal stories recounted that evening.

Despite the generic title Alcohólicos *Anónimos*, anonymity is not normally a feature of most working class groups in Mexico City. For one thing, the group location is evident, since each group announces its existence by displaying the A.A. logo within clear view of pedestrians. The logo, consisting of the double A surrounded by a circle, draws the viewer's eyes to important additional information: the name of the group and the hours when it meets. Because of A.A.'s proselytizing mission, groups feel obligated to spread the message (*"llevar el mensaje"*), as stipulated in Tradition Number Twelve (see Appendix B). The logo should ideally be hung in a place where it attracts maximum attention, particularly from *alcóholicos activos,* or active alcoholics—a category that contrasts ideologically with the A.A. members, who think of themselves as *alcohólicos en recuperación,* or recovering alcoholics.

A second feature that destroys the possibility of complete anonymity is the neighborhood character of groups. As indicated previously, Mexico City is in many ways a massive conglomeration of small villages. Especially in working class districts, buildings are low, usually no more than two or three stories high, often housing small stores, barbershops, restaurants, and shoe repair establishments on street level. People of a single neighborhood tend to know one another, to the same degree that residents of a single village know one another. Recent migrants quickly become integrated into the social fabric. The kind of impersonal life often associated with the industrial city—an image we can trace from ancient times (Caro Baroja 1963) to the twentieth century (Redfield 1947)—is absent throughout most of Mexico City. This situation worked to my advantage. Initially a curiosity in the neighborhood where Moral Support meetings take place, I quickly established myself as a familiar visitor to the scene. Within a few months, merchants and passersby would greet me warmly, even though I had not actually spoken with most of them.

The village-like character of working class neighborhoods in Mexico City means that most social activities, including those of voluntary associations like Alcoholics Anonymous, are carried out in the context of the barrio. Often, recuperating alcoholics live on the very street where their AA meetings take place. Certainly the vast majority of group members reside within a few blocks of the meeting room. Only rarely and under special circumstances do members commute even a few kilometers from home or work to meeting room.

Members of Moral Support conform to this pattern. Over the course of the two years that I was associated with the group, I was one of only two members who commuted. The other commuting member worked close to the meeting room and would attend meetings after work, then take the metro to his home half an hour away. Eventually, he changed jobs and joined a group closer to his new workplace, thereby leaving me as the only member of Moral Support who did not reside within four or five blocks of the meeting room. Four members of Moral Support live on the same block as the meeting room. In fact, as indicated, one member even provided room for the group to meet on his own property. This situation, which lasted about a decade, changed soon after I joined the group.

Because group members share a neighborhood, it is no secret to neighbors who attends meetings and how often. When the group secretary arrives to clean and prepare the room for an evening meeting, he sweeps the adjacent sidewalk. He occasionally brings furniture outside for thorough washing. He uses the street, too, to empty pails of dirty water and to dry the rags that he uses to scrub the bathroom. All the while, neighbors pass by, on their way to or from work or going about their evening chores. They often stop to chat with the secretary and other group members, as these members await the start of the meeting.

One evening, in a typical encounter, I found myself conversing outside the meeting room with the secretary, David, a *compañero* named Eduardo, and a neighbor, who is not a group member. Eduardo, a short man in his mid-thirties, pointed to a small patch of earth surrounding a tall tree right where we stood. "That used to be my bathroom," he said. "When I was drunk, that's where I'd do my necessities." "It's true," confirmed the others, smiling and nodding enthusiastically to confirm the report. We laughed at the irony of this former derelict now belonging to a group that helped to clean the sidewalk. Eduardo made this admission with no sense of embarrassment. To the contrary, he was proud of the difficulties that he had overcome. (None of us suspected then that several months hence he would return to that very tree to relieve himself.)

Ongoing encounters between neighbors and A.A. members assure that everyone on the street knows who drinks heavily; they are also aware of who attends Moral Support meetings and when these members begin to falter. Far from trying to hide their attendance, members are open about these matters. Given the close-knit neighborhood, they could hardly do otherwise. In fact, most A.A. groups in Mexico City meet right at street level, in rented rooms or storefronts. A.A. members believe that it is good to hold meetings close to foot traffic, as a sort of advertisement. They hope to attract active alcoholics into their ranks and expect that the more frequently drunks come into direct contact with the organization, the more likely they are to perceive it as an alternative.

When I first started attending Moral Support, in September 1995, the meeting room consisted of a small cottage situated far below street level, a less than ideal condition from the men's point of view. Only the roof of the cottage was visible from the sidewalk. In addition, the A.A. logo was barely visible to the public. Mounted high above the sidewalk on a wrought iron fence that defined Pedro's property, it had long been obscured by overgrown branches, thereby reducing the possibility of attracting new members. Not even the meeting hours were discernible on the sign. To get to that meeting room entailed entering private property, which any Mexican would be reluctant to do without permission. One would have to pass through the gate to Pedro's house lot, descend a long flight of stairs, and then walk across the patio to the meeting room. All this, to new arrivals, might well feel like trespassing. As at any A.A. meeting, newcomers were always welcome. But the physical layout must have proved inhibiting to potential recruits, particularly alcoholics, most of whom are at first seriously ambivalent about attending A.A.

Only gradually did I become aware that some members of Moral Support were unhappy with the meeting room, and not only because of its inhospitable location. Complaints came to a head on Thursday, October 12, almost precisely a month after I started to attend meetings. Eduardo served as moderator on the day that open disagreement emerged. Thirteen members were present. The meeting had proceeded normally and was drawing to a close. After donations had been collected, Eduardo vacated the moderator's desk so that Pedro, group treasurer and landlord to Moral Support, could count the evening's donations. Pedro sat down at the desk, as always. But, instead of counting the coins, he began fidgeting with them nervously. Suddenly and unexpectedly he announced that he had something to tell the group: he intended to raise their rent from 300 to 400 pesos per month (in 1995 equivalent to a sixteen-dollar increase, from fifty dollars to sixty-six dollars). This unilateral proclamation was met by shocked silence.

I looked around the room. The social abyss between Pedro and the rest of us was accentuated by our spatial rift. Pedro slouched his compact, wiry torso over the desk, at the front of the room. The rest of us were seated or standing at the back, huddled together around the door through which we had intended to exit. Despite his fifty-one years, Pedro's lean physique, gleaming complexion, full head of black hair, and taut, sculpted skin gave him the appearance of someone in his late thirties. As owner of the meeting room, and one of the original members of Moral Support, Pedro normally acted in a protective, nurturing manner. His air of self-assurance and strength derived in part from his status as a retired member of the Mexico City police force. In 1972, while residing just a few blocks from police headquarters in Mexico City's historic center, he became involved in a shoot-out that left many people dead. His superiors told him to flee for his life. That is when he moved to his current neighborhood, where, like the rest of the men in the group, he spent months clearing heavy rocks from the land he squatted on, until he could build on it. Twenty-five years later, at this momentous meeting, Pedro displayed the toughness and assertiveness that he had undoubtedly wielded during his years of police service. He momentarily had become a transformed personality.

The shock of Pedro's announcement slowly subsided. Pedro launched the case in his defense. He reminded everyone that he had not raised the rent at all over the past several years. The rent had gone up fifty pesos two years before, but that increase, too, came after a full two years of fixed payments. He reminded everyone that at the time he last raised the rent, he had told the group that a reassessment would be necessary every two years. Pedro explained that two years had now transpired, in fact had been up for several days already, as of October 9, the twelfth birthday of Moral Support. There was inflation to consider, he said. His electricity bill had increased; property taxes had gone up. He needed some compensation for the extra expenses. He asserted, impatiently and defensively, that the rent increase definitely would not provide him additional income: "This isn't money I can live on!"

In a working class A.A. group like Moral Support, even a tiny rent increase makes a big impact. An augmentation of some thirty percent, such as Pedro was demanding, might prove catastrophic. As the following chapter demonstrates, personal stories are replete with accounts of extreme poverty, persistent unemployment, and daily financial distress. Moral Support, like all Alcoholics Anonymous groups, takes pride in supporting its own operations. But it must do so through member donations; and these, as we shall see, are meager. By far the group's biggest budget item is rent. The proposed increase would place an immediate, perhaps unmanageable economic burden on these cash-poor men. Worse, it might adversely influence the group's ability to recruit new members. Pedro's declaration seemed to place the very existence of the group at risk. As if to emphasize this point, Emilio explained to me the following day that every effort needs to be made to retain "*los nuevos*," the new members. There were three new members, in fact, myself and two young men, who had arrived on the scene within the past half year. "We need to be there for *los nuevos!*" declared Emilio. "We have to *echarles ganas* [encourage them]! This is no time to discourage them!" Emilio's missionary zeal, which would emerge at the slightest opportunity, surfaced with special fervor over the rent issue.

At the decisive October 12 meeting, members openly and vociferously protested Pedro's proposal. Carlos, a portly, middle-aged Zapotec Indian from Oaxaca with a perpetual five o'clock shadow, raised his scratchy voice to remind Pedro that, when Moral Support was first established and in need of a permanent meeting place, he and Roberto had donated their labor to build the meeting room. Was the rent increase their reward? Pedro retorted by pointing out that he charged the group no rent at all for the first full year after the little cottage was built. "Times are bad," observed *compañero* José. "Four hundred pesos is no big deal under most circumstances," he continued, "but times are bad and we never know who will contribute to the *séptima* or how much they'll donate." To this, Pedro retorted with examples of how different groups manage rental payments. "Some require a certain payment, say ten pesos from each *compañero* at each *junta*. Some call for *una séptima extraordinaria* [an extra collection] when the rent isn't covered at the end of the month." Pedro explained that, unbeknownst to members of the group, he himself often compensated for the monthly shortfall by adding fifteen or twenty pesos of his own.

In fact, Pedro had calculated the occasion to his best possible advantage. This happened to be a rare month in which assets exceeded debits. As treasurer of Moral Support, Pedro chose this propitious day to demonstrate to the group its favorable financial situation. Even before the *junta* had begun, he had displayed our cash balance on the small blackboard hanging on the wall at the front of the room. There it was in black and white: only the middle of the month and assets already ran eighty pesos in excess of expenses. Although no one mentioned the matter openly, it might well have been my presence—my donations well above those of the others—that produced this unusual state of affairs. All it would take was one affluent member, willing to share his advantageous condition with the rest, to make the difference. In part the men resisted Pedro's demands because they were aware of the precariousness of their situation. A.A. members, as we shall see, come and go. I had been attending Moral Support for only a month. Whether I would remain and for how long were two big uncertainties. A group cannot place blind trust in the future. Survival demands financial prudence.

Now Gerardo spoke up. Of all the men in the group, Gerardo was clearly the most financially successful. Fifty-three years of age, Gerardo was a physical Paul Bunyan—husky, with thick, curly hair. He was endowed with a deep voice, a generous smile, and an optimistic disposition. His light complexion and facial features made him look more European than the rest of the men. And his small business, designing and installing fancy draperies, put him in close contact with a segment of Mexican society which shared his general appearance. "I work for Argentines, Jews, all sorts of people," he would state cheerfully. Any newcomer to Moral Support would quickly identify Gerardo and Pedro as the two most influential members. Co-founders of the group, they were its undisputed leaders. They were also occasional rivals. These are the men whom Emilio had declared would have the ultimate say on my ability to carry out a group study (Chapter One).

Tonight, Pedro and Gerardo seemed at odds, their voices reverberating from opposite sides of the room. Gerardo proposed a compromise: what if the group paid three hundred and fifty pesos, rather than four hundred? Pedro seemed irked. "Is four hundred so much?" When Gerardo reminded him that some of the men were out of work, Pedro retorted, "And I haven't worked for a year." "Three hundred and fifty," repeated

Gerardo, as if he were in a marketplace, bargaining for a sack of beans. No matter what the others felt, Gerardo now seemed to speak on behalf them all. The evening ended inconclusively, with Arturo declaring with a flourish that the group does not even need a meeting room. It can meet anywhere, one day here, another day there, even in the street if they wished. "No you can't," objected Pedro with the voice of someone who knows. "It's against the law to meet in the street. The police will come and arrest or disperse you." No one disputed this statement; as an ex-policeman, Pedro was the authority on this matter. We all went home, the situation unresolved.

Several evenings later, at the next meeting of Moral Support, I arrived to find only two other men in the room. "*No hay junta*"—There's no meeting—declared Arturo prematurely. He had occupied the moderator's desk and sounded depressed. Although several of the others arrived late, both Pedro and Gerardo were absent. In fact, it seemed as if Pedro had abandoned his property altogether. There was no light in the house. As we pondered what to do, a glass bottle, tossed by rowdy teenagers playing on the street outside, crashed down onto Pedro's cement patio. No one emerged from Pedro's house, a sure sign that the family was gone. Arturo decided to proceed with the meeting. David and others used a portion of their personal stories to express disappointment at the low attendance. They had expected some resolution of the rent dispute. Obviously, most members of Moral Support, plagued by a state of indecision or denial, were laying low.

For the next few weeks, attendance was sporadic. Gerardo and Pedro, normally model members, displayed uncharacteristically erratic behavior, arriving late, skipping meetings, delivering evasive personal stories. Young Isidoro, one of the newer members of the group, used his personal story to describe the matter bluntly: "The atmosphere has become tense." Most of the deliberations concerning the rent occurred before and after meetings, in informal gatherings, rather than through the more formal, public personal stories. It became increasingly evident that the group would move. Through it all, Pedro held a hard line. At one point, Gerardo, once again speaking implicitly on behalf of the group, had relented and offered a monthly rental of four hundred pesos, but with electricity included. Pedro steadfastly refused.

It was obvious by now that Pedro actually wanted the group removed from his property. The rent increase was a way of forcing the men out. By the end of October, they began to see his point of view and speculate as to why he would want them removed. They pointed out that, under current circumstances, it was impossible for Pedro to speak honestly and sincerely at meetings. After all, his family, residing just a few steps away in the main part of the house, might overhear his personal stories. How could he possibly express himself openly, as he should? Then, too, it was said that Pedro could earn more by renting the cottage to a family. After all, it was equipped with toilet and running water. His intransigence was explained by his desire to evict Moral Support from his home, at any cost. David expressed others' thoughts when he said, "He feels that we are on top of him ['*encimados*']." The men began to appreciate that Pedro was feeling smothered by their presence. If he wanted the group to remain, he would have negotiated. In David's opinion, the group should "use few words, speak directly to him and tell him that we are going to leave." Prolonging the agony would be worse for everyone.

But the men had more than Pedro's interest at heart. The controversy had brought their own multiple grievances to the surface. Why does the coffee disappear so rapidly? Where did the sugar go? We purchased it so recently. And what about the toilet paper? Questions like these, which the men had long kept inside, emerged in open discussion. Pedro and his family became suspect of petty theft, of stealing from the group during the long hours when none of the members were around. Direct confrontation was impossible because it would be very difficult to prove the family's guilt. The best solution was to move.

Then, too, resentment had slowly built over Pedro's role as treasurer. Like the position of secretary, which is the only other group officer, the function of treasurer theoretically rotates among the men, with a change of personnel by election every six months. The men now accused Pedro of naming himself treasurer years ago, without ever being formally elected. They claimed that he used his position as landlord as a lever to gain control of and monopolize this influential position. For twelve uninterrupted years Pedro had remained in charge of the group's finances. To be sure, he regularly provided the men a detailed accounting of financial activity. But why had he remained in office so long? By whose authority? And was the *séptima* always accurately recorded? The men were reluctant to accuse Pedro openly of embezzlement, although they mentioned the possibility to one another in private. The main, publicly aired issue was Pedro's refusal over more than a decade to relinquish financial control. Prior to the rent controversy, no one in the group had either expressed a desire to be treasurer or called an election to challenge Pedro to the post. Nor had they ever raised this complaint formally, during the course of meetings.

About a week after Pedro announced the rent increase, an incident occurred which to most of the men confirmed the wisdom of moving. At
the conclusion of a meeting, as we were chatting in our usual fashion,
Pedro's son emerged unexpectedly at the door. Calling for our attention,
he explained that in this year, 1995, the government was carrying out an
interim census, which was a less ambitious effort than the major cen-
suses of 1990 and 2000, but important nonetheless. He represented the
delegación, or borough, of which the neighborhood forms a part. He
wanted the group's permission to use the meeting room for temporary
storage of three cartons containing census forms. Several census workers would have to enter the meeting room twice a day: once at nine in
the morning to collect the forms and again between three and five in the
afternoon to store them. This routine would last about three weeks,
from October 23 until November 18. The cartons, said the young man,
would occupy little space; "They are the size of egg crates," he reassured
everyone, "about as tall as this chair here, and twice as wide." To guar-
antee that group meetings would remain undisturbed, no outsider would
be permitted to enter the room after 5 P.M. The young man concluded
his request by appealing to our *"conciencia,"* our conscience and collective will.

Throughout it all, Pedro remained obscured from view, standing just
outside the cottage door, a shadow huddled in the still night air, listening to his son's appeal. Ten of us were present. Arturo, a short, thin-
boned man who had moved to Mexico City from the tropical lowlands
of Veracruz, was consistently the most outspoken of the group. It was
therefore not surprising that he should be first to offer an opinion. The
group as a whole should not decide the matter, he said. A decision should
be rendered by the *dueño*—the owner—of the cottage, that is, by Pedro.
Possibly, this simple statement was Arturo's strategy to polarize the
situation even further. He effectively reduced Pedro to the economic
status in which he had already cast himself: that of landlord. No longer
was Pedro just another *compañero,* equal to the rest. He was a powerful
property owner. But Arturo's biting remark failed to daunt Pedro. His
son, after all, was seeking a favor of the group, the only entity that could
grant it legitimately. He suddenly emerged from the obscurity of the
night to announce that, no, this was not his decision to make. The group
should decide, which is why he asked his son to come speak to them.

Arturo responded, this time offering his real opinion. He pointed to
the Twelve Traditions, displayed on a large poster in the front of the meeting room. Look at number ten, he said. The tenth Tradition, he said, indicates that Alcoholics Anonymous "should not enter into any political

controversies." Arturo argued that the storage of census forms constitutes a political act, contrary to A.A. tenets. Like others in the group, Arturo believed that the "literature" should not occupy an important role in group affairs. But he would appeal to the authority of official Alcoholics Anonymous declarations whenever they supported his position.

The group seemed unswayed by Arturo's argument, so he took the matter further. In the first group he ever attended—as he put it, the group *"donde yo nací,"* where I was born—permission was granted to allow for others to use the meeting room. When time came for the meeting to convene, however, the room was still not vacant. Arturo declared that what now seemed to be a simple choice, that is, to lend Moral Support's meeting room to a non-member, would later cause complications. The group would come to regret the decision. Arturo, correctly sensing that he was unable to persuade his *compañeros* to side with him, stomped out of the room angrily. Although the group voted to allow Pedro's son to use the meeting room for storage of the census forms, this incident served to highlight the uncertain balance of power between Pedro and the others. Permission was granted, but only because of ongoing rental negotiations. The group was clearly wounded by Pedro's apparent disloyalty; to raise the rent at a time of economic crisis was, to their minds, cruel and unwarranted. But perhaps the group's generosity in allowing Pedro's son to use the room would persuade him to retract his decision on the rent.

On October 25, 1995, only a few days after the confrontation over storage of the census forms, a UPI report appeared in the *Mexico City Times:* "An estimated 53,000 workers began a population and housing count yesterday, organized by the National Statistics Institute to update the information gathered in 1990. The census, originally scheduled to be conducted in the year 2000, according to the Institute's program, was brought forward and coincides with the 100th anniversary of Mexico's first ever census, conducted in October 1895." The census, in fact, was more than a data-gathering event. Like so many other official proceedings in Mexico, it was an act of national affirmation. And yet, at no point in their deliberations did the men bring this aspect of the enterprise into the debate. To these men, as perhaps to most poor Mexicans, politics of any kind means the promotion of the politicians' personal advantage, which stands diametrically opposed to the people's benefit. And yet, they granted permission anyway.

If they hoped to win Pedro's favor by this act, their ambitions were dashed. Pedro remained unmoved. One of the men had heard through the grapevine that a good meeting room was available on the Avenue, a nearby shopping thoroughfare, for only three hundred and fifty pesos. But this information was soon proven incorrect. By the first of November, a new meeting room had been rented, this one for four hundred pesos a month, the same price that Pedro had requested. The rift between Pedro and the others now seemed irremediable. Emilio's opinion of Pedro was that "*No se portó como un doble A*"—He didn't behave like a double A. The general feeling was that, for the same rent, it was preferable to move, in order to avoid similar problems in the future.

"It's best that we get out of this place," David confided to me at the end of our penultimate meeting at Pedro's house. "The bathroom smells." Since no decent meeting room could be found for lower than four hundred pesos a month, non-monetary arguments became as important as those based on the rent itself. David wanted to walk me three blocks away to see the new space, but as we meandered down the Avenue, an unoccupied taxi pulled up. I was tired, it was late, already beyond my self-imposed ten o'clock curfew, so I hopped in the cab and went home. I would have plenty of opportunity later to examine the new locale.

The decision to move had been made during All Saints and All Souls Days, November 1–2, a universal Catholic holiday and Mexico's most famous national fiesta, popularly known throughout the Republic as the Day of the Dead. This is the time that many migrants, among them some of the key men in Moral Support, leave Mexico City to visit relatives in the villages and towns from which they originated. The decision to move, in fact, had been rendered in Pedro and Gerardo's absence. They had both departed the city to celebrate the Day of the Dead in the villages where they were born and raised. Without their presence, the others could act decisively, unencumbered by feelings of loyalty. The increasingly bitter rivalry between Pedro and Gerardo had turned the rent issue into a competition for personal loyalty. The rest of the men were reluctant to declare for one leader or the other, especially since Pedro and Gerardo seemed motivated above all by the prospect of winning the battle, and by the fear of losing face. Concern over the best interests of the group had become obscured by competition between the two men. Their temporary absence cleared the way for the others to decide quickly and unanimously to rent the new meeting room. This decision occurred on November 2.

By November 7, when Moral Support next met, those who had been away from Mexico City had learned through word of mouth about the impending move. However, Pedro, recently returned from his home state of San Luis Potosí, was still uninformed. Emilio, the final speaker of the evening, closed the meeting and called for a so-called *"junta de trabajo"* —a work meeting—to be held. (This is the term used to refer to any meeting or portion of a meeting specifically devoted to non-therapeutic activity, usually financial business.) Emilio proceeded to list the donors and amounts they had contributed toward the cost of the imminent move. Pedro's face fell in noticeable shock and disbelief. Throughout the half-hour work meeting, he squirmed restlessly in his chair, nervously scratching his limbs and clawing at his crotch. A few of the men felt the need gently to explain the decision to Pedro. "We just want to improve the situation," was Carlos's brave attempt. With the necessary funds to make the move now secured, there was no turning back. The next meeting would be their last at Pedro's house.

Meanwhile, this incident, coming as it did early in my research, alerted me to the complexity of group dynamics in Moral Support. I could no longer view the men as constituting an undifferentiated, egalitarian support group. The group was split by ideological divisions and an informal prestige hierarchy. Money, always scarce among these poorest of the poor, was obviously a big source of concern. But other considerations, such as group loyalty and adherence to A.A. ideals, entered into alliances as well. These were just some of the issues to which I would turn my attention in the coming months.

At the time, however, I had serious doubts about whether Moral Support would survive the rental dispute at all. Pedro had been such a key member, and his future presence at meetings so in doubt, that the very existence of the group seemed at risk. After learning of the decision to move, Pedro announced in a personal story that he had decided to return to San Luis Potosí for several months. He would be attending meetings rarely if at all, he said. In addition to raising the issue of Pedro's role in the group, the rental dispute had opened a space for other controversies to surface. Some members expressed the need to meet more often than three times a week. Others wanted more attention to *"la literatura."* The general level of dissatisfaction seemed high. And yet the relentless expression of social control, of enforced group cohesion, was obvious as well. I would take careful note of these centripetal pressures during the months ahead.

The final meeting at Pedro's house was marked by an air of serenity that comes with acceptance of the inevitable. Not one of the six personal stories even mentioned the impending move. When the meeting ended, all of us cooperated in carrying the furniture, wall hangings and other accoutrements from the old meeting room to the new. Several men lifted the heavy wooden desk. Eduardo, who had managed to secure a dolly, created an ingenious pile of seventeen chairs, which he tied together with rope and pushed through the streets on his own. Others carried the coffee urn, framed pictures, podium, cleaning supplies. There we were, at 9:30 in the evening, in full view of the neighbors, parading down the Avenue a distance of three and a half blocks to the new meeting room. A few of the men had readied the place for arrival by scrubbing and painting. If there were any doubts in the neighbors' minds as to who attended Moral Support, they were certainly dispelled on this occasion.

The meeting room promised considerably less privacy than we had experienced in the former locale. It was bright and well lit, partly due to fresh white paint. But it was clearly smaller than Pedro's cottage and had no windows. The only opening to the outside was the entrance, as wide as the room itself and separated from the street by a metal curtain, of the type used by small stores and commercial establishments throughout Mexican cities. The curtain could be rolled up halfway to allow air, light, and passage in and out; or locked in the down position to create an impenetrable barrier to the street. The closed position, it seemed to me, would create an impossibly claustrophobic situation for the conduct of any meeting. The partially open position made me uncomfortable, because it appeared contrary to norms of anonymity. But the men seemed entirely unconcerned. To the contrary, they voiced open approval. While shining my shoes, Emilio would frequently reiterate how much better off the group was now that the meeting room "is on street level, not down below."

The new meeting room exposed us to the street in a way that had been impossible before. All the sounds and smells of working class Mexico penetrated our therapeutic environment. During the several weeks when there was a neighborhood fair, we could hardly hear a word from anyone on the podium. Even Gerardo's resonant voice was no match for the blare of outdoor microphones and mariachi bands. The noise was particularly acute after the imposition of daylight savings time, when stores stayed open later than usual and workers, shoppers, and frolicking children milled in the streets around the meeting room.

And yet not one *compañero* voiced a word of protest. All the men seemed content at the new locale, grateful for their extrication from what had become an impossibly tense situation. But more than gratitude can explain their attitude. In fact, the social boundary between outside and inside among the men of Moral Support was as permeable as the physical barrier between street and meeting room. Just as the daily life of these men continually influenced the conduct of meetings, so too what went on during meetings would affect their social relations on the outside. Alcoholics Anonymous was thus integrated into the lives of these men to an extent that completely precluded true anonymity. This circumstance, reflected in the personal stories, would ultimately have serious implications for the survival of the group.

4. STORYTELLING

The central activity of the Alcoholics Anonymous meeting is speech. Any worldwide survey of A.A. would uncover considerable variation in terms of criteria for speaker selection, the rules of speech, and the meanings of oral presentations to both speaker and audience. The meeting format—the *autonomía,* as the men in Moral Support call it—is what determines the rules of speech that prevail in each group. Some groups invite guest speakers from other groups to present lengthy personal stories about recovery from alcoholism; this presentation is followed by a question-answer period. Other groups, like those I witnessed in Tzintzuntzan, permit their own members to address the group for whatever length of time they themselves deem necessary. In yet other groups, like Moral Support, members rotate to fill predetermined time slots and there exists no opportunity for open discussion.

Each recovering alcoholic responds best to a particular meeting style and these preferences are what partly determine the decision to join one group or another. O'Reilly (1997:127) describes the range of variation thus: "Some affiliates enjoy speaking, and some find it painful; speaking may bring therapeutic revelations and personal gratification to some; for others it may seem only a program obligation, a duty to be discharged with no special expectations. Speaking careers range from one or two occasions to a span of years and hundreds of engagements. There are no fast rules; there is, I think, an idea held generally that anyone serious about sobriety should speak at least once." O'Reilly's observations derive from the northeastern United States. Nonetheless, they accurately describe groups throughout the world, including Mexico.

In Mexican A.A. groups the principal speech event is called the *historial,* or personal story. As far as members of Moral Support are concerned, there is nothing more important therapeutically than presenting and listening to *historiales.* The *historial* is framed by predictable formulaic statements and the event as a whole is more or less predetermined. The moderator first calls a group member to *"subir a la tribuna,"* that is, to rise to the podium. The chosen speaker gets up from his chair, offers the moderator a simple *"Gracias, Fulano"* and takes his place at the podium. He begins by stating, *"Buenas noches, compañeros. Mi nombre es Mengano y soy un enfermo alcohólico"*—"Good evening, *compañeros,* my name is Such-and-Such and I'm an ill alcoholic." In conformity with worldwide A.A. guidelines, and in emulation of movement founders Bill W. and Dr. Bob, speakers only mention their first name. In theory, they adopt this practice in order to preserve anonymity.[1] However, they all know one another intimately and are well aware of one another's surnames, which some moderators record in the group log.

Unlike at most A.A. meetings in the United States and Mexico, the members of Moral Support do not respond to the chosen speaker by saying "Hi, Mengano" after being greeted. Rather, they remain attentively silent. The speaker follows his opening salutation by offering a few words about how happy he is to be in the company of everyone present and how supportive they have been to him. They have helped him to stay sober for another 24 hours, he states. A well-known feature of A.A. ideology, of course, is the admonition to approach each day as a separate challenge and to cherish the small triumph of having remained sober for yet another day. Long-range goals are thought to be counterproductive; they can induce a sense of despair and, ultimately, relapse.

The speaker's formulaic opening is followed by a fifteen-minute personal story, which, for some group members, is more predictable than for others. At the strike of the clock on the meeting room wall, the speaker concludes his story. His final words are, *"Gracias, compañeros. Les agradezco su tolerancia,"* or *"Gracias, compañeros, por su tolerancia"*—"Thank you, *compañeros.* I appreciate your tolerance" or "Thank you, *compañeros,* for your tolerance." Finally comes the formulaic wish, *"Muchas veinticuatro horas"*—Many twenty-four hours, meaning "May you have many days of sobriety." To the sound of applause, the speaker steps down from the podium and returns to his seat.

Within the frame of the formulaic opening and concluding remarks, the speaker at Moral Support develops his *historial,* dealing with personal thoughts and activities. As a speech event, the *historial* is virtually in a class of its own. It is not a lecture, because it lacks formal advance preparation and is only tangentially intended to instruct. Neither is it a talk or chat, because it possesses a greater degree of formality and structure than those terms normally imply. It is certainly not a conversation, given that there are no immediate responses from listeners. However, as we shall see, the personal story does often seem like an episode in an on-going conversation, given that the speaker sometimes addresses issues, topics, or specific details introduced by the moderator or other speakers earlier in the evening. Moreover, this conversation might spread over several sessions, or even weeks, as speakers refer to personal stories delivered by *compañeros* at previous meetings.

Analyses of A.A. narratives in the United States have focused almost exclusively on tales of alcoholism and recovery. This thematic emphasis is entirely understandable, given A.A.'s stated goal of helping alcoholics to achieve and maintain sobriety. Carole Cain interprets personal stories as mechanisms of identity acquisition: "as the AA member learns the AA story model, and learns to place the events and experiences of his own life into the model, he learns to tell and to understand his own life as an AA life, and himself as an AA alcoholic. The personal story is a cultural vehicle for identity acquisition" (Cain 1991:215). Thune (1977:83) points out that "If the program is to be available to them, members must establish some form of congruence between their life history and the group model." In fact, there is some evidence that potential A.A. members who are unable to identify with other recovering alcoholics decide against joining a group. One U.S. informant states, "I would sit there and listen to their stories . . . and I couldn't fit myself into their patterns" (quoted in Tuchfeld 1981:631).

Cain (1991) demonstrates that the longer a person has been in A.A., the closer his or her story comes to a paradigmatic A.A. narrative, with its special definition of alcoholism, its dramatic emphasis on hitting bottom, and spectacular accounts of recovery through membership in Alcoholics Anonymous. M.C. Taylor (1977:17), too, states that in carrying out research among female A.A. members, "I found right away . . . that the data I was gleaning seemed 'contaminated' or distorted, by a viewpoint I came to recognize as the 'A.A. line.' Over and over, the women I interviewed told me the same story. All of them seemed to sound alike." Virtually everyone who has observed A.A. groups in the United States has had the same experience. Thune (1977:79) expresses the matter well: "Most of the A.A. life histories . . . are remarkably narrow and stereotyped." "It is no accident, then," he continues (1977:83), "that new members are explicitly told to listen at meetings some weeks or months before beginning to participate actively." The idea is that newcomers "avoid speaking until they have begun to learn the concepts

and assimilate the models necessary for a 'correct' analysis of their present state and past history" (ibid.).

In Moral Support, socialization to A.A. through storytelling becomes
evident over time. But it seems not to be principally the paradigmatic
A.A. narrative that is learned by newcomers. For example, only once
did I hear any member of the group mention "hitting bottom" (*tocar
fondo*), a key concept—in fact, the turning point—in a typical U.S. personal story. A coherent life history, consisting of beginning, middle and
end, and constructed around alcohol abuse and subsequent recovery, is
rare in Moral Support. Rigorously chronological narratives do not even
characterize life history interviews, much less the personal stories that
one hears at meetings. Rather, in Moral Support small fragments of a
member's story—sometimes tentatively interconnected, sometimes entirely discrete from one another—emerge over the course of numerous
personal stories. Although it is possible for the outside observer to identify connective threads that bind a given individual's life history, this
kind of reconstruction always requires imaginative leaps.

It is not that the men of Moral Support are in any way incapable of
narrating a chronological life history. They simply have no example
to follow from more experienced members and therefore place no
particular value on molding their personal stories to the A.A. para-
digm. Nonetheless, Cain's more general point—that identity can be
transformed through personal stories—is well taken. At Moral Support,
newcomers (called "*nuevos*") soon internalize the meeting format,
including the formulaic openings and closings to the personal story.
Through imitation, they learn to incorporate within their personal stories key vocabulary, such as *Poder Superior* (Higher Power) and "*veinticuatro horas*" (twenty-four hours). They also receive instruction, both
verbally and through example, in the principles of meeting etiquette.
Longstanding members sometimes address the needs of newcomers by
using time on the podium to define proper meeting comportment.

The most noteworthy aspect of newcomer socialization, however, is
their mastery of the art of public speaking. Personal stories in Moral
Support are fundamentally performances. They require a speaker to
place himself on view and talk for a quarter of an hour, virtually without interruption, on sensitive topics of deep emotional significance. The
men of Moral Support have experienced nothing in their family, educational, or employment background to prepare them for this kind of task.
In fact, privileged as my own preparation is in these respects, I at first
found it hard to fill a quarter of an hour by speaking about myself in

front of a group of relative strangers. Only after I got to know the men a little better could I relax enough to deliver a proper personal story. I also needed time to assimilate the procedural rules and narrative themes that prevail in most personal stories. These experiences enabled me to empathize with struggling novices within the group.

Time after time, I witnessed newcomers rise to the podium, begin speaking, and sit down again after only five or six minutes. Slowly, over a period of months, they acquired the ability to elaborate their stories until, finally, they could speak uninterruptedly for a full fifteen minutes. Speakers always have recourse to one relatively easy strategy: repetition. Within a single *historial* as well as over the course of many *historiales,* speakers can repeat themselves *ad infinitum,* if they wish. But even this facile option needs to be learned. Eventually, through imitation, repetition, and other tactics, the newcomers' personal stories become indistinguishable from those of their more experienced *compañeros.*

At Moral Support newcomers invariably flub when they begin to deliver personal stories. Flubbing is in fact inevitable because newcomers are called to the podium well before they are able to learn A.A. principles and internalize the rules of public discourse. In the northeastern United States, where O'Reilly (1997:127) carried out research, "speakers in AA are chosen from among affiliates who have succeeded in remaining sober for at least ninety days. Sometimes up to a year of continuous sobriety is required for speaking; customs vary regionally, and even from group to group within a region, but six months is probably average. A newcomer's sponsor may suggest—or insist—that the 'pigeon' speak, or the newcomer may contrive independently to speak." By contrast, in Moral Support men are called to the lectern within their first two or three weeks of meetings. I myself was asked to speak at the fourth meeting, which, despite my long experience in the classroom, I found difficult enough. Working class Mexican alcoholics, who have never tackled such a task, often feel shy at suddenly being thrust into the limelight. Some men eventually master the delivery of personal stories, but for others, for whom being the center of attention is pure torture, the role is intolerable. My impression is that several newcomers to Moral Support left the program after a few meetings for this very reason.

Newcomers to A.A. need to learn not only the framing devices that set the personal story apart as a speech event. The narrative core of the personal story must also be mastered. As Edmund O'Reilly (1997:103–126) shows for the case of A.A. narratives in the northeastern United States, personal stories possess literary qualities in that they reveal an unmistakable narrative structure. They are generally divided into three parts, which are sandwiched between a formulaic salutation and coda. These include: (1) what the speaker was like before coming to A.A., (2) how the speaker discovered A.A., and (3) the personal transformations wrought as a result of membership in A.A. This story line is paradigmatic. It is modeled upon the published autobiography of founder Bill W. Narrated endlessly at A.A. meetings, the paradigmatic story, with its infinite variations, promotes a view of A.A. as therapeutically effective, indeed virtually indispensable to recovery from alcoholism. In Pollner and Stein's words (1996:211), "The 'drunkalogues' presented in AA typically recount a personal odyssey more or less conforming to the Big Book template of 'what we used to be like, what happened, and what we are like now.'"

At Moral Support, all the elements of the paradigmatic A.A. narrative are evident at any given meeting. Upon my initial arrival at the group the men certainly gave abundant testimony of past behavior, the discovery of A.A., and subsequent recovery. Repeatedly and fervently, they expressed gratitude to the organization and to their *compañeros* for having helped them overcome alcoholism. In retrospect, I realized that paradigmatic personal stories were probably delivered for my benefit. I later observed the same predigested stories emerge whenever newcomers appeared at a meeting. The men of Moral Support take responsibility for *llevando el mensaje*, "passing on the word." They believe, because they soon learn, that the best way to win converts is through effective communication of their odyssey from active alcoholism to stable recovery.

Among northeasterners in the United States, O'Reilly (ibid.:121) found that "the concentration of most AA stories is on the depiction of 'what we were like,'" that is, on the first segment of the paradigmatic personal story. The men of Moral Support, by contrast, seem to place greater emphasis on present circumstances than on the past. Indeed, they insist that detailed accounts of everyday struggles in the here and now are therapeutically more effective than vacuous statements of past suffering. Embedded within their personal stories, however, are implicit before-and-after comparisons, from which the analyst can construct a narrative. In the stories, the period prior to affiliation with A.A. represents darkness, pain and unhappiness. Although the alcoholic's subsequent recovery represents an improvement in overall well-being, he still finds true happiness elusive. Nonetheless, this developmental stage gives hope of better times to come. The early part of the story is like a vision of hell, with detailed descriptions of a life out of control. Although present circumstances never seem to live up to highest expectations, the contrast with the past is sufficiently dramatic to affirm the value of membership in A.A.

Personal stories range over a variety of themes, including grooming, behavior, and state of mind. The men first and foremost deride the way they looked as active alcoholics. Their disintegrated lives as drunks were reflected in their appalling appearance. At Moral Support meetings, as stated in Chapter Three, the initial speaker often sets a tone for the rest of the session. If he introduces a particular theme effectively, subsequent speakers pick up on it and elaborate. At one typical meeting in 1997, Nestor opened the meeting by describing his dissipated physical condition before joining A.A. His self-report led him to the topic of *compañero* Renaldo, who happened to be present that evening. Renaldo, during drunken episodes, displayed unseemly long, unkempt hair; the hair was filled with lice, said Nestor. As Nestor had raised this topic, the five subsequent speakers devoted themselves, too, to stories of unkempt hair and lice. A favorite statement indicating a former state of decrepitude is, "My hair stood straight on end (*de punta*)!" By telling personal stories of this type, the men communicate a shared state of physical decline during their years as active alcoholics.

Filthiness, in fact, appears as a leitmotif in Moral Support personal stories. Emilio recalls a time in his early twenties when he got drunk. He found himself "sprawled out on the benches, in the streets at 2, 3 in the morning." During that period, he would begin the day at 8 o'clock or so with an alcoholic drink. "I was just filthy [*mugroso*]," he declares; "When . . . I started my own business, I tried to be another person, to buy myself the finest clothing so that I could change my image, all clean with my nice white boots. But then, when alcohol possessed me . . . " Emilio's voice drifts off at this point, as if the conclusion to his sentence were obvious.

Filth also appears as a theme in Renaldo's story of his wedding, which he told in a life history interview. He looks back almost four decades to when he was twenty-six and eloped with a thirteen-year old girl. "*Me la robé*"—I robbed her, he states, referring to the term for elopement generally used throughout central Mexico.[2] Three years later, the couple got married in both civil and religious ceremonies. States Renaldo, "But all of that was . . . well, it was sort of strange. Because when we got married, I was like I am now [i.e., during the interview session], all *encalado,* covered with lime [*cal*]." (Renaldo had been carrying out light construction work just prior to my arrival at his home.)

On his wedding day, plastered in more senses than one, Renaldo had gone straight from his manual laboring job to the marriage ceremony. His bride was pregnant at the time; as he puts it, she was unable even to kneel during the nuptial Mass, as is usually required. "And I was all full of *cal*, I was *encalado*," repeats Renaldo. "And that's how I went into the church. Why should they even take pictures of me? So they all could see me like that? *Caray!* [No way!]" When Renaldo started drinking, he couldn't hold a job so his wife had to go to work. "Well, she had to go to work and that's when she seemed like the man, right?" comments Renaldo. "I stayed in the house, but drunk, and, um, she left me some money so that I could make food for the kids and sometimes I spent the money destined for the kids' food. And, well, since there was nobody who would wash them, well, they were all a filthy mess."

Eduardo expresses the same concern for cleanliness. When he first arrived at Alcoholics Anonymous, he says, "I was on the verge of dying, practically. I was all filthy, disheveled. I had grown a beard, I hadn't bathed, well, I was sleeping in the street. At one or two in the morning I was out looking for a soda, a little bit of water to mix with the alcohol that I was drinking. I mean, my alcoholism, for me it was the worst. . . . I wouldn't wish on anyone to fall in the way I had fallen."

The words the men use most to describe their own prior physical condition are *meado, cagado, mugroso*—pissed on, shit on, filthy. Anyone who knows Mexicans will testify to their pride in maintaining extreme personal cleanliness. The alcoholic body, as described in A.A. personal stories, deviates seriously from this general standard. In fact, standards of cleanliness are so high in Mexico that the men feel ill at ease when they occasionally arrive at meetings in a less than fastidious state. Hence, Arturo, who delivered the closing personal story one evening, apologized to the group for his unkempt appearance. He explained that he had come directly from work to the *junta* and had no time to wash and change before the meeting. Mary Douglas (1973:93–112) reminds us that the social order places constraints on the physical body. Except when it cannot be avoided, as in work situations, being unkempt in Mexico reflects a state of shamelessness; it demonstrates an unpardonable imperviousness to public opinion. This explains why Arturo rightly felt he had to justify rising to the podium with dirty clothing. For recovering alcoholics, a clean body normally reflects a clean, dry palate.

In Moral Support stories, drunkenness means more than physical disarray. It also brings behavioral chaos. Emilio tells about the very first time he got drunk, at the age of 15 or 16, while working for a butcher in Mexico City. He lived in the butcher's house. One day the butcher killed a pig to make *carnitas*. To celebrate, the family bought a bottle of tequila.

> Well, that was the first time I got drunk in my life. Of course it didn't matter at all how much I drank—a little or a lot. It was enough to get me buzzed. And the *señora* said, "Don't, don't give that to him, he's too . . . you know. No, no, it's not for him!" And one of her kids said no, he said, "Just as long as he doesn't get *aire*," or like vomit—that's called *aire*.[3] But then I felt drunk. They all said, "Go lay down in your room." There was a room in the attic, way up, called the servants' quarters and that's where I stayed. But that time I acted . . . well, of course, I acted like I was in my own house, with the confidence to clown around as a silly drunk. . . . Well, you know, of course I tried to be funny: "Look at the little drunk!" And in order to be more funny I went down from the room with my pants on backwards . . . you know, instead of putting the pants on the right way, like they are now, I turned them around so that this side was below and this side on top. . . . So I tried to be funny and go downstairs with my pants on backwards and roam around in the backyard being the clown, walking back and forth, wanting to fall, not to fall. This was the first time I got drunk.

In this tale, Emilio as responsible adolescent, supporting himself through honest employment, becomes reduced through drink to the level of a silly child.

Renaldo, as a drunk adult, would act in similarly puerile manner. He tells of walking the street barefoot, his sweater donned in such careless, mangled fashion that he was practically naked from the waist up. Renaldo tells this tale at Moral Support meetings. The listeners laugh. They let out, not a joyful laugh that emanates deep in the gut, but rather a tentative, nervous chuckle, a sign of embarrassed recognition. They each have a similar personal story to narrate.

The men also tell stories about how their addiction affected their family roles as children, husbands and fathers. Simón, a soft-spoken, balding man who keeps his thin lips perpetually turned down at the corners, sadly recalls his childhood. His father would ply him with alcohol. They would get drunk together, an unimaginably horrific scene for most working class Mexicans, who value highly the maintenance of a respectful distance between father and son—a distance, they believe, which can only exist if the two men avoid drinking in one another's presence. As for Renaldo, when his drinking prevented him from working, his wife had to take a job outside the home. Renaldo, now the children's primary caretaker, would buy alcohol with the money she left him for food. The children would go hungry. After they were grown, earning money on their own, Renaldo would steal from them in order get cash to feed his addiction: "Instead of bringing in money, I came to steal things here from the house. Yes, I stole. I stole *varillas* [petty merchandise]—I stole little radios, um . . . my son who is in the U.S., he was a radio technician. They brought him those little things, you know, those little radios and televisions, to repair, and I would steal them and afterwards he had to pay for all that. . . . I made him look bad." Financial irresponsibility is, in fact, a major theme of Moral Support meetings. Pedro explains to the group that, in the period when he drank heavily, he was earning a bundle of money. But, rather than save and invest, he would squander it ostentatiously. He speaks of methodically tearing thousand-peso notes into little pieces [*"cuadritos,"* he repeated over and over in telling this story to the group], which he would toss to the wind for everyone to see. Of course, by recounting this episode, Pedro, in a socially acceptable fashion, could communicate to the group that he was at one time a man of means.

In addition to alcohol-induced behavioral abnormalities, the men also tell of their abrasive, occasionally violent, dispositions while drunk. David says that people on his street used to be afraid to encounter him. "They'd see me coming home drunk and would hide, yes; because I was out of control. I liked to insult people, and, happily, this is where I say thanks to God. God looked after me and he still looks after me because if it hadn't been for the grace of God, the neighbors probably would have killed me. They were at the point of killing me because of my intolerable behavior—of course, when I was drunk." Violence during periods of drunkenness was not merely a theoretical possibility for these men. They speak of routine violent episodes that plagued their lives as active alcoholics. Eduardo remembers the frustration he suffered when the woman he lived with left him, accompanied by their daughter. "So I got frustrated," he says, "and I turned to drinking, to the false strength . . . and so then time went by, right? And in my bouts of drunkenness I'd punch people out. I got beat up a lot. A lot of the time I also beat people up, you know, but I was never afraid."

Emilio's suffering prior to entering A.A. was more than physical; it sometimes expressed itself as a vain longing for liberation from alcohol. Says Emilio, "I was a person who was, I guess, a non-believer, a non-believer because I never heard, even in passing, about A.A. or that the groups exist. My attitude was that I . . . ummm . . . well I guess I could just go on with my way of drinking, and my way of drinking was already in an advanced state. And so I was already a man of tomorrow, the man of tomorrow that never arrived, the tomorrow when I'd say, 'Enough of alcoholism, already.'"

Personal stories in Moral Support rarely delineate explicit before-and-after comparisons. The Mexican stories, as I have said, normally lack chronological sequencing; they must be reconstructed by the listener from information delivered over the course of many sessions. Nonetheless, explicit comparisons are rendered unnecessary because the storytellers are in fact on display, their words and behavior open to public scrutiny. There on the podium, engaged in what amounts to a performance, the recovering alcoholic exhibits his improved condition. He is clean, composed, articulate. His very presence at the meeting indicates a degree of responsibility and a concern for his own and others' well-being that would have been impossible during his life as an active drinker. The content of the speaker's personal story, as well as his manner of delivery, act as concluding chapters to his personal A.A. story. The message, however, is delivered through demonstration rather than narration.

Through demonstration, it is possible to show that the body has healed, that the recovering alcoholic is no longer dirty and disheveled, that he fulfills obligations to others and is capable of speaking coherently in public for a full quarter of an hour. Nonetheless, given the economic and social marginality of most men in Moral Support, there is much in their lives that in fact has not improved significantly as a result of membership in Alcoholics Anonymous. Even hygiene and appearance remain largely outside their control, because they cannot afford to maintain themselves the way they would like.

Consider the case of David, who spent most of a personal story lamenting two persistent problems: living in a house without a bathroom (he has an outdoor latrine and takes sponge baths), and suffering from ill-fitting dentures. David's mouth, in fact, displays a gaping hole in the front, where he is missing most of his teeth. For reasons he cannot explain, his dentures have long ceased to fit. New dentures, he claims, will cost as much as 9000 pesos (in 1996, $1,250 in U.S. dollars). He ponders aloud, "When will I ever get dentures? I don't even make 9000 pesos in an entire year!" Despite his woes, David maintains his optimism. A major proponent of Alcoholics Anonymous ideology, he concludes his personal story on an upbeat note. As his voice rises from a mild drone to a booming proclamation, he cries out, "These items [i.e., bathroom and dentures] are only material things! I have my health! I have a family! I have all of you! That's what counts, not material things!" For a number of the men, it is important to believe that the *compañeros* of Moral Support constitute a surrogate family, because they have in effect lost their natal and conjugal families. On Mother's Day (in Mexico, May 10), Eduardo composed a poem in honor of his recently deceased mother, which concludes, *Pues, por esa primera copa muchas veses* [sic] *recaí / Hice sufrir mi familia/ y al último la perdí*—Well, because of that first drink/ I often relapsed/ I made my family suffer/ and finally lost it [the family].

The men are clearly concerned with the negative impact of their drinking on their social relationships. Material things, nonetheless, are also on the men's minds. The general preoccupation with poverty and deprivation were among my earliest field observations. From the outset, Eduardo lamented that, even though he was still without work, he at least was not sleeping in the street. Jacinto, a man about forty years old, stated that it made him sad to think that if he had not spent so much money on alcohol, he and his wife could sleep in a room separate from the children. In conformity with the A.A. outlook, he says, "It does no good to look back with regrets because what one must do is struggle toward a better future." At the meetings I attended, Simón complained constantly about unemployment, David about underemployment, Eduardo about having nowhere permanent to live. In the group's personal stories, economic difficulties emerged almost as frequently as alcohol. Several of the men regularly reported searching for work. Only occasionally did the search have positive results and, when it did, the job they found was flawed—temporary, poorly remunerated, or filled with broken promises from deceitful employers. In trying circumstances such as these, the men, like the underemployed Puerto Ricans studied by Singer et al. (1992), might have turned to alcohol, as a way of validating their masculine identity. Instead, they vent their anguish within the A.A. meeting room, among those who share their condition.

Singer et al. (1992) provide a superb analysis of the intimate connection between male employment, gender identity, and drinking patterns. Some of the financial worries that emerged in Moral Support meetings, however, concerned problems over and above those of mere survival. In a series of personal stories, Emilio complained of having to help his teenaged son make car payments. A car that the son had bought second hand turned out to be stolen, so it was returned to the rightful owner despite the fact that the family had already paid for it. They received no compensation in return. On top of that, the family had allowed the son to buy a sparkling new red V.W. bug. The son, who works driving a minibus, is "a good boy" and "causes no problems." Soft-hearted Emilio, overcome by a sense of paternal love and responsibility, wanted to help compensate him for loss of the first car by offering to help purchase the new vehicle.

Emilio himself does not drive. He earns the equivalent of 40 cents per shoeshine, and yet manages to contribute to the loan payments. Emilio was clearly concerned about a balloon payment that soon would come due. The family was struggling with how they were to meet this obligation. A few days after Emilio's personal stories about the car, he asked me for a loan. In retrospect, it occurred to me that the stories were his way of preparing me for this request. Although I gladly complied with his request, the car payments ultimately got the best of him. The V.W., which had never been used for fear it would degenerate from its pristine state, mysteriously disappeared one day from Emilio's makeshift carport. It had been repossessed.

Most of the men in Moral Support live in shared quarters and depend on relatives for food and shelter. To a man, they deem this situation undesirable, however necessary it might be for survival. Their yearning for residential independence is another prevalent theme in personal stories. Genaro, a middle-aged man who attended meetings only sporadically, told of growing up in a household with twelve siblings. He married at a very young age and financial pressures forced him to live with his new wife in the home of his siblings and widowed mother. It seems that one older brother, in particular, made life miserable for the newlyweds. Residence in this cramped apartment became impossible for the young couple. This was the predictable theme of Genaro's personal stories. One day he reported with relief that he and his family had found a place which they could afford on their own. I never saw him at meetings again, which gives an indication of why he had attended in the first place.

A number of the men feel alone and unwanted, even in the company of close relatives. Simón struggled openly in meetings with the fact that he lived in a house belonging to his estranged son and daughter-in-law. He was so alienated from the couple that he and they were not even on speaking terms. Devoid of work or income, Simón was worried that he would be expelled from the house and have nowhere to go; during the fieldwork period, at least, he was able to remain in that unhappy home. Damián, who was recently widowed, was similarly plagued with the fear that his children and in-laws would evict him from the house which they all shared.

Amado, a soft-spoken man in his late fifties, closed the meeting one evening with a particularly moving personal story. Amado is a fruit and vegetable vendor with a chronically melancholy countenance. He seems resigned to an unhappy lot. He told the group that he drank heavily for thirty years, from childhood through most of adulthood. "*La vida ha sido triste*"—Life has been sad—he said. The worst part of it, he went on, is that his children are ingrates. One of his sons actually asked him to sell his house and divide up the property. This statement drew sympathetic laughter from the listeners, ever contemptuous of greedy relatives. The *compañeros* could identify with Amado's plight. "What has all the suffering been for?" asks Amado. Neither wife nor children have shown any appreciation for all he has done for them.

At Moral Support, delivering personal stories about financial and family problems obviously provides the men some sense of relief. They claim that they feel comfortable telling these stories to *compañeros* who share many of the same life challenges and can therefore empathize with their plight. And yet they do not use the podium to seek advice. Personal stories are used more as a means of releasing anxieties—this, as we shall see in Chapter Seven, is a conscious goal—than as a strategy for soliciting help. And yet, within the framework of personal stories themselves, an extended conversation sometimes occurs. One member introduces a particular theme or narrates a life episode early in the meeting. Subsequent speakers place their own gloss on that theme or incident, thereby publicly airing their opinions and advice. The result is a private exchange between the original speaker and one or more others, carried out in the relatively formal arena of the meeting.

Consider Eduardo, who devoted most of an *historial* to lamenting the fact that, try as he will, he cannot stop masturbating. He masturbates twice a day, he told us, in the morning when he awakes and in the evening just before falling asleep. Eduardo, who spends months at a time without female company, raised this matter casually, as if it was of no serious consequence. In fact, he almost seemed to be bragging about his libidinal energy. Later that session, Pedro rose to the podium, and fixed his gaze on Eduardo: "Instead of masturbating, you should go out and look for a young woman (*chava*)!" For the men of Moral Support, companionship is always preferable to solitude. This general principle extends to sex as much as to any other social domain.

My own personal stories met with comments delivered from the podium, as well, and these incidents were instructive. One evening I told the story of two separate encounters with taxi drivers. I negotiated

Mexico City mainly by taxi. Because in Mexico City taxi drivers are said to reflect a cross-section of popular opinion, I took every opportunity to discuss matters related to alcohol use and abuse with them. The first concerned a driver who probed for information about my work, home, family life, and place of origin. After dispensing with the basics, he turned to a more delicate matter. "*¿Toma usted?*" he asked. "Do you drink?" I responded that, yes, I do drink, but in moderation. I threw the question back at him and he replied that he drinks "very, very little, once every three or four months, when invited to a fiesta or family gathering." I waited a few seconds. Then he added, "But I used to drink a lot." So I inquired if he had ever gone to Alcoholics Anonymous. He responded that he had attended a group for a month, but then dropped out because he felt no need to continue. About that time, too, his group dissolved. But there are other groups, he added cheerfully; he would take me to one if I wanted.

After I told this story, Pedro took his place on the podium. Always quick to offer advice, Pedro reacted passionately to my remarks. This taxi driver was a liar, he stated emphatically. The truth is, the man could not stop drinking. He was not intentionally lying, affirmed Pedro, but he was deluding himself. The reality is, he could not "*entrar en la jugada*"—enter the game. It takes strength and courage to join a group and stick with the program, said Pedro. This is the only way an alcoholic can hope to recover. "In my own case," he declared, "I have been one hundred percent loyal to the group. Nothing, not work, not family, has ever interfered with my commitment to Moral Support." Pedro was not only commenting on my story, but also affirming the therapeutic value of Alcoholics Anonymous. I was a newcomer and, from the point of view of the others, required instruction and reassurance about the value of A.A. It is also possible that Pedro was trying to muster support for his proposed rent increase (see Chapter Three). Pedro's emphatic assertion of loyalty to the group came just as the men were discussing how to respond to his request. In this context, he would be eager to remind them of his unwavering support for them and their organization.

I narrated the story of a second taxi incident as well. It concerned a cab driver who took me home from a movie late one night. After inquiring about my living circumstances, the driver declared me to be a sad case: no woman to accompany me to the movies, no one at home to care for me and listen to me discuss the problems of the day. And what a boring life I must have as a professor, stated the driver. Nothing but preparing for classes, giving classes, and then returning home to emptiness and loneliness. I lead this life because I want to, he said. I could find female company easily. There are plenty of available women at the University, he pointed out.

This time it was Gerardo who reacted to my story. The sort of exchange I had had with the taxi driver makes one think, he stated as an opener to his personal story. The truth often hurts, he said, and we therefore deny it. But later the truth will come back to invade our thoughts. "Maybe that driver was right," speculated Gerardo. "Maybe there is something about your life that needs correction." This kind of confrontation is the essence of A.A. therapy, he continued. We have to view ourselves through the eyes of others before we recognize patterns that might need changing.

Commentaries like Gerardo's and Pedro's, issued within the context of the meeting, constitute unsolicited personal advice, issued in the guise of edification for the group as a whole. At any given meeting, personal stories are likely to exhibit conversational elements of this kind. Speaker opinions are directed to particular individuals although they are phrased so as to appear generally valid. Indeed, since advice is delivered so openly and confidently, it cannot help but have an impact on all the listeners in the room.

Alcoholics Anonymous groups are theoretically open to everyone. In practice, however, they display the tacit segregation by class that prevails throughout Mexican urban society. In terms of two major indices, class affiliation and gender, the men of Moral Support find themselves in objectively similar circumstances. It is perhaps for this reason that they so vehemently defend the *autonomía* (Chapter Three) of their group. Only through following the specific principles of organization and operation that guide Moral Support meetings can equality among the men be achieved and maintained. Above all, the men believe that their procedure for the delivery of personal stories assures that everyone receives fair and equal treatment. The men contrast themselves in this respect with other groups they have known in which meetings are dominated by an aggressive few, while a timid majority remain silently in the background.

The equality of the men is asserted formally at the beginning of each meeting, when the moderator reminds the group of the overriding principle that guides A.A. membership: "The only requirement for being a member of A.A. is the desire to stop drinking." Emilio put it to me another way: "What is the ticket I needed to get into A.A.? Well, all the suffering that my alcoholism caused me, that's my ticket to A.A., to enter an A.A. group." The criterion for A.A. membership states nothing about gender, ethnicity, religion, or socioeconomic status. All A.A. affiliates are equal by virtue of their alcoholic condition. The evident differences among the men in Moral Support, as well as between these men and other segments of Mexican society, are obliterated in personal stories. At the same time, the assertion of the qualities that they share and that bind them is among the most noticeable narrative strategies. I had become aware of the theme of social equality at an early stage of fieldwork, when the men tried to persuade me, via the podium, that everyone could join Moral Support and A.A. regardless of skin color or religion (see Chapter One).

However, it is not only through positive assertion that the men express egalitarian sentiments. They demonstrate a shared condition as much by what they do not say as by what they do. In "The Least Common Denominator," Colson's insightful article (1977) about a birthday party at a San Francisco senior citizen center, the author notes the pressure brought upon participants to ignore aspects of personality and status that might divide the group. The party, a secular ritual in honor of all members of the center who celebrate their birthday in a given month, is designed to foster feelings of commonality among participating elders. Public mention of anything that might act to separate members from one another, such as precise age, socioeconomic status, and ethnicity, is suppressed at the monthly parties.

Likewise, at Moral Support meetings men deliver personal stories which ignore a host of potentially divisive circumstances. Although the men are of diverse ages, personal stories make no mention of chronological age. Instead, the men openly celebrate the number of years they have remained sober, something which places them all on potentially equal footing. The men also come from different ethnic backgrounds. Group members include a Mazahua from the State of Mexico, a Nahua from the state of San Luis Potosí, a Totonac from the state of Veracruz, a Mixtec from the state of Oaxaca, several Zapotec from Oaxaca, the child of Italian immigrants, and *mestizos* from diverse states throughout central Mexico. Although all the men speak Spanish fluently, a number of them grew up speaking an indigenous language as their first tongue. And yet it is rare to hear mention of ethnic affiliation, a potentially divisive social category in Mexico. Nor do *compañeros* normally speak of skin color.

On the few occasions when ethnicity emerged as a theme during *historiales,* the issue seemed to serve an ecumenical ideal. Hence, Horacio, a newcomer to Mexico City, told of a group he had been attending on the Costa Chica, a stretch of the Pacific coast of the state of Guerrero, in which "there were two Jews and a Buddhist." None of the listeners seemed surprised or shocked. Gerardo, the only financially successful man in the group, occasionally tells of his drapery business and clients who come from every walk of life, "including Argentines and Jews." When he repeats this statement, no one in the group ever reacts. Just as ethnic differences among group members are ignored in personal stories so too are religious distinctions. There is at least one Protestant among Moral Support regulars, but most of the men are unaware of that fact. It would probably be irrelevant to them were they to find out.

Another way in which the men affirm mutual identification is to address and refer to one another by the term *compañero*. The moderator always calls men to the podium by prefacing personal names with this title, as in, "*Compañero* Damián, would you please step up to the *tribuna*?" After the speaker concludes an *historial,* the moderator might say, "Thank you, *compañero* Emilio, for your uplifting words." Within the personal stories themselves, any reference the speaker might make to a member of the group includes the title *compañero.* When a newcomer attends a meeting for the first time, the moderator might call him to the podium, in which case the moderator invariably asks, "Are you an *invitado* [visitor] or a *compañero?*" The response "*compañero*"—in this case indicating membership in Alcoholics Anonymous generally, rather than in the specific group Moral Support—immediately places the newcomer on an equal footing with the rest of the men. He is an understandable entity, an insider, hence largely predictable.

Another leveling device is repetition, especially in the constant reminders during meetings that "*Soy Fulano y soy un enfermo alcohólico*" —"I'm So-and-So and I'm a sick alcoholic." This simple but bold statement, uttered by all speakers, symbolically asserts equality among the men. It is blurted out with no sense of timidity or shamefulness. The men of Moral Support have assimilated the general Alcoholics Anonymous belief that once an alcoholic, always an alcoholic. The men think of themselves as alcoholics for life, incapable of complete cure. The only difference between them and those who imbibe, they say, is that, as members of A.A., they are *alcohólicos en recuperación,* that is, recovering alcoholics, while those who drink uncontrollably are *alcohólicos activos,* or active alcoholics. When they joined A.A., they moved from one status into the other. All the men in Moral Support share this circumstance, a defining feature of the Alcoholics Anonymous fellowship.

One evening an unknown visitor appeared at the meeting. When called to the podium, he introduced himself as *"un alcohólico social* [a social alcoholic]," rather than *"un enfermo alcohólico."* The man, who looked to be in his mid-thirties, was obviously concerned about his drinking and needy of sympathetic listeners. He explained that he does not drink to the point of "losing reason," but that whenever he does drink, his urine fills with blood. As soon as he stops drinking it returns to normal. He had not yet visited a doctor, he stated, because of what he called "the typical Mexican pattern of going to the doctor when it's too late to be cured." But he did intend to visit one soon. This man was not a *compañero.* By A.A. criteria, he was not an alcoholic of any sort because it was not the loss of control over drink from which he suffered but rather a specific physical symptom, blood in his urine. By the end of the meeting the newcomer must have recognized the difference between himself and the rest, because he never returned.

The men of Moral Support believe strongly in the Alcoholics Anonymous dictum that they suffer from a disease (*una enfermedad*), which makes them incapable of controlling their alcohol intake. Every so often, David will devote a personal story to this topic. He states that at first he thought his alcoholism was inherited, that it had a biological origin, because both his father and grandfather were alcoholic. Then he thought he was the victim of witchcraft. Finally, the truth came to him: alcoholism is *"una enfermedad"* and only with the help of God and his *compañeros* in A.A. could he hope to stop drinking. "They say that dogs don't open their eyes until two weeks after birth," he states, "but I didn't open my eyes until I was thirty-six and a half." That was when he discovered A.A.

It is not that David does not believe in witchcraft, because he does. He claims that the estranged wife with whom he shared his house for so many years once tried to poison him with a substance provided by a witch, whom the wife consulted. Emilio, who also believes in witches, mentioned during one of his *historiales* that his mother attempted to cure him of alcoholism by taking him to a *curandera,* a traditional healer. The *curandera* declared the problem to be the result of witchcraft; the witch was identified as someone envious of Emilio who was trying to undermine him by keeping him drunk. Recounting this episode, Emilio scorned the idea that his alcoholism derives from witchcraft. He declared his problem to be "an illness," one that he will never be able to rid himself of his entire life, despite prayer, medicine, or any other false remedy. This is the basic circumstance which all men in Moral Support share and which impart to them a sense of equality.

Repeated assertions of equality foster linked identities. New members only continue to attend meetings if they are able to overcome initial feelings of alienation and separateness. For David, the only member of Moral Support brought up Protestant, the struggle involved overcoming spiritual doubts, combined with feelings of envy:

> . . . from the start they schooled me in the Evangelical religion. And, I tell you, how strange—I tell you that I didn't believe in God when I arrived at A.A. It definitely made me mad when for example some *compañero* got up on the *tribuna* and shared his story, you know. He'd share his story and say, well, "Thanks to God I have work. Thanks to God I am well." At that time, when I had just started to *militar* [fight for sobriety], when I had just entered A.A., I was pretty screwed up economically, sunk in debts; spiritually, don't even talk about it; mentally really undone. It made me mad that they said, "I'm well. Thanks to God I have work, I earn good money." And there I am, all screwed up, but I didn't realize it was my alcoholism. I was in that situation because of my alcoholism. There was no other reason, because if I hadn't . . . drunk so much I could have had a palace. But since I was a stupid human being, I was a stupid person who didn't know how to live, well, I had to suffer the consequences.

David began to recover from his alcoholism by accepting God and overcoming feelings of envy. "I still can't recover economically," he concluded, "but . . . that doesn't worry me because that's material. Like I said, for me, I no longer lose sleep over material things. I want to do things that are spiritual, I want to make myself feel good inside, internally satisfied, not worry about problems and all that."

For Eusebio, meetings are especially poignant when *compañeros* echo his own experiences and feelings. He is particularly moved by Rogelio's personal story.

> Our A.A. is a place to be on the ball, with an open mind, to listen to what the *compañeros* are saying, to their *historiales.* . . . The *compañero* Rogelio also battled, he suffered a lot, too. I can understand him because his *historial* more or less compares to my own, because he also lived on the streets. I always suffered on the street. He was always there. He, we were together on the street. I didn't have cigarettes, I had to collect cigarette butts to smoke. So all that makes me remember [i.e., So I remember all that] every time he gets up and talks about his *historial*. And, really, that's how you go about curing yourself.

Eusebio affirms the belief that it is not only delivering one's own personal story, but also listening attentively to those of others, that is beneficial to one's recovery.

Empathy and identification with the experiences and suffering of *compañeros* allow the men to overcome the inevitable feelings of isolation that accompany problem drinking. By paying close attention to personal stories, the men begin to feel a part of something greater than themselves. This transcendence gives their lives meaning and motivates them to return to meetings repeatedly. The equality theme that pervades personal stories demonstrates to the men that they are not alone. It enables them to see aspects of themselves within others, and to perceive the vision that others hold of them. Openness about the past and fellowship in the present are qualities that perhaps help them remain sober. At the very least, the men themselves believe this to be the case.

5. GENDER AND THE CONSTRUCTION OF MANHOOD

The men of Moral Support strongly believe that attendance at meetings is the only way to control alcohol addiction. They therefore devote great effort to the never-ending task of preserving and expanding member participation. As we have just seen, the assertion of equality in personal stories motivates at least some of the men to continue coming to meetings. *Historiales* promote a feeling of mutual identification among the men. Over time they come to see the A.A. meeting as a space in which they can safely vent their thoughts and problems. But mutual identification is not the only mechanism by which the men are encouraged to attend meetings. A related concern is that of masculinity: one of the major tasks of the *historial* is to assert and in some cases redefine what it means to be a man in Mexico.

Matthew Gutmann's *The Meanings of Macho* (1996) is to date the definitive treatise on what it means to be a man in Mexico City. The book is particularly relevant to my own research, given that it concerns virtually the same segment of society within which my work was carried out: urban, working class migrants and their families from the Mexican countryside. The main message of Gutmann's research is that stereotypes of the violent, aggressive, and emotionally distant and insulated Mexico *macho*—images popularized in Octavio Paz's *Labyrinth of Solitude* (1961)—are unfounded. Through long-term fieldwork, Gutmann discovered, instead, a complex, nuanced definition of manhood among the men of his *colonia*, who adopt a pragmatic attitude toward men's roles and recognize the impact of the worldwide women's liberation movement on their lives.

Gutmann's chapter, "Degendering Alcohol" (ibid.:173–195), shows that alcohol affects everyone in the *colonia*, "from young girls who must fetch beer for their mothers and grandmothers to fathers, uncles, brothers, and cousins who miss work when they go on a *borrachera* (drinking binge) to friends who have to be taken to the emergency room when their kidneys will not tolerate another drop of rum" (Gutmann 1996:175). Gutmann tells of men and women drinking together, above all at fiestas. He describes cases of male violence caused by drunkenness, but also shows that alcohol exerts a calming influence on some of the men he knew while carrying out his research. Gutmann takes account of changing gender roles: "consuming one or two beers daily is a common practice for many men, whereas bingeing, though not uncommon in the 1990s, was according to most accounts more common in the past. Further, nearly all women and men I have spoken with on the subject . . . maintain that far more women today drink alcoholic beverages, and in far greater quantities, than they did in the past" (ibid.:178). Alcoholics Anonymous, according to Gutmann, is a visible presence in the *colonia*. "In this way," he asserts "alcoholism . . . has a very public presence, at least institutionally" (ibid.).

My observations generally coincide with those of Gutmann. However, even taking into account dramatic changes that might have occurred in Mexican society over the past generation, alcoholic drink in Mexico is and long has been closely connected to gender identity. Although male and female roles are in rapid flux, it is clear that men and women have long maintained distinctive ways of relating to alcohol and that these distinctions contribute to the definition of who they are. In a recent survey of physicians in Mexico City, Menéndez and Di Pardo (1996:88) report that three quarters of their respondents state that, despite the occasional exception, it is men, rather than women, who mainly suffer from alcohol problems.

Circumstances in Mexico, in fact, are not so different from those in disparate parts of the world (e.g., Child et al. 1965; Lomnitz 1969; Marshall 1979; Marshall 1982:4; Singer et al. 1992; Strathern 1982: 147). Colson and Scudder (1988:99) sum up what seems to be a cross-cultural commonplace: "in contrast to men, women are less likely to drink; if they do drink, they drink in lesser quantities, and they are less likely to become drunk in public; and drinking is most common among women who are past child-bearing age." With specific reference to Mexico, gender differences can be explained mainly on the basis of the way in which drink affects family reputation. In a word, it is not shameful for a Mexican man to get drunk, but inebriation is very shameful for a Mexican woman. This is not to say that women do not drink, for they do drink, at certain times and places: mainly within the confines of their own or relatives' homes and during fiestas. Nor does the statement imply that women never get drunk. Clearly they do. As early as 1843, Frances Calderón de la Barca, a famously keen observer of mid-nineteenth-century social life in Mexico City, noted that "there are a great many women quite as tipsy as the men" (1843). Note that although Calderón de la Barca states that women get as drunk as men, she gives no indication of the relative frequency of drunkenness by gender. Regardless of the situation in her time, almost any observer of the contemporary scene would agree that inebriation is much more prevalent among Mexican men than women.[1]

It is impossible to measure the magnitude of male versus female drunkenness, however, for two reasons: first, because women rarely drink in public establishments or on the street, while men frequently do; and, second, because women's problems with alcohol remain largely undetected. Because problem drinking is shameful for a woman and affects her family's reputation, it remains hidden as much as possible from society at large (Pérez-López et al. 1992:126). The woman alcoholic in Mexico tends to drink surreptitiously.[2] A research team based at the Mexican Institute of Psychiatry notes that, in addition to the fact that alcoholism is stigmatized among women in Mexico, "there persist moralistic attitudes toward this illness. Alcoholism impedes a woman's fulfillment of the traditional role expected of her. It represents a deviation from values connected to her conduct as wife and mother; it is associated with sexual promiscuity and with the inability to provide a good example for her children" (Pérez-López et al. 1992:126; my translation). Because of the double standard, precise quantitative comparisons between male and female drinking are impossible to obtain.

In a questionnaire-based study, the National Survey on Addictions in Mexico determined that, in Mexico City, only 17 percent of men stated that they do not drink alcoholic beverages, while 40 percent of the women make that claim (ibid.). (The parallel with the Mexican American sample collected by Corbett, Mora, and Ames is striking. State the authors [1991:217], "Over 40% of the wives reported never having had a drink and under 17% of the husbands.") Further, among those who do drink, men admitted to a much higher frequency of alcohol intake, and more abundant intake, than women. Because it is probable that many Mexican women drink secretly, these figures are likely unreliable. However, no reasonable observer would deny their general validity: clearly, many more men in Mexico City drink alcoholic beverages, more frequently and in greater quantity, than do women.[3] Not surprisingly, the National Survey on Addictions in Mexico (Pérez-López et al. 1992:

128) also discovered that in Mexico City over ten times more men than women are alcohol dependent.

Although quantitative measurements of drinking patterns in Mexico are inherently unreliable, there exist reasonably good data on the gender composition of A.A. groups. By all accounts, members overwhelmingly are men. In 1991, a study team reported, on the basis of a survey, that men constitute 91% of the A.A. members in Mexico City (Rosovsky, Casanova, and Pérez 1991:138). "In the rest of the country," states the senior author, "this proportion is even bigger" (ibid.). The 1991 survey demonstrates that the number of women in A.A. has increased slightly over time; but, as the study team laments, "there still persist discriminatory attitudes of machismo and paternalism toward women, which makes women's participation difficult" (ibid.:142). Nonetheless, given that it is an enormous, complex metropolis, Mexico City is endowed with resources equal to urban centers throughout the United States. There exist both exclusively female and mixed male-female A.A. groups in Mexico City for any woman who wishes to attend. In fact, about half of the groups surveyed in 1991 included women among their membership (Pérez-López 1992:127), whether in exclusively female or mixed male and female groups. In some of the mixed gender groups, however, women meet alone once a week, where they apparently feel freer to express their experiences than they do when men are present (ibid.:128).

Officially, no Alcoholics Anonymous group can or should claim social exclusivity based on gender or any other aspect of social identity. A.A. meetings always begin with the proclamation "Alcoholics Anonymous is a group of men *and women* [emphasis mine] who share their mutual experience, strength, and hope to resolve their common problem and help others to recuperate from alcoholism. The only requirement to be a member of A.A. is the desire to stop drinking." However fundamental this principle, it seems that recovering alcoholics, like the rest of humanity, often find solace among people like themselves. Hence, in Mexico City, as elsewhere, special interest groups have developed within Alcoholics Anonymous, including, among others, gay and lesbian groups, *gringo* groups, and, of course, women's groups.

It is instructive to examine the sociodemographic profile of men and women in Mexico City who attend Alcoholics Anonymous meetings. According to survey results, the age of male and female members is about the same. The vast majority of A.A. affiliates fall between the ages of 30 and 50. The educational level also varies very little by gender: almost half of both male and female members (44 percent) never went far-

TABLE TWO. Sociodemographic Profile of A.A. Members, Mexico City (Male N = 498; Female N = 50)

Age	% Men	% Women
Below 21	0.8	2.0
21–30	18.5	14.0
31–40	35.3	34.0
41–50	31.6	36.0
Above 51	14.1	14.0
Educational Level		
Primary School	44.0	44.0
Junior High School	22.7	22.0
High School	11.8	10.0
Commercial School	11.8	18.0
Marital Status		
Unmarried	19.2	21.2
Married	65.9	25.1
Free Union	5.5	12.8
Separated or Divorced	8.1	31.9
Widowed	1.3	8.5

Source: Pérez-López et al. 1992: 127.

ther than grammar school; about 20 percent of men and women have had formal education beyond high school.

The most revealing gender differences emerge in the figures on marital status. Over 65 percent of the male members are married, while only 25 percent of the women are. Eight percent of the male members are divorced or separated; but nearly a third of the women have had a broken marriage. Only the figures for those who have never been married are the same for men and women, about a fifth of the total for each gender. Although the published survey results do not specify, it is likely that it is the young men and women in the sample who account for this similarity. Overall, the sociodemographic profile shows that a much higher proportion of women A.A. members in Mexico City than men are single.

In Alcoholics Anonymous, a woman can overcome the social isolation that is an inevitable byproduct of her drinking problems. The study
team believes that it is the female drinker's social isolation, more than
anything, which impels her to affiliate with A.A. For such women, they
say, A.A. "becomes their new family and their new friends. The chores
that they carry out are typically associated with female roles: serving
the coffee, cleaning, greeting members as they arrive at meetings, and
assisting hospitalized alcoholics" (Pérez-López 1992:129). In essence,
many of these unmarried women treat the group as their surrogate family; they become married to the group, symbolically. Indeed, in some
cases, a woman in a mixed gender group "is looked upon as a person
who needs protection and guidance, and frequently she gets amorously
involved with *compañeros*" (ibid.). Not infrequently, young women
new to a group establish kinship-like ties with older, more experienced
women. The Mexican Institute of Psychiatry research team noted that
among women in A.A. there is a symbolic reproduction of socially ap-
proved roles, such as wife, mother, little girl, seductress, sister, or close
friend (ibid.).

Although fewer than a tenth of A.A. members in Mexico City are
female, women by far predominate in Al-Anon, the twelve-step support organization designed for relatives of alcoholics. To accommodate
women's traditional work schedules, Al-Anon meetings tend to be held
in the mornings or early afternoons, thereby allowing women to take
care of their families in late afternoon and evenings and avoiding the ne-
cessity of going out alone after dark (Rosovsky, Garcia, et al. 1992:
591). The first Al-Anon groups in Mexico were English speaking and established themselves in Mexico City in 1960. In 1965, the first Spanish-
speaking group was founded. By 1990, there were 220 registered groups
in Mexico City alone.

A study team found that Al-Anon meeting room decorations in Mexico City reflect the differing styles ("'feminine' styles," in the words of
the authors [ibid.]) of each social class: "vases, embroidered cloths,
furry toys, and little baskets made by the group members themselves
from bread dough, yarn, beads, ribbons or lacework are all objects often found in lower- and middle-class groups. . . . For upper-class social
groups the places are larger, furnished with comfortable easy chairs and
carpets and decorated soberly" (ibid.). Testimony from Al-Anon study
groups indicates that not a single member attended meetings because of
the alcoholism of a female relative. All said they were there because of
men, principally husbands (ibid.:594). This is one indication that female

alcoholics in Mexico, though considerably less numerous than men, have a much weaker support network than their male counterparts. Women in Alcoholics Anonymous often report feeling abandoned by their families (ibid.:601), a situation reflected in part by the virtually complete absence of family members of female alcoholics in Al-Anon groups throughout Mexico City (ibid.:600).

According to long-standing, worldwide tradition, Alcoholics Anonymous has always seemed more appropriate for males, Al-Anon for females. After all, the two founding members of A.A. were men, most of the A.A. literature is written by men, and "men in all countries have constituted and still constitute the majority of members" (Mäkelä et al. 1996:170). The founding fathers of the movement, Bill W. and Dr. Bob, adhered, in contemporary parlance, to family values, incorporating conservative gender roles. Dr. Bob, in particular, was unhappy about the prospect of women being admitted to A.A. (Robertson 1988:37). For these and other reasons, "AA, Al-Anon, and later Alateen developed around modern nuclear family roles, AA being primarily for the father, Al-Anon for the mother, and Alateen for the child. Gender polarization was thus a reality: women were in Al-Anon and men in AA" (Mäkelä et al. 1996:171). This situation, obsolete in many countries, has largely persisted in Mexico throughout the 1990s.

In fact, for working class Mexican women, it is possible that a lesser-known twelve-step program—Neurotics Anonymous (Neuróticos Anónimos)—is more popular than Al-Anon. In Mexico City among the most popular definitions of neurosis is the inability to control one's temper. A person who expresses anger openly and at the least provocation is known as "*neurótico(a),*" or "neurotic." Hence, for the men of Moral Support, a woman who continually scolds her husband and children is neurotic; she is the perfect candidate for membership in Neuróticos Anónimos, an organization whose logo is displayed prominently throughout the city. The men of Moral Support believe that women become neurotic largely as a reaction to male drinking problems, although men themselves are subject to this condition as well. However, the men of Moral Support believe that neurosis is largely a female affliction, which can be allayed by attendance at Neurotics Anonymous meetings. These beliefs are yet another indication of the way men and women in Mexico City relate differently to alcohol.

The beliefs also demonstrate that the men of Moral Support are well aware of the afflictions that they bring upon their families, particularly their spouses. Kaja Finkler (1994) applies the apt term "life's lesions" to bodily pain brought on by emotions, including anger. Her study of gender and morbidity demonstrates that, among Mexicans, "moral indignation is often expressed in anger (thus intensifying the experience of life's lesions) which in Mexico is culturally recognized as sickness producing" (ibid.:18). Says Finkler, "The central 'trouble' impinging on marital relations is a man's drinking habits. Undoubtedly a woman suffers most from her husband's bouts with alcohol. Drinking is most often accompanied by physical and psychological abuse, and in those instances women experience angers and sickness" (ibid.:63). Finkler continues: "In Mexico the circumstances that lead women to 'make angers' and are culturally perceived to be sickness-producing abound: when children who ought to obey their parents do not; when husbands who ought to be faithful betray their wives; when husbands get drunk but ought not to; when husbands dissipate their meager earnings on drink and other women and the wife is left with no money for daily expenses," etc. (ibid.:45). One of Finkler's principal informants, Josefina, states of her husband that "He always turned a pistol on me when he was drunk. At such times he wanted to kill me. When he was not drunk he was nice" (ibid.:108).[4] The connection between drunkenness and violence in Mexico, as elsewhere (e.g., Pernanen 1991, Parker and Rebhun 1995), is longstanding. An earlier report from rural central Mexico indicates that "most violence involves either temporary or chronic intoxication" (Romanucci-Ross 1973:137).

The men of Moral Support are supremely conscious that their alcohol problems once exacted a terrible emotional and physical toll on the women closest to their hearts—above all, mothers and spouses, who suffered in ways very similar to Kaja Finkler's "women in pain." The men of Moral Support differ from many other Mexican men in that they are openly repentant. Participation in Alcoholics Anonymous provides an outlet for their remorse, a space in which the expression of regret is interpreted as strength rather than weakness. In the mid-1990s, Eduardo experienced a terrible loss, when his sister and mother died within six months of one another. Just afterward, Eduardo was able to tell me,

> Recently, in my last drinking bout, [I lost] my mom, right? My sister and my mom. . . . Well, I have felt bad, because once you lose the moral support of a mother—right?—of a sister, well, you feel bad. Especially with how much I made my mother suffer, you know, with my drinking habit. . . . Oh, I felt so bad. I would have celebrated

eleven years in A.A. and, well, I relapsed again. And who bore the burden? My children, my woman, my mom, my *mamá,* because she was the one who took care of me, too—so much! On the eighth of November my mom dies. . . . Physically I didn't hurt my mother. But, morally, it was another story. Morally, I was always drunk. And she wondering if I had eaten or not, if I was drinking or not, where I was sleeping, what I was doing. All of that drained her, robbed her of sleep, robbed her of well-being. And that's why they say that an alcoholic is a thief. By nature a thief. Because he robs tranquility, he robs his family of their sleep.

When Eduardo spoke of his remorse on the podium, his voice cracked and he burst into tears, an indication, as we shall see in subsequent chapters, of sincerity, courage, and strength.

Among working class Mexican men, like those in Moral Support, sobriety and the abdication of arbitrary power over spouses is often interpreted as feminizing behavior. Whatever they feel inside, it is rare for men openly to express guilt over mistreatment of women. In Alcoholics Anonymous, by contrast, men feel free to abstain from drink and ask women in public for forgiveness. Far from casting their masculinity in doubt, this behavior seems to enhance it. In A.A., the men come to realize, in David's words, that "if the head of household is drunk, there is unhappiness, there is suffering, there are tears, there is illness, there is misery. All that is what alcoholism produces. Alcoholism destroys homes." [5]

In Moral Support, membership is highly flexible, making it difficult to state precisely the number and social composition of the group. There is one valid generalization that can be made, however: all the members, without exception, are male, despite the moderator's pronouncement at the beginning of every meeting that "Alcoholics Anonymous is a group of men and women. . . . " In this respect, as we have seen, Moral Support is representative of the vast majority of A.A. members in Mexico City and the entire Mexican Republic. Only once did we get some indication that a woman might join the group. Arturo told us that he had met a woman alcoholic and convinced her to attend a meeting. She would join us the following week. The atmosphere in the meeting room was charged with excitement. There was nothing but enthusiastic anticipation at the prospect of acquiring a female member of the group. And yet, on the evening when Arturo was to have brought her to Moral

Support, he arrived as alone as always. The prospective *compañera* soon disappeared from memory.

On several occasions, I brought women friends, visiting from the United States, to view the meeting. Initially, they were taken for alcoholics and treated as any new member would be, with words of welcome and encouragement from those delivering personal stories. On each of these occasions, I took the podium and explained that the women were just friends who were curious to observe the group that was the subject of my research. The men would simply smile in mild amusement at their innocent error. I once asked Emilio why women never attend Moral Support. His reaction was to reiterate the A.A. pronouncement that any man or woman who wishes to attend meetings would be welcome to do so. I responded that, in fact, new men do arrive from time to time, but women are never present. He explained, "If it's hard for a man to stop drinking, it's even harder for a woman." Although Emilio was unable to elaborate further on this intriguing statement, it suggests that he acknowledges the sense of shame and the absence of family support which weigh on the female alcoholic in Mexico. These conditions make it particularly difficult for women to admit they have a drinking problem, usually the first step in seeking help.

For men, including the men of Moral Support, there is no easy solution to alcohol addiction either. Drinking alcoholic beverages is an inherent part of the male role in Mexico. Christine Eber, a specialist on gender and alcohol, finds evidence that, from ancient times through the Mexican colonial period, men were given "more leeway to drink" than women (1995:23). This pattern has persisted to the present day. In fact, I would say that Mexican men have more than mere leeway to drink. Drink is virtually a prescribed feature of religious ritual and ritualized encounters of all kinds in which men frequently participate. In fact, as is true elsewhere in the world (e.g., Marshall 1979:97), drinking alcohol on certain occasions not only distinguishes men from women, but also differentiates between youth and maturity. As in so many societies in which so-called binge drinking is the norm, young Mexican boys are prohibited from imbibing, especially in the presence of their elders. A lad's coming of age is marked largely by his tacit authorization to drink liquor openly.

The most obvious examples of prescribed male drinking come from the religious realm. Throughout Mexico, male drinking is and long has been essential to the ritual process (e.g., Brandes 1988:174–178; Taylor 1979:61; Madsen and Madsen 1979; Warren 1985:92). In fact, this relationship extends beyond Mexico to much of Latin America (e.g., Doughty 1979:73–74; Heath 1958; Leacock 1979; Nash 1985:208). At Mass, it is the priest—without exception a man—who takes communion by drinking wine.[6] During rites of passage, particularly baptisms and weddings, it is principally the male celebrants who publicly exchange bottles of liquor and consume them as a formal part of the ritual process. Speaking of the central Mexican town of Tlayacapan, located less than two hours from Mexico City, Ingham (1986:151) states that "drinking is a typically male behavior. Women may drink a little at fiestas, but rarely to intoxication, and what sipping they do usually takes place apart from their menfolk. Men, by contrast, may drink heavily at fiestas, during Carnival, on weekends, or just about any time, for that matter." At the fiesta of the Tastoanes in Zapopan, on the outskirts of Guadalajara, male clown figures who are able to perform their role to the spectators' satisfaction are "rewarded with a jug of huariche, which is a local term for hard liquor, usually mescal or tequila" (Nájera-Ramírez 1997:19). The ceremonial role of male folk healers and public officials in Mitla, in the state of Oaxaca, "lends itself to continuous drinking" (Parsons 1936:187).

Among the main arenas for male drink are life cycle rituals and community fiestas, that is, village and town celebrations, normally held in honor of an especially venerated saint. During community fiestas, male cargo holders, or *mayordomos* (religious and/or civil officeholders, who assume these posts on a rotating basis) are expected to distribute and imbibe large quantities of alcohol. A particularly rich anthropological literature describes the duties of cargo holders in the Indian villages of highland Chiapas, where alcohol occupies a central ritual role (e.g., Bricker 1973, Cancian 1965, Nash 1985, Vogt 1993). In Chiapas, too, legal disputes are often settled through the presentation of bottles of liquor by the offender to the victim. With the exception of litigation between long-married spouses, it is always men who give and receive alcoholic beverages in these transactions (Collier 1973:24–27, 100–103).

Throughout Mexico, during family and community festivals alike, hired musicians, who are almost always male, are supposed to be provided with food and alcoholic drink (e.g., M. Foster 1984:138, Nutini 1984:152). There are occasions, as in Tzintzuntzan, Michoacán, when women are supposed to imbibe alcohol as part of their ritual role. However, as Mary Foster (ibid.) points out, they often find this role distasteful. Their solution is to "tie a waterproof bag under their clothing into which to pour an unwanted drink, dump it secretly on the ground, or invent some way to be called home suddenly in order to avoid inebria-tion." During All Saints and All Souls Days (November 1–2) through-out Mexico, family members place items favored by the deceased on gravesites and home altars. Liquor often figures among these offerings in altars dedicated to deceased male relatives, but never females. Even if it is known that a deceased mother or sister had favored a particular alcoholic beverage, the family would never announce that preference through public display. It could only bring shame upon the deceased and her relatives.

Mexican men often demonstrate friendship through drink. Lomnitz (1977:175ff) and Gutmann (1996:177) both show that male friendship in Mexico City is intimately bound to alcohol consumption. When young and prohibited from imbibing alcohol, Mexican boys often play at being drinking buddies. In Tzintzuntzan, I have observed young men, entirely sober, wobble down the street with arms around one another's shoulders, pretending to be drunk. Girls never play at this game. When they are teenagers or newlyweds and forming friendships, men will say to one another, "We'll have to get drunk together some day!" It is in-conceivable that a woman could use this technique to forge a friendship. Gutmann (1996:173) observes in Mexico City that "Every day, and even more so on holidays, men are found sipping *las copas*—alcoholic beverages—in the streets. . . . " He adds a cautionary note (ibid.:174) by asking, "What of those men who were at home and sober through-out that day? Were those men, at least implicitly, less manly than those who were drunk in the streets?" The answer is, of course, no. They are not less manly. But drinking in the streets is normal, predictable, and far from scandalous for men. For women the situation is just the reverse.

In drink, as in the sexual and other domains, the range of permissible behavior is wider for men than for women. For that reason, men use drink in the mediation of social relations, as a means of increasing and decreasing social distance. The effect of alcohol on men's behavior is un-predictable. Gutmann has shown (ibid.:178) that some short-tempered men become mild-mannered under the influence of alcohol. I have even observed drunks let down their guard and become downright amorous with one another, uttering propositions that would be inconceivable for these men when sober. In Mexico, trust and intimacy between men seem to grow under the influence of drink. However, alcohol sometimes exerts the reverse effect, transforming temperate men into aggressors. According to Gutmann's observations (ibid.), intoxication "may lead to violent outbursts revealing long-simmering feuds or to tender confessional moments. In either case the parties involved are capitalizing on the belief that drunks should be held less responsible for their words and actions." That is, drinking is time-out behavior, rather than being woven seamlessly into daily life, as is the case, for example, in most of Spain and the European Mediterranean (e.g., Brandes 1979, Gilmore 1985, Hansen 1976, Lolli et al. 1958, Blum and Blum 1964).

Given the centrality of alcohol in the life of the Mexican male, it is no wonder that problem drinking is the leading cause of death among males in the so-called productive years of life (35–65). Mortality from alcohol results directly through cirrhosis or indirectly through accidents and homicide (Menéndez 1990:9). Moreover, data show that it is above all poor men—particularly rural migrants to the city who work in construction and other manual jobs—who suffer the most from alcohol excesses (Menéndez and Di Pardo 1996:173). However, these problems are not unique to the city. In the peasant village of Morelos, Romanucci-Ross found a strong correlation between masculinity, violence, and drink. States Romanucci-Ross, "That men are more involved in violence and killing reflects not only the divergent codes of behavior . . . but also the exclusive right of men to non-ceremonial drinking and drunkenness (women drink moderately and only at fiestas). The tie-in between aggressive violent behavior and alcoholism is nearly complete, in my opinion—that is, the aggressor is almost always either a heavy drinker or an alcoholic and is in most cases intoxicated when the aggression is committed" (Romanucci-Ross 1973:136).

The overall evidence leaves little doubt that throughout Mexico, on a daily basis and during fiesta celebrations, alcohol consumption is more central to men's lives than to women's. This situation is hardly unique to Mexico. Mac and Leslie Marshall (1990:3), authorities on gender and alcohol, declare that "In some human societies women are not supposed to drink at all, and even in most of those where women may drink they are enjoined to consume smaller amounts and to drink less often than men." In Mexico, as in most parts of the world, drink and drunkenness are not exclusive to men. Nor does a man necessarily lose his male identity if he abstains. However, manhood and drinking are closely enough linked in ideology and observable behavior that men—at least, most men in the Mexican laboring classes—come to associate imbibing and inebriation with male identity. Male ritual roles and norms regulating friendship are too deeply ingrained for them to reject or ignore this feature of life. Similarly, the roles and norms guiding female comportment offer such a striking contrast that it would be easy for a man in such circumstances to question his manhood should he decide to abstain.

The men of Moral Support are, from a statistical standpoint, good candidates for alcohol abuse since they belong to those segments of society which have been identified, by Menéndez and Di Pardo (1996:173), as producing a high concentration of alcoholics: male migrants to the city, between thirty and sixty years of age, who work in construction and at other manual labor.[7] The life histories and personal stories of the men of Moral Support show that, while active alcoholics, their male identity was clearly dependent upon alcoholic drink. In the sober state, they have had to struggle with what it means to be a man. In effect, to identify as competent men, they have had to redefine the meaning of manliness and manhood. However, this process of redefinition in no sense involves complete abandonment of the behavioral patterns that they maintained as active alcoholics.

In Mexico, one of the key ways in which manliness is expressed is through friendship, particularly in the creation of strong bonds with other men. Lomnitz (1977:175–180) found that in Mexico City during the 1970s, male construction workers developed exclusively male friendships. They called their friends *cuates* (literally, "twins"). *Cuates* are first and foremost drinking buddies. Although *cuates* potentially share a number of activities—among others, card playing, viewing television together, playing soccer, going for walks, or simply conversing—their most significant activity from a symbolic point of view is drinking. In Cerrada del Cóndor, the district where Lomnitz worked (close both geographically and socially to the world of the men in Moral Support), "the *cuate* group is the effective community of a male in the great city" (ibid.:178). *Cuates* develop a trusting relationship, accompanied by a release from the ceremonial formalities of interpersonal relations that prevail throughout most segments of Mexican society. Lomnitz found that it is "the act of getting drunk" (ibid.:176) that above all brings about this bond, since "getting drunk together represents a high degree of trust" (ibid.:177). As one of Lomnitz's informants put it, "Getting drunk is a liberation, people get rid of their inhibitions. When you are sober you cannot say the kinds of things you can say when drunk; these are your truths" (quoted in ibid.:176). Another man in Cerrada del Cóndor told her, "I do not drink so I don't have any friends" (quoted in ibid.: 177). With respect to the meaning of getting drunk together with male buddies, the situation in Mexico City is, in fact, not so different from that found in other large urban centers throughout Latin America (see, e.g., Lomnitz 1969:47–71; Roberts 1973:29).

The men of Moral Support, some of whom were young alcoholics in the 1970s, use the same terminology as Lomnitz's informants and do so tellingly. Repeatedly, in personal stories, recorded life histories, and daily conversation, group members refer to former male friends from their days as active alcoholics as *cuates.* They distinguish *cuates* from their new male companions, those from Alcoholics Anonymous in general and Moral Support in particular, who are known as *compañeros.* *Cuates* emerge in life history narratives as evil creatures, luring their so-called friends into cantinas and seducing them to have yet another drink. *Compañeros,* on the other hand, represent recovery from the insalubrious effects of alcohol.

Given that Alcoholics Anonymous proclaims alcoholism to be a mortal illness, the men of Moral Support think of their former *cuates* as nothing short of harbingers of death. David speaks bitterly of the treatment he received from former drinking companions. In the process of separating himself from their company, he states, "I had to withstand humiliation from my buddies because then they'd see me and [say] 'Hey, come over here and have a drink.'" His response, a culturally appropriate one, was to refuse on the grounds that "I'm on medication." But the drinking buddies would taunt him by accusing him of being cowardly: "It's that they'll hit you . . . you're afraid . . . your wife will scold you . . . you've become an *hermano,*" literally a "brother," or Protestant fanatic. When I asked David whether the term *hermano* means "Protestant," he responded,

> Exactly, they think that because I stopped drinking that I'm a Protestant or I'm an Evangelist, etc. You know? So that's what I had to suffer, because it's unbearable. They're unbearable things, that they're just poking and poking you with the intention of making you fall back down, fall back into drinking again for your own dignity, for whatever reason. Because they told me over and over, "No, it's that those at home will punch you" or "They'll scold you" or "You're a . . . " or "You've become an *hermano*" or "repentant drunk," you know, things like that. Because, those people didn't get it, they didn't understand and I more or less by then I could envisage that what I was saving was my skin, it was my life itself. That's what I was saving, without worrying about theirs, because they wanted to live like

that. But I didn't want to live like that anymore. I wanted to release myself from the hell into which I had sunk, that mud hole that was alcoholism, that quicksand from which so many times you desperately want to escape and can't. You can't because you don't know how to do it. But in my own personal case, A.A. came to me. They held my hand and little by little helped me out.

After more than a decade of sobriety, David still has to deal with invitations to join former buddies in a drink. But, as he says, "It's stupid, for example, that I as [a member of] Alcoholics Anonymous, instead of seeking out beneficial friendships, should enter a cantina. Because, thank God, I don't even step foot in a cantina anymore, and even less in a *pulquería,* and even less in a *piquera.* Right? Because that's not my scene anymore."

Renaldo, with his sixty-four years of age and seventeen years of sobriety, recalls that he started drinking at the age of sixteen. At first he would drink alone, frequenting cantinas located in a nearby town. All this occurred in his native state of Guanajuato, immediately after the government opened the first highway leading from the small *ranchería* of Hinojosa to the city of San Miguel de Allende.

San Miguel de Allende was far from there, from where I lived, from Hinojosa. More or less, hmmm, walking it was more or less two hours from there. And, well, when they opened the highway—because there weren't any highways before—we didn't know anything about busses at that time, we didn't know what a car was, we didn't know what a radio was, nothing, nothing. All of that was, hmmm, as they say, dead; it didn't exist. It was only later that we started to see all of that, when they opened the road. . . . And that was when I started to go to the cantina.

The little *ranchería* of Hinojosa, as it turns out, had cantinas of its own. But Renaldo would walk the two hours to San Miguel de Allende to avoid being detected. "I didn't like to drink there [in Hinojosa] because I was ashamed. I was ashamed that they would see me drinking and so, in order for them not to see me, well, I went all the way to town. I'd come back late at night." At age sixteen, states Renaldo,

I started to go, but they didn't let me in, they threw me out. They didn't let minors enter the cantina and I asked permission to enter. I told them I was going to take a piss, right? But then, while I was there, I'd have a tequila. Right? In my hometown, they drank tequila a lot. And, well, that was where I started. Afterwards, when I grew up, they let me in. Once I was eighteen years old they let me enter the cantinas and, hmmm, that was where I started to get caught up in alcoholism. . . . And, well, I started to like it. . . . Actually, when I started to drink, I didn't have friends. I was alone, right? Afterwards, I needed company to drink. Afterwards, I got together with friends to drink and drink and, well, *echar relajo,* as they say . . . that is, to be laughing there in the cantina, to be, hmmm, playing, playing pool. And, well, you've seen that there are cantinas that have pool tables. And there are a lot of ways to make a scene there, . . . to start to laugh, to start to shout, to start, well, to make noise, to start to fight, to start to do many things. . . .

Renaldo, like others in Moral Support, draws a picture of drinking as a social act. It is not always a harmonious act, as is clear from his words, but it is usually an act carried out in company. Once he had come of age, his solitary drinking ended and he began to share drinking bouts with friends. As a migrant to Mexico City, already married, Renaldo's drinking got even worse. "That was when I started to drink, hmmm, with fervor—you know? Because here is where I got together with people who were alcoholics and, well, I ended up being that way afterwards. They were *alcoholizados* [literally, alcoholized, i.e., hooked on alcohol], good at drinking and, well, I started to hang around with them."

David and Renaldo are typical of the men in Moral Support. Friendship—specifically male friendship—was the foundation of their drinking careers, just as friendship is what helped them to escape. When David first attended an A.A. meeting, he fought against the program.

I thought that there [at the group meeting] they were going to give me an injection, you know, to tell me that this is how you go about stopping to drink until you definitively stop. But, no, it was completely the opposite. They told me that if you want to quit drinking, come and listen, join with us, join up with the triumphant ones. I didn't understand anything, I didn't understand a thing, because . . . because I was blocked by my alcoholism—mentally blocked, physically destroyed, morally undone . . . and, economically, don't even mention it! Because, really, as I told you a moment ago, alcoholism is the mother of all evils; out of all the evils that exist, alcoholism beats them all. You know, all that negativity. So I started going [to meetings] with this friend and little by little it started to affect me. Of course, I had to discipline myself, I had to make an effort, I had to make the sacrifice not to hang out with the people I used to hang out with, because the people who I used to drink with . . . of course, I had to separate myself from them for a reasonable time, you know.

Now an established member of Alcoholics Anonymous, David looks back on his initial encounters in A.A. and summarizes what the men in his group provide him. He tries recapturing their words: "Here [in A.A.] we're going to help you, here we're going to give you the arms to defend yourself out there, so that you can say 'no' to the first *copa* [alcoholic drink]."

Of course, according to A.A. ideology and beliefs—including those of Moral Support members—it is the first drink, even a mere sip of alcohol, that inevitably leads to relapse. The goal of the A.A. program is to help individuals prevent themselves from taking even one drink during the next 24-hour period. At the start of every day, each A.A. member reestablishes this time-limited horizon for the maintenance of sobriety. To look too far into the future, which means for a period longer than 24 hours, is presumed to be an overwhelmingly burdensome goal, which can only backfire. As one of the framed placards on Moral Support's walls reads, "*Poco a poco se va lejos*"—"Little by little, you go far." But this slow journey is accomplished, not on one's own, but rather with the support of the A.A. fellowship. As Vaillant (1995:259) suggests, "willpower and self-control can be enormously enhanced if they are derived from belonging to a group."

Scholars have pointed out that Alcoholics Anonymous meetings can become as addictive to the recovering alcoholic as was alcohol itself. One compulsion is replaced by another; the person who successfully abstains possesses a "gift for substituting people for alcohol" (ibid.:259). The men of Moral Support tell of experiences that confirm this analysis, but only partially. Although they describe drinking bouts in which they are left alone on the streets to binge until they run out of money, or fall down in a drunken stupor, their drinking episodes were almost always initiated and flourished in the company of male drinking buddies, the *cuates*. The decision to become sober leads them to abandon not only alcohol, but also these companions.

The Alcoholics Anonymous group consisting of the newly acquired *compañeros* becomes a substitute not so much for alcohol as for the former drinking buddies. One group of men replaces another. Moreover, it is difficult to say which group occupies more of the alcoholic's time and thought. To be sure, the active alcoholic saps more of the family resources and reaps deeper unhappiness among his wife, children, and other relatives, than does the recovering alcoholic. But to carry out the Alcoholics Anonymous program properly requires a great deal of time away from home. Moral Support meetings occupy three evenings a week. Several of the men attend two groups which meet on alternating nights, so that they are away from home virtually every evening of the week. Whether drinking or sober, the men of Moral Support like to establish connections with other men, who relate to alcohol in the same way they do. The quality of life at home for these men might well improve under the influence of the A.A. program. However, the actual number of hours they spend with the family is probably not much greater than it was prior to group membership.

There is no doubt, however, that the men of Moral Support perceive Alcoholics Anonymous as the salvation of the family. David, whose own family was torn asunder by his drinking problems, expresses the A.A. ideal.

> I told you about *compañeros* who have arrived [to A.A.] almost destroyed, who almost don't have their lives anymore. And now, thanks to A.A., which exists not just in our country but throughout the world, we have that great hope to save ourselves from the claws of alcoholism, to be good citizens, to be good spouses, to be good children, to be good workers. So this is what you win from being a member of Alcoholics Anonymous. They move you from one place to a more positive place. Yes, so that is so nice, that is marvelous. Above all, as I told you awhile ago, the family [of an A.A. member] lives in tranquility, now that the wife is no longer wondering what time her drunkard will arrive home, in what state he's going to return—if he isn't going to come home beaten up and batter his own wife and kids. Or if he'll bring home money for the household expenses. Because . . . a drunk can't fulfill his responsibilities.

To fulfill responsibilities is one of the great precepts of Alcoholics Anonymous. And one's duty to family members—parents, spouses, children—is paramount. Of course, says David, men sometimes lure their wives into drink. "That is a grave error," he proclaims, "because afterwards it's not going to be one alcoholic, one drunk, but two. And if these two are heads of a family, it will be hell for the kids, a life of traumas, of sadness, of tears. . . . "

David's marriage, like that of so many alcoholics, was destroyed by his drinking. When drunk, he mistreated his wife badly. After joining

A.A. he tried to win her back, but she was already lost to him. During most of my field stint, the two shared a house and kitchen, arranging their schedules to assure minimal contact. If they encountered one another within the confines of their tiny home, they did not even speak. Eduardo had a similarly sad experience with a common-law wife. She left him because of his alcoholic episodes, despite the fact that she had just become pregnant. Eduardo narrates:

> So we broke up. She left my house, she left her poor home. I am from the state of Tlaxcala; my *pueblo* is Tamales. So, well, with that woman I had a girlfriend. And . . . in reality, you know, it makes me so sad to remember that. Because all I did was ruin the life of that poor woman, of my wife. In reality, my intentions were good. But alcohol destroyed me completely. . . . Afterwards, she broke up with me, you know, she had to work for awhile. I didn't give her alimony, because they didn't force me to and I didn't want to, me being the asshole [*culero*] that I am. I was angry because she had left my house, you know, and she only came looking for me after she had the child. So then afterwards she met another man and I think they live around here in Mexico City, I don't know where. The problem is that, from what I learned, what they told me, right? that guy treated her really badly. Because then she became alcoholic, too, and she drank and she drank. They fought a lot. He beat her.

Eduardo describes himself as neglectful and irresponsible toward his family, attitudes born of his drinking career. His story is shot through with images of violence. He harbors lingering feelings of hostility and self-recrimination, sure indications, by A.A. standards, that problems deriving from his alcoholism are still unresolved.

One of the main tasks of Alcoholics Anonymous is to help recovering alcoholics overcome such internal conflicts and deal with their past. After all, Step 8 of the A.A. twelve-step program stipulates that the recovering alcoholic should make a list of all persons harmed and be willing to make amends to all of them. Step 9 directs the recovering alcoholic to make amends to such people, except in cases where doing so would injure them or others. Eduardo's story reveals that he has yet to attend to the fulfillment of these steps. In fact, even while sober, some *compañeros* maintain—even boast on the podium—that they treat their wives in a stereotypically macho fashion.

Raúl provides one such case. Raúl is a shoe repairman, whose tiny shop is located just down the street from the Moral Support meeting room. He is a stocky man about forty-five years old, always neatly groomed, but driven by an aggressive, combative impulse unlike anyone else's in the group. During my months with Moral Support, Raúl faded in and out of meetings. On one occasion, after a lengthy absence, he was called to the podium and spent most of his personal history condemning his wife. The two of them had had a bad argument, he said, so he abandoned her and his children for eight months. That experience taught her a lesson, he said. She had to go begging from her brothers and sisters for beans and tortillas. He had warned her, "Your brothers and sisters are not going to support you, because they have their own children to take care of." He seemed pleased to report that his prediction proved right. They did not provide for their abandoned sister. At this point, Raúl displayed the cruel, almost sadistic, side of his personality. Instead of eating "nice cuts of beef" on Sundays, he said, the children ate *"puros chilaquiles"*—only *chilaquiles,* a poor man's dish, made of leftover, dried out tortillas. Rather than putting on new clothes at the beginning of the school year, the children wore hand-me-downs from their cousins, second-hand clothes and shoes. That taught her a lesson, Raúl repeated. He seemed as unconcerned about his children's welfare as about the well-being of his wife. To end his tale, Raúl reported that he and his wife have reunited. He had taught her a thing or two.

Raúl, as I have said, is an unusual case. Others in Moral Support speak with deep remorse about the injuries caused to parents, wives, and children in their periods of alcohol abuse. Through involvement in A.A., they hope to redefine family relationships so as to maximize equality and mutual respect between spouses. This endeavor naturally involves a redefinition of what it means to be a man. The men of Moral Support know that, as recovering alcoholics, they have to abdicate as authoritarian rulers at home. They should share in household tasks and take responsibility for their children. To signal the new form of relationship, the men have dropped the common Mexican label *"esposa"* to refer to the wife. Instead, they make a point of referring to their wives as *compañeras.* This designation, they believe, automatically elevates their wives to a position equal to themselves.

In fact, by using the term *compañera,* the men symbolically conflate all categories of female partners. The term *compañera* refers without distinction to women who are legally married as well as to those who live in common-law unions (*uniones libres*). Long-term romantic companions are also potentially *compañeras.* Formal church marriage is normally more prestigious than a common-law marriage and results in a man acquiring a wife, or *esposa*. Hence, to substitute the term *compañera* for *esposa* is symbolically to eradicate a two-tier system, elevating those men who are formally married by a priest above those who are not. The term *compañera* helps to produce the common denominator that the men share as an ideal (see Chapter Four).

The term *compañera* also equates the female partner with the male *compañero* in A.A. Symbolically, this usage elevates a man's significant other to a status beyond that of sexual partner, wife, and mother. It transforms her symbolically into a kind of friend, placing her on an equal footing with the men in the group. Likewise, to equate one's *compañeros* in Moral Support with the *compañera* at home is to convert the men into quasi kin. Symbolically, they become a kind of family. In the space of half a year, Eduardo suffered the death of two close female relatives: "my sister died the 26th of June, my mother the 8th of November," he says. "I was left alone and today I only have my *compañeros* from A.A. who are all of you—my friends, my true friends." The men of Moral Support regularly equate friendship with family. Friends become like symbolic family, family like symbolic friends. This symbolism is reflected in the use of the terms *compañero* and *compañera*.

Over and above linguistic usage, Moral Support takes on the quality of a family for its members. According to A.A. ideology as interpreted by the members of Moral Support, neither family relations nor friendship should be sullied by acts of dominance and submission. All human interactions should reflect feelings of equality and mutual respect. To the members of Moral Support, family relations ideally should be infused with an element of friendship and friendship with an element of family. Hence, at the conclusion of my fourth group meeting, just as I announced my intention to carry out research on Moral Support, David offered words of encouragement. "You are welcome into the group," he assured me. "You have a family here, because we are like a family." The men of Moral Support do more than substitute one group of males for another when they join A.A. For at least some of the men, the group is a surrogate family. More importantly, the men use the group meeting as a principal arena for expressing and redefining gender identity.

Recovering alcoholics like the men of Moral Support cannot bolster their male identity by sharing drinks. In an abrupt reversal of norms, which George Vaillant interprets psychoanalytically as a reaction formation (Vaillant 1995:243), these men have come to consider drinking and getting drunk as the antithesis of manliness. That which they previously loved and cherished is now hated and rejected. Vaillant considers this emotional turnaround "essential for abstinence" (ibid.). Without it there is a high risk of relapse.

Although the men of Moral Support can no longer express their masculinity through drink, there exist alternatives. One is repeatedly to assert a redefinition of masculinity which excludes alcoholic consumption. David seems to require constant reassurance. Each time he delivers a personal story, he states that Alcoholics Anonymous breeds "*hombres de verdad, hombres enteros, hombres íntegros*"—"real men, whole men, complete men." He and several other men in the group use the podium to declare, "*Soy manso, pero no soy menso*"—that is, "I am tolerant and understanding, but not cowardly." Arturo, whose small size and thin bones seem at odds with his strong will and fearless assertiveness, explained this formulaic expression to me. You have to be tolerant, he said, but you can't let people step on you. When people try to take advantage of you, you have to know how to "*sacar las uñas*"—that is, "show your claws." Arturo claims to suffer from "*neurosis*," his term for uncontrollable anger. On several occasions, in disputes over policy issues, he stomped out of the meeting room angrily. Arturo is definitely not *menso*—cowardly—although his impetuousness tends to undermine his political effectiveness within the group.

I sat with David one morning on his weathered sofa in the tiny parlor of the house he shares with his estranged wife. He mentioned that before entering A.A. he used to be a *machista*—that is, a sexist. I asked him to explain.

> Look, being a *macho* in our country . . . well, you hear much said about Mexican *machismo,* the *macho*. The *macho* is a person with no interest in feelings; he's the kind of person who is interested in nothing but what he does and he says. And, really, that can't be. . . . He likes to give orders rather than to do something himself, far from providing an example by putting his own words into practice. . . . And, before arriving at A.A., I was that person. I only liked to give orders, to say, "How come you haven't swept? Why haven't you dusted? Why haven't you made the bed?" Or, "Bring me this" or "Take this for me" or "Do this thing for me." And, really, that's wrong.

David clearly has a capacity to empathize with women's heavy lot. Empathy was an emotion that he lacked before entering Alcoholics Anonymous.

David believes that, since entering A.A., he has changed his ideas and habits. Living alone, separated from his wife, has forced him to learn to take care of himself.

As I told you, it's not easy to live alone; it isn't agreeable to live alone. Take me, for example. I'm alone. At this moment, having your company serves me well, but, independent of this, I am happy. I feel happy because, as I mentioned to you, I go about my chores here, sweeping, watering the plants, dusting, washing clothes. Before I never did these things; it was because of my *machismo* that I didn't do them. I thought that chores were only for women and this is a serious error . . . to think that chores are only for women to do is a grave mistake, one that I was personally committing.

Being a man, to David, has little to do with abstaining from traditionally feminine activities like housework. Male identity seems to derive from self-sufficiency, competence at taking care of oneself. This criterion represents a radical departure from his former point of view.

Personal stories, which tend to ramble from topic to topic, regularly touch on the theme of household work. The redefinition of wives and live-in partners as *compañeras* implies a new sexual division of labor. Hence, the men claim that they collaborate at chores in a way that they never did before joining A.A. It is clear that a few of the men are happily married, a significant improvement over the family strife of their drinking years. Gerardo, by far the most affluent of the group, takes his wife and children on a long road trip every Sunday. Renaldo participates with his wife in church activities. Emilio, who, along with his wife and children, shares a single house with his brother's family, lives in apparent harmony with them all.

However, the majority of married men in the group continue to suffer problems with wives and children. It is clear that the group meeting provides them a forum for airing their difficulties. Amador is one such person. Amador is in his late fifties and runs a small fruit and vegetable stand in the immediate vicinity of Moral Support. Descended from Italian immigrants, his translucent, paper-white skin and thinning light brown hair give him an entirely different appearance from the other men. Amador almost never smiles. He stoops slightly, bears a sad countenance and speaks so softly that it is hard to know whether he is depressed or just very tired. But kindliness, gentleness, and empathy shine in every statement he utters.

On the podium one evening Amador told his story. He drank steadily for over thirty years, from childhood. Life has been for him no more than *"un suspiro,"* a sigh. It has slipped away rapidly, he says. It has been *"triste,"* sad. The worst is that his children have turned out to be ingrates. Amador wonders whether his suffering has had any positive consequence at all. Neither his wife nor children show appreciation for what he has tried to do for them, he claims.

Jacinto also vents marital problems through the personal story. When he was an active alcoholic, he says, he and his wife would walk down the street and she would comment, "Doesn't that couple look nice? Don't they look like they really love one another and enjoy being together?" And he would say, "That's the way they are. You and I are different." Now that Jacinto is in recovery, he claims that it is his wife, not he, who is difficult to be around. They do not get along. And as they stroll together, he is the one who now yearns inwardly to feel as happy as the couples they pass on the street. But he keeps this wish a secret, revealing it only to the group, never to his wife. Jacinto worries about compulsive masturbation and confesses his concerns to the group every time he delivers a personal story. However, he never explicitly connects sexual habits to marital infelicity. Jacinto believes that his masturbation is pathological. Rather than being symptomatic of marital unhappiness, it is a problem in and of itself, to be conquered and eliminated.

On the podium Renaldo tends to repeat himself and speak in generalities. Occasionally, however, he departs from this defensive strategy to deliver moving, detailed accounts of his alcoholic past. Once, as his personal story was drawing to a close, he departed from his well-worn tales and his voice suddenly became dark. He told of returning home one day to find his wife with another man. The intruding lover escaped with Renaldo in pursuit. As he ran, Renaldo hurled stones at him with the intent to kill. But the man jumped over the adobe wall surrounding Renaldo's property and got away. At this point in the story, the clock on the meeting room wall sounded, indicating that Renaldo would have to yield the podium to another speaker. In a completely uncharacteristic move, Renaldo exceeded his fifteen minutes and continued to talk. The incident was obviously traumatic, and Renaldo was drawing cathartic release from telling about it. After repeating the story several times, he ended with the rhetorical question, "When would I ever tell this story in the cantina?" The implied response was, "never." Only to his *compañeros* in A.A. could such confessions like this be made. Renaldo on other occasions confessed about how he would come home drunk from the *pulquerías* where he used to hang out. His wife would get so angry that she would beat him. When he first started attending A.A. meetings, he says, he used to think to himself, "How can I admit that my wife would beat me?" But he now claims that speaking openly about these events has helped him to stay sober.

The personal stories that concern family problems imply an acceptance of traditional gender roles and values. Women should be faithful, they should not beat their husbands. Husband and wife should be happy together and enjoy a mutually satisfying sex life. In Renaldo's case, being cuckolded was a deeply shameful, emasculating experience. To tell this story to the group involved enormous courage for the incident was a grave assault on his masculinity. On the other hand, he was sure to narrate to the men his reaction to finding his wife with a lover: he thrashed out violently in an attempt to kill, which is exactly what traditional male norms would dictate. As for Jacinto, it is obviously hard for him to confess his marital unhappiness. However, his repeated, even casual, public confession of compulsive masturbation at least communicates to the group that he is sexually active, again important for any self-respecting male.

Masturbation emerges in other men's personal stories as well. Eduardo claims to worry about excessive masturbation. He says that he was "very young" when he started to masturbate, eleven years old. Although now, in his mid-thirties, he considers himself much too old to be masturbating, he nonetheless masturbates compulsively several times a day. Unlike Jacinto, Eduardo seems to be bragging, rather than distressed, when he talks about masturbation. Although Eduardo claims that masturbation makes him anxious, his jubilant tone of voice belies this assertion. Eduardo's confession implicitly serves as an announcement of his lively libido. Unmarried and romantically unattached, Eduardo consciously or unconsciously uses the personal story to communicate that he does not settle for complete sexual deprivation. Pursuit of pleasure is a necessary quality for any fully developed male.

Haydée Rosovsky (1991:2) notes that sexual bragging is a normal feature of personal stories at Mexican A.A. meetings. Observations from Moral Support accord with her findings. David claims repeatedly in personal stories that, after more than a decade of sobriety, his alcoholism is well under control. He no longer needs A.A. to keep sober. Instead, he says, the group helps him control other negative impulses, which linger despite his many attempts to overcome them. The strongest of these impulses, he says, are "*envidia*" ("envy") and "*lujuria*" ("lust"). Without entering into explicit details, David's public statement reveals him to be a normally functioning Mexican male. Other *compañeros,* like Pedro for example, have no reticence about speaking about their extramarital affairs in public. Pedro routinely brags about his uncontrolled sexuality. At the age of thirteen, he had sex with a fifteen-year-old girl. Ever since then, he claims, he has thought about sex continuously.

Emilio is to all appearances happily married. And yet his personal stories reveal long-term relationships with other women. As he puts it, this is the one problem that he has never been able to conquer. He has always been "*mujeriego*"—a womanizer—he confesses, with an air of combined pride and regret. Periodically, Emilio's personal stories concern the internal struggle he suffers at the end of the workday: should he visit "*una vieja*" (an "ol' lady") with whom he is carrying on an affair, or should he attend his A.A. meetings? Attendance at the meeting in and of itself bears witness to his moral strength, which operates as additional evidence of his masculinity. Emilio presents himself as a man battling to keep his libidinous drives within bounds. Sometimes his efforts succeed, sometimes not. In either case, his masculinity is affirmed. Accounts like those of David and Emilio, told as public confessionals to a group of men, reproduce gender relations outside of the meeting context. In effect, they are sexual boasts. When narrated in personal stories, however, the boasts appear disguised as moral weakness. The open admission of that weakness is itself sufficient evidence of courage to demonstrate the manliness of the speakers. Moral Support speakers who use the podium to disclose uncontrolled sexual activity have nothing to lose. The confession inevitably reinforces their gender identity, despite their abstinence from drink.

Unmarried members of Moral Support confront a particularly grave form of sexual insecurity. Either they reside alone, which to most working class Mexicans is a pitiful fate for any human being, or they live with married children and suffer the threat of being evicted by their own families. Their unhappiness and insecurity frequently emerge in personal stories. True, these men theoretically accept—even embrace— a redefinition of gender roles. They state that they strive for equality. They selflessly abdicate their traditional position as uncontested family power holders and demonstrate a willingness to carry out household tasks normally restricted to women. And yet, no matter what new beliefs they might profess, these men have failed to fulfill an essential male role: to be the head of a household. They are not masters of their own home. It is probably for this reason that these are the men who use personal stories most explicitly to raise issues of gender identity.

For all but two or three of the men in Moral Support, living circumstances are anything but ideal. Those who reside alone or as dependents in the homes of relatives have a natural motive to leave the house: for human companionship, in the one instance, or escape from domestic unpleasantness, in the other. For the unhappily married men, life outside the home is preferable to unhappiness within. The group provides all these men an escape into the public sphere. At the same time, for every one of the members of Moral Support, attendance at meetings provides a culturally validated refuge away from family life, which is the principal feminine domain.

It is important to bear in mind that Moral Support consists only of men. This circumstance contributes to a perpetuation of certain patterns that they used to follow in the company of male drinking buddies. Open admissions of uncontrollable sexual activity and of the violent defense of one's honor are among the familiar themes carried over from pre–A.A. days. The repeated use of obscene language is another male speech pattern brought into the meeting room. One *compañero* starts almost every personal story with the confession, *"Sigo siendo culero"*—"I'm still an asshole"—a statement he would be unlikely to make in the company of women and children. The curse word *pinche*, which bears no particular lexical meaning but might be translated as the adjective "fucking," appears in almost every sentence of some personal stories. The common Mexicanism, *chingar* ("to fuck"), emerges with similar frequency. And there are other speech patterns—including casual references to genitalia and erotic behavior—which, together with stories of sexual conquests and fantasies, impart a macho tone to Moral Support meetings. Even when the men confess personal weaknesses, the use of obscene language —especially language that draws attention to their own physical endowments—operates to counteract the message. On the podium one evening, Emilio stated his constant nervousness at having to rise to the podium to speak. *"Me tiemblan los huevos"*—"My balls quiver"—he said. Pedro explained the fear he felt at giving up drink and joining Alcoholics Anonymous, explaining *"Me costó un huevo, hasta los dos"*— "It cost me a ball, even both." Only in exclusively male company may such statements be made. The assertions themselves highlight the unmistakable sexual identity of the speakers.

Paradoxically, too, the macho tone is reinforced through confessions of spontaneous homosexual desire under the influence of alcohol. Horacio, a stocky man in his mid-thirties, first arrived in the group about a month after I. Born and brought up in Mexico City, he lived most of his adult life on the Costa Chica, in the state of Guerrero, where he married a woman from the black community long established along that part of the coast. There he helped found an Alcoholics Anonymous group, which started out with five members. Horacio spoke movingly of his early suspicions that A.A. would fail to keep him sober. But he was proven wrong, he said. After this preamble, Horacio launched into an account of his "crazy" behavior as an active alcoholic. Whenever he got drunk, he would undress, stand nude in front of his *cuates*, spread his arms, and declare, "*¡Quiero hombre!*"—I want a man! Iván, about the same age as Horacio, was convinced to join A.A. by his wife. She urged him over and over to find a "*grupo*," but for a long time he resisted, claiming, "Look, I can go for two weeks without drinking, can't I?" The wife would reply, "But you always relapse." And so he was convinced. Iván's main recollection is that the atmosphere in the *pulquerías* was "disagreeable." One detail in particular, he said, confused him. When men were urinating, they would grab one another's penises. On such occasions, he would think to himself, "Hey, what's going on here?"

The men laugh nervously when listening to confessions of homosexual desire. Recorded life histories reveal many more such encounters than those which emerge during meetings, in the formal, public setting. One man even boasted in private to me that he has had sex with fourteen men, specifying at the same time that it was he who was always the partner to penetrate. As is well known, in the Latin American context, for a man to play the active role in homosexual encounters in no way reduces his masculine identity (e.g., Klapp 1964:412, Paz 1961). States Joseph Carrier (1995:15), "There is some evidence that homosexual contacts between males are thought no better or worse than other kinds of sexual outlets lacking social approval; however, the provision here seems to be that that understanding is extended essentially only to those playing the role of insertors in anal intercourse." A similar attitude prevails in Nicaragua, for example, where "it is anal passivity alone that is stigmatized" (Lancaster 1992:242).[8] It is uncertain whether the confessions of homosexual contact that emerge in Moral Support interviews reflect widely shared experiences or whether they are even true. But they do perform a symbolic function. By portraying homosexual wishes and encounters as part of their dark alcoholic past, the men distance themselves from this kind of behavior in their present.

The relentless affirmation of heterosexuality gives the impression that the men protest too much. This pattern is particularly noteworthy given the exclusively male membership of Moral Support. In a close-knit, intimate setting such as A.A. meetings, where men confess weaknesses, where they cry in front of one another and admit their faults, they strive to marshal whatever linguistic and behavioral mechanisms they can to demonstrate incontrovertible masculinity. As a result, a hyper-masculine atmosphere prevails in the Moral Support meeting room.

The need to express hyper-masculinity becomes all the more apparent when regular Moral Support meetings are compared with so-called *aniversarios*. *Aniversarios* are meetings which commemorate annual achievements. They are of two types: (1) those which honor a group member's years of sobriety, and (2) those which celebrate the founding of Moral Support. Anniversaries begin with an open meeting to which group members invite their families and others who might be interested. Following the meeting, there is a party. Anniversary meetings are very different from those that occur normally. In addition to the *compañeros* themselves, the meeting room is crammed with women and children. Always present, too, are male relatives and occasional non-related guests, most of whom are unknown to anyone but the members who invited them.

The presence of so many outsiders, particularly women and children, changes the character of the meeting radically. Although anniversary meetings last one and one half hours—the same duration as other meetings—they are held during the daytime, usually Sunday afternoon, rather than at night. The men select Sunday because that is when relatives and other guests normally have the greatest freedom to attend. Prior to the meeting, the men select a coordinator for the event, always a member perceived as gifted in the performance of that role. Personal stories are generally shorter than the usual fifteen minutes. In addition to group members themselves, numerous guests ask to speak on behalf of the celebrant; with a total hour and a half available, personal stories have to be brief in order to provide a chance for all who wish to speak. Among the most common guest speakers are grown children of the celebrants as well as former members of the group, who have moved from the neighborhood and joined other groups closer to their new places of residence. It is ungracious, indeed inconceivable, for a moderator to deny any visitor the opportunity to express his or her appreciation of the celebrant. As a result, almost twice the normal number of personal stories need to be crammed within the hour and a half meeting.

The brevity of personal stories during anniversary meetings also derives from the inexperience of the visitors, most of whom have never before spoken in public. Women's personal stories rarely last more than a minute or two. Daughters of the celebrant usually confine themselves to platitudinous, but heartfelt, statements of pride in their father's control over alcohol consumption. After wishing him well, they urge him to keep up the struggle ("*seguir echando ganas*"). Not only the women's personal histories, but all that is said in public during anniversaries, are sanitized. Except for the occasional slip of the tongue from one group member or another, the stories are cleansed of curse words and free of sexual themes or innuendoes.

Because of self-imposed censorship, even regular members of the group seem to have less to say when they deliver anniversary addresses. Their personal stories are considerably vaguer, more confined to generalities and statements summarizing the official A.A. ideology and program, than is the case during regular meetings. If any single theme dominates, however, it is the mistreatment of women: *compañeros* take the podium during anniversary celebrations as a way of indirectly apologizing to their families for irresponsible, occasionally violent behavior during their years as active alcoholics. Uttered in a softer tone of voice than usual, these sorts of apologies are not directed toward particular family members, but rather phrased in generalities, to avoid the past victims' possible embarrassment. The celebrant himself rises to the podium last of all. He takes the opportunity to thank *compañeros* and guests for their supportive role in helping him to stay sober.

The parties that follow an anniversary meeting always include a birthday cake, decorated to indicate the celebrant's years of sobriety. Women in the celebrant's family usually serve food—tamales, rice, and other standard Mexican dishes—as well. It is invariably women, and never the men themselves, who prepare and serve the food to all the guests. In this respect, anniversary fiestas reproduce traditional gender roles. In fact, group members who live alone or who are alienated from their families are at a serious disadvantage. Incapable of preparing food on their own, they can hope for no more than a purchased birthday cake and soft drinks during their anniversary.

During anniversary celebrations, Moral Support members and guests strive to replicate the atmosphere that one would find at most Mexican fiestas. However, alcohol is such an integral part of virtually all fiestas, and affects people's behavior so predictably and radically, that no A.A. event could ever achieve the kind of loose gaiety that characterizes most Mexican celebrations. According to a Mexican proverb, "*Si no hay borrachos, no hay fiesta*"—Without drunks, there's no fiesta. Moral Support anniversaries, like fiestas that prevail outside the world of Alcoholics Anonymous, include eating, drinking, singing, dancing and sociable chatting. Several of the members of Moral Support bring musical instruments to the party and play for the guests' entertainment. During the period of my field stint, there was even one occasion when a small mariachi band was hired, with funds collected from Moral Support members themselves in celebration of the group's anniversary.

But, despite the best efforts of participants, anniversaries at Moral Support are relatively somber affairs. They are also relatively brief. Rather than stretching late into the night, as would be usual for community or life cycle celebrations in any Mexican village or town, they last only a few hours. By 10 P.M., group members and guests have cleaned the premises and dispersed to their respective homes.

There are at least two crucial ways, among those not yet mentioned, in which Moral Support anniversaries actually replicate regular fiestas. For one thing, they publicly reinforce non-kin-based social bonds. This is the one type of occasion when the men unfailingly address their sponsors as *"padrino"* (*"godfather"*) or their sponsees as *"ahijado"* (*"godson"*). This is the event, too, in which *compañeros* all give one another the *abrazo*—or ritualized embrace—in front of all the guests. The embrace generally occurs immediately after the ceremonial meal and just prior to the cake cutting. Gerardo's seventeenth anniversary celebration occurred soon after my initial arrival at Moral Support. As he stood at the table next to the uncut birthday cake, all the *compañeros* lined up to give him the *abrazo*. Still only a mere acquaintance of Gerardo, I offered him my hand. My *padrino* Emilio intervened: "Go ahead, *compañero*," he said, "give him an *abrazo!*"

There is a further replication of Catholic fiestas in Moral Support. *Aniversarios*, like any major fiesta celebrations, are open to virtually anyone who wishes to attend. Anniversary celebrations spill out from the tiny meeting rooms onto the patio and street outside. Just as for any fiesta, folding tables and chairs are erected for the comfort of guests and these are situated outdoors for everyone in the neighborhood to see. There can be no anonymity under such circumstances. Nor is anonymity sought by members and guests. Open identification of A.A. members is perhaps the greatest difference between A.A. groups in Mexico City and those in U.S. cities and towns. As elaborated in the following chapter, this lack of anonymity has serious consequences for the nature of meetings and fate of groups.

6. BLURRED BOUNDARIES AND THE EXERCISE OF SOCIAL CONTROL

In theory, it should be possible to state how many members belong to Moral Support, or, for that matter, any other Alcoholics Anonymous group. However, precision is almost impossible to achieve. For one thing, Alcoholics Anonymous, as its name implies, tries to preserve the anonymity of its members. Hence, it retains a roster of affiliated groups rather than membership lists per se. Each group has its own procedure for recording member attendance. At Moral Support, the moderator writes the names of the evening's speakers in a log, so as to help future moderators choose speakers. But the log only records the names of six speakers for any given evening. The total number in attendance goes unrecorded.

Even if one could record the total attendance, it would prove impossible to reconstruct total membership over any given period of time. A man might be absent for a month or more and still consider himself a member of Moral Support. Or he might not. Several of the men have a history of leaving Alcoholics Anonymous for months, even for a year or more, and then returning, without ever experiencing a relapse. At least two of the men in the group attend more than one group in a given week. These patterns, replicated throughout Alcoholics Anonymous in Mexico City, make it impossible to determine actual A.A. membership at any given moment. In fact, the calculation of precise membership is almost irrelevant to an understanding of Alcoholics Anonymous. More significant is the ongoing process of change which each group experiences over time.

In the case of Moral Support, meeting attendance usually varies from three to twenty. Normally there are eight to twelve men present. But the men consider these numbers far from ideal. Indeed, considering that there are sometimes insufficient numbers for a full roster of six speakers, the men suffer ever-present anxiety about group survival. This is one of the reasons why they exert persistent pressure on one another to attend meetings. Alcoholics Anonymous guidelines of course encourage regular meeting attendance as the best means to maintain sobriety. However, the existence of the group is also a salient issue. For this reason, inside and outside the context of meetings, the men issue constant reminders to one another that meetings are central to the A.A. program and to their health.

In addition to uncertain meeting attendance, Alcoholics Anonymous groups in Mexico City sometimes seem to teeter on the brink of extinction. Mexican groups experience a constant process of fission and fusion. As a survival mechanism, when its membership shrinks below a critical mass, a group can try to combine with one or more others. More often, however, dissention within a group's ranks results in the creation of several smaller groups, each of unsubstantial size. This situation, familiar to all the men in Moral Support, potentially places each group at risk. Groups splinter for a number of reasons, among which competing ideologies and personal animosities are the most prevalent. Active alcoholics who seek out Alcoholics Anonymous almost always enter recovery by joining an established group, rather than starting their own. When enough members within an established group become dissatisfied, the group splits in two, with the parent group remaining the larger, at least initially.

Occasionally a split occurs because several members, who live near one another but relatively far from the parent group, decide to start a new group for matters of convenience. Moral Support was "born," as the men put it, because the group which the founders attended was located further from their homes than they considered ideal. In fact, two groups in the neighborhood splintered off from the "mother" group, as the men call it. One was founded by three *compañeros,* who felt they constituted enough of a critical mass to start their own A.A. chapter. The second was started by a physician from their neighborhood, who lured some of the men away from the mother group. Emilio was one of these men. He joined the doctor's group, not because he was dissatisfied with the mother group, he says, but because of convenience. It appears that he was also attracted by the doctor's charisma.

According to Emilio, it was shortly after this group's founding that problems began to emerge. One incident in particular destroyed the trust that members had placed in one another. The group needed a bookcase to store its meager belongings (sugar, coffee, tea, cups, and the like), so members contributed twenty pesos (about U.S. $3.00) apiece toward its purchase. But the treasurer, responsible for collecting the money, ran off with the money and was never to be seen again. At the same time, members protested at the fact that meetings were constantly disrupted. The group met on the second story of the house where the doctor maintained his practice. Patients would routinely interrupt to call for his help and he would respond by leaving. Emilio complains bitterly to think that the doctor would try to carry out both missions simultaneously: to attend to patients and participate fully in meetings. Emilio's frustration grew and he eventually left to join Moral Support. Others followed his example. The doctor's group completely vanished from existence.

This kind of A.A. group formation and dissolution is a common occurrence in Mexico City. All Alcoholics Anonymous units theoretically strive toward a common goal, the sobriety of the members. However, because A.A. chapters are so numerous, attendance so unpredictable, and groups constantly at the risk of extinction, chapters often find themselves in competition for membership. The flight of members from the doctor's group is not unusual. The group's weaknesses—member irresponsibility, anxiety over money, and invasions into the meeting space from the outside world—are common problems among working class groups in Mexico City, including Moral Support. When the situation becomes sufficiently intolerable for members, there is always another group waiting to receive them. Hence, groups must attend to their members' concerns and constantly guard against possible defection.

Perhaps the most surprising feature of Moral Support and other working class Alcoholics Anonymous groups in Mexico City is that their membership is anything but anonymous. This is not to say that *compañeros* expect their personal stories to be revealed outside the group, for they do not. In fact, when someone gossips by divulging presumably confidential information, the men come to harbor enduring resentments. At the same time, no one even pretends that the identity of individual members can remain a secret. In working class Mexico City, everyone in the neighborhood knows who belongs to an A.A. group. Everyone in the neighborhood, too, is aware of when an A.A. member does or does not attend meetings. Further, every group member knows every other member's full name, ethnic origin, place of residence, and family circumstances. Despite this lack of anonymity, members of Moral Support and other Mexican groups follow the international A.A. guideline of using only the first name when introducing themselves during meetings.

In Mexico City, with its myriad close-knit, village-like neighborhoods, anonymity is impossible to maintain. Recovering alcoholics choose their group mainly on the basis of neighborhood. Most often, a member's A.A. group is very near his place of residence. Very occasionally, a man belongs to a group far from home, which is a choice he makes based on convenience to the workplace. As pointed out in Chapter One, neighborhoods in Mexico City replicate the small towns, villages, and tiny *rancherías* all over the Republic from which many of the recovering alcoholics originate. The intimacy of social life in these neighborhoods effectively eradicates the possibility that the identity of A.A. members can remain secret.

In the case of Moral Support, the men make no attempt to hide their affiliation. Group members begin congregating by the meeting room entrance, where they chat until 8:00, when the meeting begins. I have witnessed this ritual dozens of times. On each occasion passersby, returning from work or errands, greet the men openly and enter casually into their conversations. There is never any awkwardness in these interactions. Nor do the men consider it inappropriate to speak with neighbors while they wait for the meeting to begin. During the meeting itself, a member might have to leave temporarily to carry out urgent business. He slips in and out of the room while others are delivering personal stories. This behavior, hardly ideal from the standpoint of A.A. guidelines, demonstrates how little the men care if neighbors identify them as affiliates of Alcoholics Anonymous.

Anniversary celebrations (see Chapter Five) provide further evidence of the lack of anonymity. At Moral Support, where the meeting room is small and opens directly onto the sidewalk, visitors cannot possibly all fit inside. Members therefore keep the entrance open throughout the proceedings, allowing any observer easily to hear and watch the delivery of personal stories. *Aniversarios* are by no means private occasions. In fact, if anyone's view of the meeting is blocked, the crowd willingly adjusts the seating and standing room to permit the visitor an improved range of vision. Just as there is insufficient room for everyone to observe the meeting comfortably, there is even less quality space for the food service that follows. In order to accommodate visitors, the celebrant's family erects long folding tables and chairs, situated on the sidewalk and street immediately outside the meeting room. For several hours, *compañeros* and visitors alike move seamlessly between the meeting room and the street, eating together and socializing. Anonymity under such circumstances is neither possible nor desirable.

In fact, given the ostensible anonymity of A.A. groups, there exists a remarkable permeability between the Moral Support meeting room and the world outside. For one thing, the meeting room is not a secret venue. It is clearly indicated by an outdoor sign, which includes the A.A. logo, group name and meeting hours. The sign operates as intentional advertising. Occasionally, meetings are punctuated by the unexpected arrival of newcomers. More than once, in my experience, drunks actually walked into the room and sat quietly through the meeting while rocking in their chairs in a stupefied state. Once a drunk even continued drinking during the meeting. The men tolerate this kind of behavior; it is even the source of mild amusement. They smile knowingly and glance at one another as the drunk reels back and forth in an attempt to remain seated. Indeed, as we shall soon see, the men often seem less indulgent of one another than they do of drunks, who, they know from personal experience, are unable to exercise control. As long as the visitor is not disruptive, he is allowed to remain.

The permeability of the boundary between inside and out is reflected in the ambiguous physical separation between meeting room and street. When Moral Support moved its meeting room (see Chapter Three), the new locale seemed to be designed exactly as small stores in Mexico City are. It was fitted with a corrugated steel curtain, which could be dropped to the ground for closing or raised nearly as high as the ceiling for exposure to foot traffic outside. The curtain, and in fact the entrance to the room, was as wide as the room itself. During meetings, the curtain could not be closed completely without producing an intolerably stuffy atmosphere. So the men kept it halfway open, about five feet above ground level, an inconvenient placement requiring members to crouch slightly in order to allow passage. More problematic was the fact that, with the metal curtain open in this fashion, the meeting completely lacked privacy. Conditions seemed to me chaotic under these circumstances. Dogs wandered in and out. Children, at play in the street outside, would enter the meeting room unexpectedly, seat themselves at will, and silently listen to the men deliver personal stories. When they got bored, they would calmly leave. If the children happened to arrive during coffee and tea service, they would be served along with the men. Invariably they would proceed to entertain themselves by banging the metal spoons rhythmically against their cups, which produced a distracting, nerve-wracking noise. At every meeting, groups of young boys would camp at the entrance, peering into the room as they joined members in listening to the personal stories.

Feeling besieged by this distracting behavior, the men decided to erect a more permanent barrier. As a temporary solution, until they could amass the necessary funds, Gerardo said that he would fasten a cloth along the bottom rim of the metal curtain—"*color naranja*" (orange colored), he added in jest, "*algo llamativo*"—something attention-grabbing. The provisional response was to attach plain white material, which had been used as window coverings in the previous meeting room, to the edge of the metal curtain. The men would gain entrance to the room by lifting the fabric aside. Of course, this answer was imperfect as well. Dogs continued to enter and leave the room while meetings were in progress. On one occasion, as I sat quietly listening to a personal story, I felt something pushing against my leg. This time it was not a dog. It was a young boy. In a feeble attempt to remain inconspicuous, he had crawled into the meeting room to retrieve a soccer ball that had come rolling inside. At least once every two or three weeks some stranger would push back the cloth curtain to inform one of the men that he needed to see him immediately. The two men would converse audibly right at the meeting room entrance. With his business concluded, the *compañero* would rejoin the meeting as if nothing unusual had occurred.

It was clear that I was more affected by these distractions than the other group members were. The need for erecting a more permanent barrier between street and meeting room had been openly expressed and the group was patiently saving toward this goal. But the men seemed to feel no sense of urgency. In fact, most of the time, the presence of animals, children, and drunks was met by furtive smiles and jocular glances. The problem had to be corrected, we all knew; but, as far as the men were concerned, it was clearly tolerable. In fact, they were much more able to concentrate on the meeting than was I.

One Saturday evening at the end of November, Gerardo appeared with a glistening green plastic Christmas tree about four feet tall. He decorated the tree with colorful ornaments and placed it next to the podium. Its numerous flickering lights flashed rhythmically to the sound of a music box playing well-known carols—"Jingle Bells," "Silent Night," and the like. The tree and its electronic attachments operated throughout the entire meeting, a situation that persisted for weeks afterward. At the end of February, I mentioned as casually as I could—without trying to seem judgmental—that we might want to silence the carols, given that the Christmas season was long past. Gerardo seemed disappointed but complied. I was clearly the only person in the meeting room distracted by the music, which actually competed in volume with the voices of the speakers. The tree and flashing lights remained standing for a full eleven months, until the following October.

For a long time after the move to the new meeting room, incursions from the outside world only seemed to increase. Although a proper door was never erected, it took only five months before a *cancel*—an adjustable, removable heavy plastic screen—was wedged into the space between the raised metal curtain and the sidewalk to provide a better barrier than the draped cloth. At the beginning of each meeting, the group secretary would install the *cancel;* it would be removed after everyone had gone home. This improvement at least prevented passersby from peering into the meeting room. However, it accomplished very little in the way of sound control. Hence, meetings continued to be punctuated by the enthusiastic cries of young boys playing soccer right outside our room. The familiar whistle of the knife sharpener, bicycling along the street, and the bellow from the stove of the *camote* peddler,[1] wheeling his cart on the sidewalk right by the meeting room, remained as audible as ever. During the annual neighborhood fair, temporary stalls selling food and offering games of chance were set up on the Avenue half a block away. A Ferris wheel, merry-go-round, and other amusement park rides were erected as well. For the better part of a month, music blared from loudspeakers throughout the night and penetrated the flimsy Moral Support walls, to the point where the personal stories could barely be heard. Similarly, on religious feast days, like the day of the Virgin of Guadalupe on December 12, the blast of skyrockets and firecrackers almost completely drowned out the meeting. In the neighborhood where we met, virtually no building was insulated against street noise.

It is doubtful that the men would have preferred enhanced silence and privacy. Once the *cancel* had been installed, the question of sealing the meeting room from the street never again emerged. The men, raised in large families and residing in crowded circumstances, appeared blissfully unaware of loud sounds or other interruptions emanating from the world outside the meeting room. Not even the musical Christmas tree inside the room itself seemed to disturb them. Neither spatially nor socially, then, were the men of Moral Support isolated from the neighborhood at large.

Although noise never bothered the men, the social permeability between street and meeting room did prove to be an occasional problem. By social permeability, I refer to a certain seamlessness or fluidity of interactions that occur inside and outside the meeting room. As we have already seen, a good number of the men are bound to one another by ties that exist alongside their common membership in Alcoholics Anonymous. Because the men live in the same neighborhood, they encounter one another every day. The men of Moral Support are relatives and *compadres* to one another. Eduardo is distantly related to David: Eduardo's father and David's mother-in-law are first cousins. Eduardo is also Donaldo's brother-in-law. Eduardo for a long time shared a house with his sister and Donaldo. When they expelled him from their house, he moved in with David. David, in turn, is baptismal godfather to three of Donaldo's children, which makes David and Donaldo *compadres*. They even address one another as *compadre* (rather than simply *compa*, which might be taken as a short form of *compañero*) during A.A. meetings. Whenever David or Donaldo acts as meeting moderator and calls the other to the podium, the speaker responds by saying, "*Gracias, compadre*," rather than the usual "*Gracias, compañero*." The men of Moral Support are tied to one another through friendship, as well. Eduardo and David were drinking partners—*cuates*—before they became *compañeros* in A.A. The same is true of Renaldo and Pedro. In many ways, then, the men have shared and continue to share social worlds.

The intertwining of members' lives, past and present, exerts a significant impact on Moral Support meetings. The complex relationships among Eduardo, Donaldo, and David provide the best evidence of this kind of impact. Eduardo, as I have said, is an unmarried man who for a long time resided in the home of his sister, brother-in-law, Donaldo, and their two children. As long as Eduardo and Donaldo were sharing a house, there was no evidence of conflict between these men. When Eduardo's sister died suddenly, however, Donaldo's son and daughter pressured him to remove Eduardo from their house. Eduardo willingly moved, but became obsessively resentful. David took pity on Eduardo, invited him to stay with him, and expressed open sympathy with Eduardo's scorn for Donaldo and his children. Donaldo, David, and Eduardo all reside on the same street where Moral Support meets. Inevitably, their feelings toward one another emerged within the meeting room.

Eduardo and David seemed to harbor unbridled hatred for Donaldo, a man who, at least on the outside, seemed blessed with an unusually mild-mannered, soft-spoken disposition. Donaldo was to all appearances a gentle person. But the gentleness sometimes seemed to me excessive and might be interpreted as either timidity or obsequiousness. If

Eduardo could be believed, however, Donaldo's shortcomings were far more serious than false humility. He was downright scary. Eduardo, clearly angry at having been expelled from Donaldo's house, waited impatiently and in vain for a personal story in which Donaldo openly confessed to the wrongs he had supposedly committed.

Eduardo's list of Donaldo's heinous deeds was long. He claimed that Donaldo has never confessed that he, Donaldo, once tried to choke Eduardo. Donaldo never has told in a meeting how he beat his wife—Eduardo's sister—with a wooden pole so that she would rise from her sickbed to cook for him. Nor has he informed the group that once, when there was no toilet paper in the bathroom of their home, Donaldo was so disrespectful that he used his wife's underpants to clean himself and simply left the soiled garment tossed on the floor. On one occasion, too, Eduardo came home drunk. Donaldo, with whom Eduardo was still living, gathered all Eduardo's possessions and threw them in the street. He locked the door so that Eduardo could not enter. This incident occurred while Donaldo was already a member of Alcoholics Anonymous. Eduardo believes that he should have shown greater compassion. These complaints gushed out of Eduardo in a personal story that he delivered to the group in Donaldo's presence. After that fateful meeting, Donaldo threatened Eduardo by telling him that "This controversy is going to be settled, not in the meeting, but in the street!"

Weeks passed without Donaldo returning to the group. Eduardo began to muster his courage for what he saw as an inevitable confrontation. As time passed, and Eduardo's anxiety grew, he would describe in detail how he intended to defend himself against his brother-in-law. He would kill Donaldo if necessary, he said. Eduardo claimed to be from a family of men who are not afraid to fight. "My father was an assassin," he said, adrenaline practically seeping from his pores as he spoke. "He killed a man and I am capable of doing that, too." Eduardo already pretended to know where he would escape to, if necessary. He evidently imagined he would have to carry out what in Mexico is a common post-murder stratagem: as a defense against reprisal, the assailant disappears for years, sometimes forever, from the scene of the crime to a faraway hiding spot.

Eduardo confided these feelings to me during a taped life history interview. The interview took place on a sunny Saturday morning in Eduardo's one-room stucco cottage located down a long flight of stairs from street level on David's house lot. Eduardo's anger was palpable. He was eager to prove his courage to me, and probably to himself as well.

As he spoke, he unbuttoned his shirt to show me a scar on his chest about an inch and half long. Then he unbuckled his belt and pulled down his pants to display a scar nearly six inches long on the inside of his right thigh. With his index finger, he indicated wounds all over his face. All these wounds come from fights, he said, and he claimed to be ready to fight again, this time against Donaldo. Later in the course of the interview, as the narrative turned to the same subject, Eduardo pulled out from his left pocket an enormous switchblade knife. He pressed a button and the blade swung out. "I use this knife to open sardine cans," he said ominously, "but I can use it for something else as well."

The disintegration of relations between these two relatives and *compañeros* stunned my senses. Aside from being unfailingly soft-spoken and polite, Donaldo is elderly, overweight, and slow of movement. Eduardo, by contrast, talks tough. However, he is capable of great tenderness. To remind him of his mother's love, he sleeps with a pillow that she embroidered for him. In his small, crowded room he keeps a saint's image nailed to the wall, nearly at floor level. There he lights a votive candle daily in honor of his recently deceased sister and mother. Eduardo, unemployed during most of our acquaintance, always had a hard time surviving. He proudly showed me a plastic toy bear, which he revealed with great glee to be a fully functioning radio. Like other possessions of his, he found this one on the street. He also came upon a small paring knife lying on the ground and feels satisfied that he has been able to use it for years.

After the interview in which Eduardo aired his resentment against Donaldo, he and I walked a block to the Avenue where we had a bite to eat. From there we strolled a short distance to the Moral Support meeting room. On the way, Eduardo stopped at a tree with low, thick branches. From the branches he pulled out a partly full beer bottle. He emptied the bottle on the ground and explained that earlier that day he had found the bottle across the street from our meeting room. He hid it in the tree for later retrieval. "That's my carfare for a day," he declared with a smile. Eduardo, who is thirty-eight years old, lives as close to the economic edge as seems possible.

Immediately after being expelled from Donaldo's house, Eduardo rented a series of inadequately equipped rooms and ate with relatives who would occasionally feed him. Following several months of a semi-nomadic existence, David took pity on him and invited him to live in the unoccupied cottage on his property. David says that, unbeknownst to Eduardo, he took him into his home as a way of repaying Eduardo's mother and sister, who would frequently offer him food when he was in need, especially during drunken episodes when his wife would ignore him. Even when Eduardo's mother and sister issued no formal invitation, they always treated him with kindliness and respect, he says. David would show similar generosity toward Eduardo, their spurned son and brother, even though they were not alive to witness this act of charity.

In the controversy between Eduardo and Donaldo, David bore no personal grudge against Donaldo. He simply expressed sympathy for Eduardo, whom he believed to be severely wronged. David also supported Eduardo because he is Eduardo's *padrino,* or godfather, by virtue of having brought Eduardo into A.A. *Padrinos* are supposed to show protectiveness and loyalty toward their godchildren. David minces no words. He calls Donaldo *"un parásito"* and *"una mala persona"*—a parasite and a bad person. Considering that Donaldo is David's *compañero* and *compadre,* this statement represents particularly strong condemnation. Having been criticized from the podium, and feeling little support from other members of Moral Support, Donaldo remained absent from meetings for several months after Eduardo had publicly aired his accusations.

Eduardo not only used the podium to express resentment against Donaldo (and, in fact, other group members). He was also the occasional victim of others' complaints, similarly aired in meeting. I was told that, prior to my joining Moral Support, Pedro had devoted part of a personal story to criticizing Eduardo. Eduardo had set up house with an unwed mother, an act which Pedro considered highly unwise. In an attempt to bring Eduardo to his senses, Pedro issued an insult from the podium; he called Eduardo *pendejo* ("fool"), a highly pejorative term. Eduardo has never forgiven him the insult. "What business is it of his?" asks Eduardo. "That's my personal life and he has no reason to mix into it. Those kind of things are for me alone to judge."

Eduardo's resentment, as it turns out, had a permanent impact on the future of the entire group. It was Eduardo who discovered the availability of the new meeting room. He became one of the most outspoken proponents of abandoning Pedro's cottage, which the group had rented from Pedro for over a decade (see Chapter Three). Eduardo stated that he had always been uncomfortable meeting at Pedro's house. His status, like that of everyone else in the group, was ambiguous while in that house. On the one hand, as a *compañero,* he should have had the freedom to speak his mind, which includes issuing personal criticisms. On the other hand, because the meeting took place on Pedro's property,

Eduardo felt somewhat like a guest in Pedro's home; as such, to criticize Pedro would have been improper. Eduardo claims that he feels much freer to speak candidly in the new meeting room. Eduardo admitted, however, that he was worried that Pedro would try to destroy Moral Support. "Why should he do that?" I asked. "Because we're no longer in his house and he can no longer rob from us. He no longer has the key to the meeting room to walk in whenever he wants and help himself to our supplies!"

The bond between Eduardo and Pedro is obviously no better than that between Eduardo and Donaldo. In both cases, a rift had developed because of criticisms leveled at a *compañero* during the delivery of personal stories. Eduardo seemed permanently scarred by Pedro's public criticism of his personal life; he harbored enduring resentment against Pedro for his cruel indiscretion. While delivering a personal story, Pedro had called Eduardo by name, insulted him, and offered him unsolicited advice. However, Eduardo was not above such behavior himself. Eduardo's attack on Donaldo was direct. During a personal story, he told the group about specific occurrences and explicit grievances against Donaldo, whom he openly named. For this, Eduardo incurred Donaldo's ire. In Moral Support, there exists a blurred boundary between the meeting room and world outside. Each domain impinges on the other, sometimes producing an atmosphere of enhanced supportiveness for the men, but at other times exacerbating the divisions between them.

Pointed attacks directed against specific individuals are relatively uncommon during meetings, however. For the most part, criticisms that emerge during personal stories are issued in the form of general statements, iterations of organizational rules and norms. Because Moral Support is a small group, in which everyone knows one another intimately, there is rarely a need to refer to the offender by name. Members assume that the rule or norm invoked during a personal story is one that has been broken recently by a particular *compañero,* even though he goes unnamed. *Compañeros* employ personal stories in this way as a convenient pretext for accusing someone in the group of allegedly reprehensible behavior. Often, as we have seen, the criticism operates as a commentary on behavior that occurred outside the context of the meeting room. With even greater frequency personal stories become the principal medium through which *compañeros* reflect on comportment that occurs during the meeting itself. Personal stories are therefore potent mechanisms of social control. They are also the central strategy by which the group strives to perpetuate its existence.

One of the men's abiding concerns is attendance at meetings. Moral Support conforms to Mary Taylor's definition of a "flexible involvement self-help group." The author explains (Taylor 1977:181): "Flexible involvement self-help groups provide some degree of external control over members' behavior, but because members' involvement in such groups is somewhat time-limited, such groups rely on processes to develop or enhance members' self-controls, so that they may be able to regulate their own conduct when not actually physically present in the group." By flexible involvement, Mary Taylor seems to refer to the periodicity with which meetings convene—a feature of all A.A. groups—rather than to irregular attendance by individual members. However, both these conditions prevail in Moral Support. While irregular attendance creates few, if any, problems in large groups, it can cause a minor crisis in small ones like Moral Support. According to the Moral Support meeting format, a minimum of seven members is necessary to allow for a normal meeting: six speakers and one moderator. Meeting procedures require alteration if there are any fewer attendees, and this is an accommodation that no one in the group likes to make. Further, a small turnout yields low morale and raises the possibility of group disintegration.

There are *compañeros* who have been with the group for a half-decade or more who periodically disappear and resurface without criticism. This is the case, for example, with Roberto, who one *compañero* compares to a soccer player, restless and always on the move. Roberto tires quickly of groups. He therefore spends several months with one group, a month or two with another, and so on, moving among several meeting places, among them Moral Support. The men tolerate this kind of erratic behavior, not only because Roberto adheres to the A.A. program and remains sober, but also because he has defined himself successfully as a peripatetic group member, a team player who needs to experience a diversity of therapeutic environments. The group tolerates David, too. He misses about a third of the meetings, but on a predictable basis. Because David works long hours on weekends, and commutes two hours in each direction, he is unable to attend the group on Saturday nights. This circumstance is fully understandable to group members, to whom poverty has taught that earning a living takes precedence over all else.

The case of Renaldo is very different in that he disappears from meetings, but suddenly and at random intervals. Most of the men accuse Renaldo of being "*codísimo*," miserly in the extreme. They say that he predictably stops coming to meetings whenever there is a general call for extraordinary funds—when a group anniversary celebration is imminent, for example, or during and immediately following the group's move from one meeting place to another. Some group members use their personal stories obliquely to issue a general criticism against unnamed *compañeros* who do not contribute their share to the common kitty. In reality they are referring only to two or three of the men, who are undoubtedly aware that the accusations are directed toward them. Upon hearing these personal stories, Renaldo responds by distancing himself from the group. During one of his personal stories he confessed, in a sad tone of voice, *"De veras hay compas que no me llenan"*—"Truly, there are *compas* who don't satisfy me." He complained specifically of men who use the podium to criticize others. "Then after a while, I feel better about the situation and return."

Emilio, as hard on others as he is on himself, uses the podium to campaign vigorously against absences from meeting. Speaking to me in private, Emilio explained that Renaldo sets a bad example. He is one of the *"viejos,"* or old-timers, of the group, and the old-timers have the responsibility to be "exemplary." Emilio claims that he attends meetings, not to respond to the expectations of the group, but because he knows he should attend and feels bad whenever he cannot. "I go because of my conscience," he says. As usual, this conversation revealed Emilio in his role of *padrino,* socializing his godson—myself—not only in proper modes of behavior but also acceptable motives for conduct. The contrast he drew between his own and Renaldo's motives was his way of instructing me, first, that I should attend meetings regularly and, second, that I should be internally driven to attend, not merely responsive to public opinion. A third, perhaps subsidiary message was that it is wrong to be miserly.

As recovering alcoholics, the men of Moral Support stress the importance of self-discipline. Aside from staying sober, self-discipline reveals itself in punctuality and attention to time limits. Members strive to arrive at meetings punctually, but sometimes cannot, due to chores and work obligations. No one would criticize justifiable lateness. However, some members arrive late chronically and without legitimate excuse and this behavior does arouse commentary from the podium. Chronic lateness not only indicates lack of self-discipline. It also virtually disqualifies a member from assuming office as secretary, moderating a meeting, or carrying out any number of other activities on behalf of the group as a whole. Lack of punctuality therefore leaves a member open to the accusation of irresponsibility and selfishness, an unwillingness to sacrifice personal comforts for the general good.

Chronic latecomers and absentees suffer from having to listen to personal stories in which their unattractive behavior is derided. They also, at least in theory, deserve to be punished by being called as infrequently as possible to the podium. As demonstrated in the following chapter, the men of Moral Support consider it a right and a privilege to deliver personal stories. Every member has a right to deliver personal stories because they form the basis of A.A. therapy; it is a privilege to be allowed to deliver stories because the very act of delivery is indicative of a certain worthiness. The men believe that those who do not live up to proper behavioral standards, such as punctuality and regular attendance, should pay a price in the form of listening quietly and patiently as others deliver personal stories. This punishment is particularly harsh considering that the personal stories often include indirect criticism of those in the audience. By contrast, the men believe that good attendance and punctuality should be rewarded by frequent turns at the podium. What prevents this system of rewards and punishments from operating is the frequent scarcity of members in attendance and the need for a quorum of seven members. More often than not, the need to "*llenar hueco,*" that is, fill in gaps in the evening program, forces a moderator to call on a supposedly undeserving *compañero*. When an insufficient number of *compañeros* are present to complete the full roster of six speakers, it is justifiable to call on anyone present, including chronic latecomers and absentees.

Sometimes, however, moderators themselves suffer from their *compañeros'* criticisms. When moderators fail to select speakers according to acceptable guidelines, the men bring this matter to the group's attention in the form of personal stories narrated during subsequent sessions. Courtroom-style dramas are enacted over this issue. Consider an incident that occurred shortly after Moral Support changed meeting rooms. Three men, who seemed to be newcomers, began attending Moral Support sessions. One of them, Mateo, had attended A.A. meetings elsewhere, but relapsed. This was his second serious attempt at recovery.

During Mateo's first week at Moral Support, David and Arturo—both seasoned A.A. members who had sustained multiple years of sobriety—moderated the meetings on alternate evenings. Both moderators made the mistake of calling the new *compañero,* Mateo, to deliver personal stories.

The following week, Pedro rose to the podium and assailed "the previous coordinators" for their poor judgment. They had selected a new *compañero* to speak during two sessions in a row. Pedro mentioned no specific names. He simply stated that "Mistakes have been made," which placed *compañero* Mateo's sobriety at risk. Pedro pointed to the fact that Mateo was not present; calling on him prematurely had probably driven him away. Delivering two personal stories in a row was too much pressure for a newcomer to bear, Pedro said. As Pedro completed his story, Mateo with uncanny timing walked innocently into the meeting room and sat down, unaware that he had been the subject of controversy. His very presence had proven Pedro wrong, at least in the short run. Later, in private, Arturo advised me bluntly to ignore Pedro. "Don't listen to him," he said. "Pedro is always that way. I was the person moderating the *junta* and I called Mateo to the podium. People say that he [Mateo] arrived at the meeting drunk. But he was not drunk." Emilio interpreted the incident in less personal terms, and proceeded to explain, without reference to specific individuals, that newcomers should remain seated for at least five sessions before being asked to speak. (In fact they usually are called to the podium sooner than that.) They need to listen to others in order to absorb the A.A. message. They must learn, through experience, that listening is as crucial to recovery as is speaking. Only then will newcomers be motivated to continue attending meetings.

At Moral Support, moderators are expected not only to select the most appropriate roster of speakers, but especially to make a good choice of speakers to open and close the meeting. The men believe that the first and last personal stories of the evening are particularly critical for setting a positive therapeutic tone. The opening story should inspire subsequent speakers to confront their limitations and transgressions with complete candor. The opening, too, needs to provide a model for others in the group by strictly respecting the quarter hour time limit and by raising themes that are of general value to the group. Above all, opening stories should not criticize *compañeros* or blame others for one's personal defects. Rather, they should reveal, with ruthlessly honest detail, the failures and successes of the day and the lessons these experiences convey. The final speaker of the evening is supposed to provide an upbeat conclusion to the meeting. His personal story should communicate enough encouragement and support to sustain the members' sobriety until the next meeting. Because of their special role, the first and last speakers need to be excellent orators: stimulating, engaging, sincere. They also should be exemplary group members, that is, among those who are regularly present and punctual. Given the inevitable differences of opinion as to who is or is not a good orator, it is not always easy for a moderator to satisfy everyone's expectations. When moderators fall short in their speaker selection, members use the podium to let them know.

New moderators need to be socialized to the task of speaker selection. The day after I served as moderator for the first time, Emilio praised the wisdom of my choices and articulated group ideals. "It was good that you chose Arturo to close the session," he said. "Either Arturo or Gerardo would have been fine, because both men speak their mind. Both have loud voices." A loud voice is considered motivational. People with soft voices should be placed in the middle of the session, says Emilio. Emilio was upset one evening because Donaldo, who rarely coordinates (Donaldo is nearly illiterate and needs help carrying out the moderator role), selected Jacinto to close the session. "Jacinto should not close the session [*cerrar la junta*]," exclaimed Emilio. "He speaks too softly. Jacinto belongs in the middle."

On another occasion, I was publicly informed that I performed the moderator role poorly. It was midway through the session and we had already heard three speakers. To select a fourth, I followed what I thought to be the usual procedure: I looked a newcomer squarely in the eyes and asked him to identify himself as *visitante* (visitor) or *compañero*. When he answered "*compañero*," I called him to the podium. I was feeling proud of myself for having questioned the newcomer in this fashion. The inquiry seemed to signal my heightened sophistication as group member. However, I had overlooked Simón, a particularly touchy *compañero*, who was also in the room and had not been called to the podium. In the evening's final personal story, Emilio stated that "There were mistakes made in the "*coordinación*"—moderator performance. Simón had not been called upon for the past two sessions, he said, and Simón's turn was long overdue. I checked the logbook sitting open on the desk before me. Simón in fact had spoken during the previous session, thereby minimizing his claim to the podium on this particular evening; but I remained silent. I felt humiliated by the public reprimand, all the more so because it was unjustified. Simón graciously approached me at the end of the meeting to reassure me that he attends meetings not merely to speak, but to listen as well. My feelings somewhat assuaged, I nonetheless went home that evening smarting from the cruel impact of social control.

One evening the meeting ended in a particularly unpleasant fashion. Pedro had moderated. He selected Roberto, a known curmudgeon, to close the session. When the meeting ended, Gerardo was red in the face from fury. Hardly able to contain himself, he pulled me aside to explain his point of view. "The coordinator selects the *compañero* who closes the meeting. And the closing [*cierre*] has to be very good. This was not a good closing." Indeed it was not. Roberto, who attends Moral Support only sporadically, spent most of his personal story complaining about the group. In other groups, he said, when you rise to the podium, you introduce yourself by saying, "*Buenas noches, compañeros, soy Roberto*"—"Good evening, *compañeros*, I am Roberto." The group responds by stating in unison, "*Buenas noches, Roberto.*" That makes the speaker feel good, he said. Not in Moral Support, he continued. At Moral Support, "Everyone just sits there staring at you with blank faces. Everyone looks depressed. There's no life to the occasion." Raising his voice for emphasis, Roberto then blurted out, "A bit of change! A bit of change! We need to enliven the place! I want to hear what the newcomers [*nuevos*] have to say, not just listen to the same old tired stories that put everyone to sleep. The *nuevos* should have a chance to speak!"

Roberto's personal story met with much weaker applause than usual. The men sitting next to me remained stone faced; far from applauding, they hardly twitched a finger. Gerardo explained why Roberto's personal story had failed. "A good closing needs to be uplifting, he said. It should make everyone walk out of the meeting feeling good. It should move people to keep coming to *juntas* and stick with the program." A Moral Support meeting is analogous to an orchestrated performance. To be effective, particular actors need to be assigned the roles for which they are best suited. If the director of the production—that is, the moderator—fails in this task, he becomes the target of criticism. The criticism, in turn, reminds everyone of the ingredients required for a successful meeting. In this particular meeting, both Roberto and the coordinator, Pedro, had failed in their assigned tasks. From the men's point of view, Pedro should have selected a worthier speaker than Roberto to close the meeting. Once chosen as speaker, however, Roberto should have played his proper role, that is, to conclude the evening with an uplifting, inspirational message.

Moderators and speakers are not the only men who get assailed during meetings. So, too, do listeners. The proper role of listeners is to lend undivided attention to personal stories. In a small group like Moral Support it is easy to detect when *compañeros* are distracted and behave impolitely during the delivery of personal stories. It is bad enough when outsiders, like children from the street, enter the meeting room and tap nervously on their coffee cups. Much worse, according to the men, is disturbing behavior on the part of the *compañeros* themselves. Eduardo is among the worst offenders. On one particularly annoying occasion, he began the evening by spilling his coffee, which required a cleanup while someone was speaking. As subsequent speakers delivered personal stories, Eduardo blithely cleaned and cut his fingernails with a noisy clipper. He only stopped when Pedro, seated directly behind him, poked him in reproach. Eduardo continued to fidget with the clipper throughout the evening. Several weeks later, David, whose speech was laced with malapropisms—told me, "Our group is marvelous, but we need to eliminate *distorciones*," by which he meant distractions. "For example," he continued, "when people clip their nails or clean their combs or do other disturbing things, it is distracting and disrespectful to the speaker." David also criticized the group secretary for collecting and washing the coffee cups while the last speaker was delivering a personal story. The secretary strives to complete his duties in time to return home at the same hour as the other men. But carrying out his chores should not intrude on the serene conduct of the meeting.

Newcomers have to be socialized to the role of listener, just as to other facets of meeting participation. When an elderly newcomer innocently sat in meeting, copying the Twelve Steps and Twelve Traditions from wall posters, he was eyed critically by others in the room. At the end of the meeting, after the *séptima* was collected, Gerardo discretely handed the unwitting transgressor an A.A. publication, listing the Steps and Traditions. This kindly gesture was probably enough to instruct the newcomer, in a gentle, indirect fashion, that he should not take notes during meetings, for the newcomer never repeated that behavior again. Nevertheless, a month later, a speaker took the opportunity to criticize "people who write during meetings." The next day Emilio, squatting on his stool and looking up at me as he shined my shoes, bluntly supported the speaker's opinion: "We're not at meetings to do homework!"

Note taking is not the only offense of listeners. At Moral Support meetings, the men occasionally fall asleep. They put their feet up on chairs and stretch. They push furniture around to get to the bathroom. These and other distracting activities all receive critical commentary during personal stories. When *compañeros* listen to publicly aired complaints about their behavior, they remain calm on the outside, but become angry within. Even though their names are rarely mentioned, they feel victimized. They know as well as everyone does that, in a group as small and intimate as Moral Support, there can be no mistaking their identity.

Group officers also get criticized for poor performance. Perhaps the most vulnerable office is that of secretary. The secretary, as readers recall (Chapter Three), arrives early to unlock the meeting room and prepare it for the evening meeting. The secretary is also known by the title *servidor,* or server, because he is the person who prepares and serves coffee and tea throughout the meeting. As the final act of the evening, he cleans and locks the meeting room. The men are acutely aware of the state of the meeting room, so that the least oversight on the part of the secretary in carrying out housekeeping duties evokes criticism. Emilio accuses Eduardo of being a *"puerco"*—a pig. He picks his nose and grinds dirt from his fingernails in public, says Emilio. And Eduardo dirties the washroom of the meeting room by spitting on the wall. It is the duty of the secretary to clean that mess, says Emilio, but that task never gets done properly. The toilet remains dirty, the plastic-covered chairs unwashed, the floor unswept. Emilio even spent a rainy day, when he could not work at the shoe shine stand, in cleaning the meeting room, thereby compensating for the secretary's inadequate discharge of duties. Emilio claims to have cleaned the chairs with soap and wiped the accumulated grime from the pictures and posters on the walls. Resentful at having to work at someone else's job, Emilio used his next personal story to complain openly about the secretary's irresponsibility.

The following week I arrived at the meeting room some twenty minutes before the meeting began. David, the secretary, was outside, scrubbing the bristles of a broom. He lost no time in explaining to me that he arrives at 7 P.M., a full hour before the start of the meeting, in order to clean the room properly. Then, without mentioning names, he said that he had been criticized for performing his job inadequately. To justify himself, he said, "I might not wash the floor every three days, but I do wash it every week." I had not attended the meeting at which Emilio issued his criticism. But David, probably respectful of my special relationship with Emilio, would not divulge his name. All he would say is that it was someone "with many years in the program." What is worse, said David, the criticism was leveled on a Saturday evening, precisely the one occasion when David, bound by work obligations, is unable to attend. He finds this kind of backbiting particularly hurtful.

That evening, the central theme of the personal stories was group service. Gerardo opened the meeting by reminding everyone that service is a big responsibility and that the person in charge should read the "Manual de Servicio," published by A.A. In Moral Support, a group which positively denigrates the role of *"literatura"* in the therapeutic process, I had never before heard this publication mentioned. Gerardo went on to explain that the secretary has to arrive a half hour early and leave a half hour later than everyone else, in order to allow time for the performance of duties. He added that *compañeros* should sympathize with the plight of the secretary because the secretary finds himself in a weak position vis-à-vis his family. Past experience has taught family members to distrust him. To a wife and children, a late arrival home arouses the suspicion that the man has not been at a meeting, but rather at a *pulquería* or other drinking establishment, spending money irresponsibly. Gerardo's analysis made David feel better, even though everyone is aware that he has no family to go home to.

Money itself is probably the greatest source of unhappiness and critical commentary in Moral Support. For this reason, the group treasurer also comes under particular scrutiny and suspicion. Throughout the years that the group met at Pedro's house, including the first months of my fieldwork, Pedro himself served as treasurer, collecting the *séptima* and special contributions at the end of each meeting and assuming responsibility for the maintenance of financial records. From the outset, I was impressed by the clear, concise way in which he explained the distribution of funds to the men and oversaw the collection of supplementary funds for extraordinary expenses. He would list assets and expenses on the blackboard in large, bright numbers. He answered the men's questions and addressed their concerns with unfailing patience and diplomacy. However, like all officers of the group, he was not immune to the silent force of social control. A number of the men told me that they were wary of his performance as treasurer, because he had named himself to the post at the very time the group started meeting at the cottage next to his house. The general opinion was that he had abused his role as landlord to acquire a potentially powerful post. As soon as the group changed meeting rooms, the men seized their opportunity to appoint a new treasurer, this time through election.

When Emilio let it be known that he would willingly serve ("I wouldn't have any problem with serving as treasurer," he said), he was elected. However, he explained that he would need to be absent on certain occasions and therefore should share the post with another *compañero*. David volunteered, at the same time warning the men that he would not tolerate auditing. He announced to the group that there was a tendency to audit the treasurer by checking his accounting. Overseeing the treasurer's work, stated David, is contrary to the spirit of trust that should accompany the job. Pedro disagreed vehemently, because, as he correctly stated, there are some in the group who cannot add. "They write 30 instead of 300 and when the sum should read 320 it reads 290 and so forth." With that, Pedro left the room and David continued grumbling. There was no resolution to the matter. Stated Simón, "Well, if someone takes ten pesos from the collection box, that deed will haunt them." Despite Simon's optimism, everyone's memory was focused at that moment on the doctor's group, to which Emilio and others had belonged and which had dissolved partly because of problems of embezzlement.

Although theft seemed possible, no one during the period of my fieldwork was ever accused of stealing money from the group. However, finances were a constant source of worry and conflict. Disputes over money arose from time to time, but never got resolved, thereby producing an underlying atmosphere of suspicion. On one occasion, Simón offered to have the Moral Support sign repaired. The job accomplished, he claimed that it cost 50 pesos, and tried to collect that amount from the group when *compañeros* discovered that, in fact, it had only cost him 40. Simón complained bitterly, but group treasurer Emilio did not capitulate, for he suspected Simón of trying to extort 10 pesos.

The most common financial grievances, however, arise among those who consistently donate disproportionately large amounts of money to support the group. Several of the unemployed men rarely contribute anything. They use personal stories to apologize for their grave economic circumstances and solicit the group's understanding. Simón explains in a personal story that he is unemployed and has no money, except what his children give him to buy food for himself and his *compañera*. He claims that he is ashamed to admit that he cannot afford to donate to the *séptima,* but there is no alternative. Most of the men have only part-time employment and give a peso or two each meeting. A few gainfully employed *compañeros* are famous for disappearing at the moment the collection basket makes the rounds at the end of each meeting.

The men who donate regularly to the group accuse the others of being lazy misers, unwilling to work even when employment is available. They point out that Eduardo wanders the neighborhood aimlessly, neither looking for work nor worried about his lamentable situation. When he is not on the streets, they observe, he stays at home, "like a dog." "How can these men hold their head up?" asks one *compañero* who regularly contributes 5 or 10 pesos a session. "That should be the minimum donation," he says. Instead, the men deposit a few centavos, or one or two pesos at most, into the basket. At the end of every month, the group is required to make an emergency collection of funds in order to meet the rent and electricity bill. This is precisely the moment that a few men predictably disappear. Others, confident that without their generosity Moral Support would collapse, become resentful and secretly plan to abandon the group.

When Moral Support mounted a special collection for moving funds, Gerardo provided leadership. As with all extraordinary donations, the names of donors and the amount of each donation was listed on the meeting room blackboard. Gerardo had given 50 pesos; several other men had contributed up to 30 pesos apiece. To encourage further donations, Gerardo devoted a personal story to boasting about his own generosity. He derives satisfaction, he says, from donating money to his pueblo in San Luis Potosí. He likes to treat his *compañeros* to food and drink on the occasion of his anniversary celebration. He also always contributes to his neighborhood fiesta. His face suddenly radiant with a wide smile, he summed up his feeling about the matter: "*Me gusta cooperar*"—I like to donate. By holding himself up as a positive example, Gerardo possibly hoped to shame the men into donating for the imminent move. Whatever their motivation, the holdouts managed to contribute money in enough time for the group to move from one meeting place to the other on schedule. Nonetheless, this financial campaign, like every other in Moral Support, proved to be a dramatic struggle.

Personal stories provide an arena for the airing of group alliances and rivalries. Consider what happened when a young newcomer walked into the meeting room one day while Pedro was at the podium. The young man, well socialized to Mexican norms of politeness, felt he had to shake everyone's hand before being seated. This is precisely how any well raised individual would behave upon entering a stranger's home. Although the newcomer's comportment had distracted attention from the speaker—all the more so because he arrived late—the men tolerated it, because they assumed that he was well meaning. To criticize his behavior might drive him away.

One evening, two weeks after he began attending meetings, the newcomer walked in late and, as usual, shook everyone's hand before taking a seat. Pedro, again at the podium, could no longer contain his anger. He interrupted the personal story to state firmly that it is a "disturbance" for a person who arrives in the middle of a meeting to shake everyone's hand. What is proper, he continued, is for the latecomer to enter the meeting room unobtrusively and be seated in the quietest, least noticeable manner. Pedro's words, taken at face value, might be interpreted as supportive advice to the young man, or even as a general reminder to the entire group of proper meeting behavior. Clearly, this newcomer needed guidance. However, there was anger in Pedro's voice. He had in effect scolded the young man and the impact on him was obviously devastating.

Gerardo, acting that night as moderator, noticed the newcomer's reaction. As soon as Pedro took his seat, Gerardo commented softly, "I don't know why, but there is something I like about the *saludo* [greeting, handshake]." Gerardo pointed to the poster of the Twelve Traditions hanging directly behind the moderator's desk. He continued, "Look carefully at the Twelve Steps and you'll see that even the literature talks about how positive the handshake can be." To conclude, Gerardo reiterated, "I don't know what it is, but I just like the *saludo*. There's something good about it."

That statement ended the small drama. Brief as it was, this interaction demonstrates some of the main reasons why recovering alcoholics remain in the group as well as why they are driven away. These men, whose lives were so disrupted by their addiction and who see their alcoholic past as disorderly and chaotic, are driven by rules. They interpret strict adherence to rules as necessary for continued sobriety. The same may be said for their delivery of personal stories, which, as we see in the following chapter, they consider their principal therapeutic medium. The men are inspired to *"llevar el mensaje"* (literally, "carry the message"), that is, to proselytize and bring within the fold of Alcoholics Anonymous as many sufferers as they can.

The exchange over handshaking that took place between Pedro and Gerardo represented a perhaps inevitable clash between competing A.A. principles. On the one hand, Pedro was upset by the newcomer's deviant behavior. The young man consistently arrived late and disrupted the meeting. He prevented the speaker and listeners from concentrating on business at hand. His behavior had become intolerable. It needed correction and Pedro took it upon himself to carry out this unpleasant deed. On the other hand, as Gerardo's reaction indicates, newcomers need to be supported emotionally and instructed if they are to remain within the A.A. fold for any sustained period of time. Gerardo's statements were designed with this goal in mind. While Pedro upheld one set of rules, those necessary to the smooth functioning of the meeting, Gerardo supported another, those designed to attract newcomers to the group.

But this confrontation not only reflected a momentary incompatibility between particular norms and rules. It also involved a fundamental clash between two strong-willed members. Pedro and Gerardo were known within Moral Support as *padrinos*. They were the group's main founders and, among all the men, were financially the strongest. They also had the most forceful personalities. Both men are articulate, entertaining, often insightful orators, who express well-defined, cogently argued opinions. As such, their words carry unusual weight. These two men are the de facto leaders of Moral Support, regardless of which members hold formal office. They are also in competition with one another for leadership. It is this competition that emerged over the newcomer's behavior. Gerardo's concluding statements were not only designed to provide the young man with supportive words, but also to challenge Pedro.

Unfortunately, not everyone can withstand public criticism. Pedro and Gerardo are accustomed to confronting one another in public and are strong enough to withstand the critical words of their *compañeros*. They are also accustomed to the occasionally cruel process through which members of Moral Support exert social control. But the innocent newcomer, half the age of most of the men in the room, was completely unfamiliar with Moral Support rhythms and routines. A drug addict as well as alcohol abuser, this young man was in a weakened mental and physical state when he arrived at Moral Support. He must have found Pedro's words devastating, for he left that meeting never to return.

Flight from the group, whether temporary or permanent, is a common reaction to public humiliation. The men of Moral Support repeatedly state the general A.A. principle that groups should not *"meterse en controversias"*—get involved in controversies. They denounce what they consider the all-too-common practice of speaking about *"terceras personas"*—third parties, that is, anyone but the speaker himself. They interpret personal conflict that emerges in meetings as a breach of the Twelve Steps, which they point to whenever criticizing *compañeros* who violate the rules, as they conceive them. Sometimes, by using personal stories to invoke the letter of the rules, the men simultaneously violate the spirit of the rules. The recovering alcoholic's insistence on following group guidelines accords with assuming a responsible social role. However, lapses, real or imagined, are inevitable. More often than not, these lapses evoke humiliating rebuke, issued from the semi-sacred position of the podium. Often, if not driven from meetings altogether, the victim's response is to denounce the emergence of "controversies" and remind *compañeros* that discussion of "third parties" should be curtailed.

At times the victim of an attack proves unable or unwilling to defend himself. In such instances, a *compañero* will sometimes come to his rescue. One evening, Simón was called to the lectern and immediately began a personal story by lashing out against Eduardo. Referring to Eduardo by name, Simón reproached him publicly for smoking. He looked Eduardo straight in the eyes and told him that he smells bad, that smoking will harm him, and that he is making a big mistake to smoke. Eduardo remained quiet throughout the assault, a faint smile plastered on his face. He pretended to remain calm, although I could tell that he was seething inside. José's personal story followed. He defended Eduardo, not by referring explicitly to what Simón had said, but by stating simply, "First I will clean out my own house, then I'll worry about others. We are not here to criticize one another but rather to examine ourselves."

This lesson, reiterated often in Moral Support meetings, provides a modicum of support to the victims of public criticism. Unfortunately, the wounds can take literally years to heal. The humiliation and anger are sometimes so strong that you can feel them swirl through the meeting room air. They occasionally cause *compañeros* to disappear from Moral Support for months. And they place the stability, even the very existence, of the entire group at risk.

The men of Moral Support on the whole strive to conform to the guidelines of the international Alcoholics Anonymous movement. But, in an attempt to inform newcomers of the rules, gain prestige among *compañeros*, or simply express malice, their self-righteousness sometimes destroys the nurturing and supportive atmosphere that can prevail in the meeting room. For most of the men, personal confrontation is trying. They therefore use the podium as a disguised way of criticizing those *compañeros* whose behavior seems wanting. This situation is seriously complicated by the almost complete lack of anonymity among the men, who are relatives, friends, neighbors, and former drinking buddies. At Moral Support the boundaries between meeting room and street, inside and outside, family and *compañero*, are indeed ambiguous. The result is that problems among *compañeros* that originate at home or in the neighborhood get aired on the podium. At the same time, difficulties generated during meetings have repercussions for the way these men treat one another in the world outside.

7. ILLNESS AND RECOVERY

The men of Moral Support accept what has long been the most widely accepted definition of alcoholism, that is, alcoholism as a disease. There can be no doubt that excessive alcohol consumption causes disease and contributes significantly, through accidents, to mortality rates. At the turn of the previous century, Mexican pro-temperance physicians were well aware of the potentially injurious effects of alcohol, to which they attributed virtually every physical and social malady. Consider, for example, the introductory words of Dr. Fernando Ponce (1911:3), who wrote a long book on the subject.

> Thirty years practicing in the medical profession has taught me that in the entire Mexican Republic there is a group of illnesses which attack individuals of both sexes, of all ages, and without regard to social class; that these illnesses . . . are generally incurable; that the infirm individuals who unfortunately visit all types of physicians, [because they are] attacked by maladies of the type I am referring to, almost always succumb, despite enormous struggle to save them; and, finally, that all these infirmities have as their origin the use or abuse of inebriating drinks.

Among the maladies which Ponce attributed to alcohol are premature aging, shortened life span, heightened susceptibility to infectious disease, insanity, loss of motivation and aptitude for work, family unhappiness, suicide, delinquency, and numerous others. Ponce apparently did not consider alcohol consumption a disease in and of itself, but rather the cause of numerous biological and social ills.

Eduardo Menéndez (1990:9), a medical anthropologist and author writing on alcohol and society in Latin America today, states that "Alcoholism, in both its direct form (cirrhosis of the liver, alcoholic psychosis) and indirect form (accidents, homicide), constitutes one of the primary causes of death in Latin American countries, such as Mexico, Chile, and Argentina. These consequences show themselves above all in men between 20 and 64 years of age, to such an extent that in Mexico men in the so-called 'productive years' die over and above any other cause through the use and consumption of alcohol." Like Ponce, Menéndez portrays alcoholism not as a disease but as a cause of serious physical and social maladies.

Menéndez is of course much more moderate in his attribution of maladies to drinking than Ponce was. Nonetheless, the conditions he outlines, far from improving over the past generation, seem to have worsened. Menéndez (ibid.:19–26) takes pains to demonstrate that, while mortality rates in Mexico have decreased substantially over the past half century, and life expectancy has increased, there has been an alarming augmentation in rates of cirrhosis during the same period. In 1998, cirrhosis and chronic liver disease were the third leading cause of death in Mexico among 15–64-year-olds (Pan American Health Organization 1998). Statistics (World Drink Trends 1997:9) show that in the period 1961 to 1996, Mexican annual ingestion of pure alcohol—that is, of the total alcohol content from distilled and fermented beverages—increased from 1.1 to 3.4 liters per capita. During the same period, per capita beer consumption rose from 22.3 liters to 53.4 liters (ibid.). Considering that beer is, and for decades has been, the overwhelming beverage of choice in Mexico (Bennett, Campillo et al.:1998), these figures give some indication of why so many Mexicans over the past generation have sought help from Alcoholics Anonymous.

However, if we consider the proposition that alcoholism *is* an actual disease, in contrast to being the cause of disease, we enter contested terrain (e.g., Menéndez 1990; Piazza and Wise 1988). Pertti Alasuutari (1992:2) points out that the definition of alcoholism as a disease "*shifts attention from the* [drinking] *situation to individuals and their drinking habits or style*" (italics in the original). The term alcoholism, he correctly states, "distinguishes between normal and abnormal (or pathological) drinking" (ibid.). The prevailing conception of alcoholism, in fact, "sees drinking as the result of craving and the inability to refrain"; it furthermore "portrays heavy drinking as a long-standing problem which can be managed and handled, but not cured" (ibid.). Alasuutari's analysis of drinking ideology and behavior does much to support his contention that, as a named, identifiable, discrete infirmity, "Alcoholism is a Western culture-bound syndrome" (ibid.). Largely owing to the nearly ubiquitous adoption of Western medicine, this syndrome has become an accepted medical fact throughout the world. The globalization process assures that the disease model will continue to diffuse at an ever more rapid pace. It has certainly become a well-established feature of Mexican medical systems, largely due to the influence of Alcoholics Anonymous.

According to E. M. Jellinek (1960:10), the scholar who most avidly has promoted the medical model of alcoholism, "One of the greatest roles in bringing the illness conception to the widest reaches of public opinion was played by the fellowship of Alcoholics Anonymous." Jellinek (ibid.:12) also points out that *"a disease is what the medical profession recognizes as such"* (italics in the original). Given that the medical profession has fully embraced the disease concept of alcoholism, physicians have provided expert validation of worldwide A.A. ideology. In Mexican A.A. groups, the disease model is evident not only in repeated assertions that *"el alcoholismo es una enfermedad"*—"alcoholism is a disease." It is a viewpoint also reaffirmed in meetings, when each speaker introduces himself as *"un enfermo alcohólico"*—"an ill alcoholic." The very word *historial,* which I, following Carole Cain (1991), translate as "personal story," derives from the world of scientific medicine. An *historial,* in Mexican Spanish, is the term used to indicate a patient's case record, as in the instance of a hospital log (Paul Hersch-Martínez: personal communication). In the context of A.A., the *historial* is the alcoholic's detailed account of trauma and recovery.

At Moral Support it is impossible to sit through a meeting without hearing at least once that "alcoholism is progressive, incurable, and fatal" [*"progresivo, incurable, y mortal"*]. This expression, uttered so frequently and in such a formulaic fashion, almost achieves the status of a mantra. The belief in alcoholism as an incurable disease is part of what motivates the men to continue attending meetings, long after they have ever had even a sip of alcohol. They have come to believe that they are, once and forever, alcoholics. María Eugenia Módena (1999:388) points out the implications of this type of self-labeling:

> Alcoholism, alcoholization, and the alcoholic complex construct an identity. . . . The alcoholic, . . . in contrast to other chronically ill people, engages the totality of his person within his [drinking] career, from the entirety of his roles to his feelings and fantasies. Borrowing from the concept "total institution," alcoholism is a "total illness"

which implicates the very Ego of the subject, who feels and thinks about the world in terms of the presence or absence of alcohol. (my translation)

The sufferer's presence at A.A. meetings acts as repeated affirmation and reinforcement of this totalizing identity.

The acceptance of one's identity as an alcoholic means that the sufferer may never take another sip of alcohol, lest he relapse. In the scientific world, there is considerable disagreement over whether and to what degree the former alcohol abuser places himself or herself at risk by enjoying an occasional drink (see, e.g., Alasuutari 1992, Satel 2000). A.A. believers, however, admit no such doubts. According to Paul Antzé 1982:280),

> AA teaches that recovery begins only after a special experience of despair, an experience that finally compels the confession of illness. Ironically, members believe that the alcoholic is ready for change only when persuaded that all efforts at self-control are hopeless. To this end, AA "Twelfth Steppers" (members working with drinking alcoholics) often attempt to push their prospect toward despair. A favorite technique is challenging the candidate to "try some controlled drinking," the expectation being that he will fail miserably, and that in the depression that follows he will take the first of AA's Twelve Steps: "We admitted that we were powerless over alcohol—that our lives had become unmanageable."

One of the strictest tenets of A.A. ideology states that, given the alcoholic's diseased condition, he will lose control if he drinks even the tiniest sip of alcohol. Since A.A. prohibits experimentation with controlled alcoholic consumption, attendance at A.A. meetings prevents recovering alcoholics from engaging in this kind of risky behavior.

The men of Moral Support have internalized this message thoroughly, and articulate it readily—at least during periods when they are actively engaged with the group. Only by attending meetings, says Renaldo, has he been able to stay completely sober for seventeen years. "I know that if I have even a sip it might mean my death—the death of me." "That will be my death," repeats Renaldo over and over, his voice rising to convey his horror at that thought of this gruesome possibility. Most of the men, in fact, believe they owe their lives to Alcoholics Anonymous. Concluding a taped interview, Emilio states, "Thanks to A.A., I got my life back. Thanks to A.A., I'm having this conversation with you. If it hadn't been for A.A., Emilio would not exist any more in this life."

Eduardo, too, dangles the prospect of certain death in front of anyone who dares to drink, alcohol abuser or not.

> Just last night, after we left the meeting, I was with some friends there and we started to talk about alcoholism and one of them says, "Listen, Duardo," he says, "Didn't you used to feel gross, being plastered like that?" I said, "Yes, I felt gross, believe me. But, just as you guys are drinking calmly, there was a time when I could drink calmly. But alcoholism is necessarily progressive and fatal. If you continue taking those shots once a week, afterwards it's not gonna be once a week. It's gonna be once every four days, five days, and you're gonna go like that for entire weeks, or after weeks, entire months. Then it'll be the whole year, like happened to me. Be careful, you bastards [*cabrones*], because alcoholism is progressive and fatal, by definition. If you don't stop it in time, you will die."

Like some of the men, Eduardo seems to conflate alcohol consumption per se with alcoholism. To him, drinking is inherently addictive and bears fatal consequences.

The men derive a sense of solidarity from knowing that they all suffer equally from a common affliction. They are also certain that they will share this condition throughout life. "See," Emilio explains, "there are only two places where you can stop drinking: in the grave or in Alcoholics Anonymous. If there were another way to stop drinking, well, lots of people wouldn't be suffering. But there isn't. There are intellectuals, there are doctors, there are the . . . well, the people with plenty of studies behind them, but unfortunately alcoholism doesn't choose social classes. It affects us all the same: the literate, the educated, everyone in general."

In Moral Support, of course, basically one social class is represented: proletarian. Acceptance of a variety of explanations for alcoholism would threaten to divide these men along other than class or educational lines. At the very least, each etiology would suggest a distinct kind of treatment. For those suffering from a specific genetic abnormality, one remedy would be indicated; for those impaired by status incongruities, child abuse, or the effects of poverty, alternative solutions might prove appropriate. The virtue of a disease model is that it allows uniform treatment. That, unfortunately, is also its shortcoming. In Moral Support, the shared, unquestioned belief in the disease model of alcoholism constitutes a source of fundamental equality among the men. It is one of many ways (see Chapter Four) in which they come to identify with one another.

However, their testimonies and life stories indicate an awareness of competing theories of alcoholism, especially those based on inherited or acquired traits. For the men of Moral Support, various causal factors, which are not always compatible with one another, seem to co-exist.

While giving me a shoeshine, Emilio, who is ethnically indigenous, stated that he blames his alcoholism in part on racial prejudice. Born and brought up in a tiny village about an hour's drive from Cuernavaca, capital of the state of Morelos, Emilio moved to Mexico City at the age of thirteen. He barely spoke Spanish at the time. For this, he was ridiculed mercilessly. Among other insults, he recalls being called *indio de pata rajada*—"Indian with the cracked foot." Indians wore *huaraches,* or leather sandals with soles made of rubber automobile tires. Emilio explains that this garment leaves one's feet raw and cracked. The Indian's damaged feet were transformed into a stigmatizing symbol and, from there, into an ethnic slur—in effect the bodily imprint of poverty and social marginality. "*Pata rajada*"—cracked feet—was the label that urban *mestizos* would apply to poor migrants from indigenous regions in Mexico. "That was what they called me," says Emilio, "and for me these things were traumatic." It has at least occurred to Emilio that this and similar experiences might account for his alcohol abuse. He is probably unaware that, over and above making a living, his occupation as shoe shiner has helped him integrate into urban, mestizo life and overcome childhood traumas. He now devotes most of his waking hours to keeping his customers smartly shoed. By shining shoes for a living, Emilio in effect symbolically rejects the extreme poverty, ragged clothing, and, most importantly, cracked feet that identified him in early life as a despised Indian.

Despite Emilio's awareness of his suffering and the impact it might have had on his drinking, he embraces the Alcoholics Anonymous interpretation of alcoholism as a disease. Emilio is disdainful of the popular view that alcoholism is a "vice." Membership in Alcoholics Anonymous, he says, taught him to believe otherwise.

> When I didn't know about the group [i.e., the A.A. group], I said that it's a vice. But it's not a vice, because with a vice you could say, "I have a vice." Because I like to eat fruit cocktail so much, because it's good. But the day arrives when it bores me and I don't crave its fla-

vor anymore, right? And that's what I see as a vice, [something] that you eventually stop craving. And this [i.e., alcoholism] is a disease . . . a sickness growing within the human organism. I mean you could say this is related to the blood because lots of times the alcoholic . . . uh, the alcohol mixes with the blood. Yeah, it mixes with the blood so a lot of the time you no longer have blood, you have alcohol in your veins. And that's why you get that illness that's called, ummm, hepatitis . . . or, ummm, cirrhosis. Because when a human being gets it, cirrhosis, it's not blood anymore. It's water. The blood converts, it converts into water from drinking so much alcohol. That's it. So when it's that illness, cirrhosis, there's no cure. There are very few people who survive with cirrhosis . . . and he who has that illness shouldn't drink alcohol again in his life. By doctor's orders he can't ingest any alcohol anymore. . . . And for the person who relapses, who doesn't heed the doctor's advice (because this is life or death we're talking about, yeah) it's a straight, straight path to the grave.

Emilio clearly articulates the A.A. model of alcoholism as a disease. He also believes that, via the blood, this disease leads to other maladies, namely hepatitis and cirrhosis, the latter fatal.

David's ideas about the etiology of alcoholism changed when he joined Alcoholics Anonymous:

When I stopped drinking I was thirty-six and a half years old, but the truth is that I started drinking at around twenty. At twenty I began drinking and, well, of course, like they say in A.A., alcoholism is an illness. And in my case, well, I can testify—I can say with certainty—that alcoholism is an illness, an incurable illness that is progressive and fatal—inevitably fatal. So, at the time I arrived at A.A., well, I really didn't know that alcoholism was an illness, that alcoholism was the mother of all evils, that alcoholism is the panacea [*sic*] of all evils, and I had no idea of that because of oversight, out of ignorance, out of whatever. I never knew that alcoholism affected us physically, mentally, and spiritually, economically. I simply drank since I saw that everyone else drank. I thought that drinking was something that you needed to do to be a man, to be a man. I really, well, I was mistaken, you know, because that was a lie. Because I also drank because I said it was hereditary, you know, that I had inherited it because my father, my grandfathers, and my uncles drank. And actually they did all drink.

David's account indicates awareness that some people believe in the hereditary transmission of alcoholism. He also reveals that he drank to feel part of something bigger than himself—a group of men.

David suspects, too, that social and emotional factors might have played a role in his childhood development. "Since I was a small boy, I have always been in trauma, always felt traumatized. I had an inferiority complex. My parents were very poor, they suffered a lot, they were lacking. We lacked many things." Alcoholics Anonymous was David's salvation. "I never knew that there was a place where you could stop drinking," he says, "that there was a place where they could take my hand and support me in so many ways—in this case to support me, give me understanding, [a place] where I feel love, true affection. That I was someone who mattered, that I was an important person."

What is clearly important to David, apart from the ability to stop drinking, is the sense of security and belonging that he derived as a member of Alcoholics Anonymous. After more than a decade of sobriety, David claims, "Now I'm not worried . . . that I need to drink. I'm not interested in it because I don't want to. I don't want to drink because my mind has finally been released. It has escaped from that obsession." And yet David is one of the most faithful followers of Moral Support. His reason: "Look, I have to keep going to Double A because—given that alcoholism is progressive, incurable, and fatal—I'm not cured of alcoholism. What I'm doing is holding my alcoholism back through therapy."

Each of the men in Moral Support eventually has to confront the question of why they suffered from alcohol abuse. Alcoholics Anonymous provides them a medical definition of their problem: they were born with a proclivity for uncontrollable drink. This proclivity is permanent. They can hope only to keep it under control by refusing to drink a single drop of alcohol—what they refer to in personal stories as "esa primera copa" ("that first glass")—ever again. Only through regular attendance at Alcoholics Anonymous meetings can they achieve lifetime sobriety.

It is the main task of Alcoholics Anonymous to assure that its members refrain from taking "esa primera copa." Theoretically, that first drink signals their ultimate demise. One drink inevitably escalates to two, two to three, three to four, and so on, until the victim finally dies. The alcoholic might try various remedies—vows to the Virgin, pills, self-control. But all these attempts will fail. Only Alcoholics Anonymous, say the men, can save them from self-destruction.

It is important to recognize that not all self-help groups, much less therapeutic approaches, advocate complete abstention for the recovering alcohol abuser. Alasuutari (1992:130), for example, analyzes a Finnish guild whose members "do not make total abstinence part of an ideology and policy." States one of Alasuutari's informants, "We're allowed to deal with the issue of drinking the way each of us wants to. If a guy wants to reduce his drinking, so let him try. AA stands for unconditional abstinence only, but with us everyone makes his own program" (quoted in ibid.).

The A.A.–derived beliefs that prevail among the men of Moral Support echo those which Howard Stein has identified as characterizing those propagated by the medical community of the United States, where the disease model of alcoholism flourishes and from which it is exported. Stein (1982:368) points out that

> the treatment for this disease possesses an all-or-nothing quality that is simply absent from the treatment of other disease-entities. One would not think twice if a patient with bacterial pneumonia or coronary heart disease had a relapse and showed the full spectrum of original symptoms—if not worse. . . . Not so the alcoholic. One slip and he falls into perdition and disgrace, quite a burden for a mere disease. "The alcoholic" is either wet or dry; there is no intermediate ground. In one sweeping act, he must quit, "go cold turkey," to demonstrate his wish to recover. Likewise, one drink and he is as "confirmed" an alcoholic as he ever was. . . . the alcoholic is under close scrutiny by others and learns to monitor himself with unbridled vigilance. . . . Whatever he may lack or think he lacks in an observing superego is more than compensated by those who appoint themselves to watch over him. He constantly hears and reminds himself that "It takes only one drink, and you'll end up right where you were," or "one drink, and you're finished." "The alcoholic" is thus ascribed awesome, dangerous power, and at the same time is sternly reminded of his helplessness before the desire to drink.

According to Stein, the disease model imposes a never-ending awareness on the sufferer, which constantly draws attention to his flawed condition.

The men of Moral Support are no less affected by being labeled alcoholic—and labeling themselves alcoholic—than anyone else: they perceive themselves as at once responsible and not responsible for their drinking behavior. This inherently contradictory perception, as Stein

(1982) points out, is one of the "paradoxes of inebriation and sobriety" which automatically derives from the belief that alcohol is a disease.

According to the model of alcoholism propagated in Alcoholics Anonymous, the active alcoholic necessarily finds himself in a state of mental and physical disarray. So how and when does the decision come to seek help? The critical turning point, according to the paradigmatic A.A. narrative, occurs when the active alcoholic "hits bottom" (O'Reilly 1997: 22). That is, the victim's life becomes an impossible nightmare, moving him to a state of utter degradation and despair. As Bateson puts it (1971), he is in a state of radical defeat. This condition produces in the alcoholic an ability to see his miserable existence for what it is and motivates him to seek help. Hitting bottom constitutes a crucial part of the overall conversion experience. It is what impels the alcoholic to recognize his powerlessness, accept help, and embrace sobriety.

The term *tocar fondo*—or hitting bottom—appears in only one taped interview from Moral Support, namely in Emilio's life history, in which he provides a moving account of the abyss into which he had fallen prior to his introduction to A.A. One day, after a two-week binge, his wife and sister-in-law, who were worried about his seriously weakened condition, took him to see a neighborhood doctor.

> And what's more, I didn't know that the doctor was in Alcoholics Anonymous . . . On that day, when they took me, I was, well, desperate. Desperate. And what I wanted was something like a magic wand, that by simply going to the doctor I'd get rid of it. That thing was like a desperation that I just couldn't handle anymore; that desperation, those destroyed nerves. So he was seeing another patient in his office and I could tell that he took the time to talk. . . . I could tell that he did things with calm, with a lot of patience. And my desperation was so immense that—I didn't say it aloud, right?—but I said it to myself that, well, since that guy [patient] isn't sick, if I come here sick, how can he just stand there chatting? How come [the doctor] is not attending to me? OK, so then the doctor was kind enough to see me and the person he had been talking to left. He knew right away that I was sick, but sick from alcoholism, which is a chronic illness, right?

Emilio continues by telling how afraid he was of receiving some unidentified serum intravenously: "I was afraid. . . . The truth is I wanted to get out of there." And then the doctor revealed to Emilio that he himself had suffered in the same way. "But the truth is," says Emilio, "I didn't believe him, because, well, he looked to me like a normal guy. Normal. And I couldn't imagine that he had also been an alcoholic like me."

While the I.V. was being administered, the doctor told Emilio about A.A. and invited him to return to the office to learn more about it. In effect, the doctor sought an opportunity to *"pasar el mensaje"*—convey the message—to Emilio. Passing on or conveying the message is a paradigmatic part of the A.A. conversion story. To proselytize in this fashion is the responsibility of all A.A. members who meet anyone in need. This mission, as stipulated in the twelfth Tradition (see Appendix B), in fact, derives from the evangelical Protestant origins of A.A. (Chapter Two).

Emilio did not return to see the doctor at that point. Instead, he continued to drink, until his condition deteriorated to the point that he began to hallucinate.

I mean, I heard voices. I felt like I was being followed. . . . At night I couldn't sleep. I dreamed about animals that never in my life will I see. I thought I heard people speaking to me and I'd turn around and say, "Who is it?" . . . I got those sweats, those terrifying sweats. . . . I felt all those things. . . . I went on drinking and my wife became fed up with me. She didn't want to have anything to do with me anymore. Around that time, she told me, "You know, Emilio? If you're so happy drinking with your friends, well, don't come to this house anymore." Or, rather, "Your brother [with whom Emilio and his family share a house] has ordered you not to enter this house. And, look. If you're so happy drinking with your buddies, why don't you just go die there? But you can't come here to the house anymore. You're too screwed up, you're someone who doesn't care about himself at all. You're a negative person, negative because you've left us with nothing to eat, negative because you ignore your obligations. You don't know whether you have two kids or none at all. All that matters to you is your alcoholism. So why don't you just go out there and die?"

At that point, Emilio left his neighborhood for another part of the city where he worked selling chickens and where he'd get drunk three or four times a day.

Against the wishes of the rest of Emilio's family, his sister-in-law pleaded with her son—Emilio's nephew—to bring Emilio home. Explains Emilio,

My nephew took pity on me, but this was because of my sister-in-law, who told him, "Know what? Go look for your uncle. How can we let

your uncle just go and die out there, without us caring?" . . . And so
when I saw my nephew I was in front of a *pulquería,* where they sell
pulques. . . . sad, I guess and, well, wasting time there. By then I was
really dirty, I mean in every aspect of my life. I had no direction, no
faith. I guess I must have lost all hope. And the truth is, I believe that
[was] what I really wanted . . . if that were my fate, that God take me
away from the suffering. I wanted to die, but it didn't happen. And so
I was sitting in front of the *pulquería* and I saw my nephew coming.
And when he arrived, he was carrying a book bag, because he was in
middle school. And so he sees me and says, "Uncle!" And so I look
at him. And since he always liked me and I have always cared for him,
[there was] the love between uncle and nephew. "Uncle, what are you
doing sitting here? Let's go home." "No, why should I go home if I've
been kicked out? They say I don't belong at home anymore." And the
nephew says, "I don't care. Let's just go home."

Emilio agreed to accompany his nephew on the condition that the
nephew buy him a bottle of tequila. The nephew bought him a bottle
and took him to some public baths to get clean. "At that moment I was
very dirty," says Emilio, "my whole body was dirty. I was drunk, well,
in all aspects of my life I was bad off."

Emilio's nephew prepared him a *cuba libre* to drink while he was
showering—"because a drunk like I was, if he didn't drink a *cuba* of alcohol, well, the water could hurt him." Emilio explains that the alcohol
helps the alcoholic resist the bad effects of cold and hot water. Without
alcohol, he says, the effects of the shower might have been fatal.[1]

Back at the house, they gave Emilio one more drink. But that was to
be his last. "That day was going to be my day. It was going to be my last
day of drinking alcohol, and that's how it was." The family tried to persuade Emilio to visit the doctor again, but he refused. Explains Emilio,

I'm describing the path I took when my alcoholism was at its most intense. I had already hit bottom. And that bottom was when I was begging so I could drink and I didn't care about my two kids anymore, I
didn't care about my wife. I no longer gave them money for food. I
devoted myself so completely to alcoholism that I was laying on the
sidewalks. I had a lice-ridden jacket, my hair stood up on end, and
my face was grimy. I mean, I was a zero, I wasn't worth anything anymore. . . . What I'm trying to tell you is, that was when I had hit bottom. And today I'm in A.A. That's called a ticket that you pay. What

is the ticket I needed to get into A.A.? Well, all the suffering that my alcoholism caused me. That's my ticket to A.A.

Because Emilio refused to go to the doctor's office, the family convinced the doctor to make a home visit. There, at Emilio's house, he administered an I.V. again. At the end of treatment, the doctor said, "Tonight we're going somewhere. . . . I'll come by to get you and we'll go to a place where you stop drinking."

Although each man's story is a variant of the same miserable circumstances they all found themselves in before entering Alcoholics Anonymous, Emilio's story is unique in that he actually uses the classic A.A. term "hitting bottom." Hitting bottom is not a moment that can be determined through the uniform application of specific criteria. Rather, it refers to a moment in time that can be determined only in retrospect, during the recovery process. To interpret your past in terms of "hitting bottom" is to have assimilated A.A. ideology and understood one's own life history in terms endorsed and promoted by A.A.

To hit bottom is reach a point where one recognizes one's limitations and powerlessness. Presumably, many alcoholics—those who die on the street or who somehow muddle through life at half speed—never reach bottom. Reaching bottom in this sense is a blessing, because it impels the alcoholic to seek help. It is the moment that immediately precedes receptivity to the A.A. program. In this sense, to hit bottom is to allow oneself to place one's fate in another's hands. It is a quasi-religious experience, if we accept Edward Sapir's definition of religion. According to Sapir (1949:347), religion is "the haunting realization of ultimate powerlessness in an inscrutable world, and the unquestioning and thoroughly irrational conviction of the possibility of gaining mystical security by somehow identifying oneself with what can never be known." It is precisely this sense of powerlessness, what O'Reilly (1997:23) calls "the unmediated recognition of limits," that results from having hit bottom.

Predictably, conversion stories among the men of Moral Support almost always include a rescue team. A close relative, friend, or former drinking buddy intervenes to save the alcoholic when he is most desperate, hence, at the point of greatest receptivity. When the doctor administered Emilio's I.V. for the second time and announced that he was going to take Emilio to a place where he would stop drinking, Emilio thought to himself, "Where is he going to take me? Where will it be? . . .

Well, maybe they'll give me tea with alcohol so I'll get better." Emilio continues,

> At that moment I did want to drink in order to feel, well, a bit of a tranquilizer in my body. . . . Since he cared enough to take me [to A.A.], you know, I thank him. I am grateful today that I, well, that I am Emilio, right? Because I have been born again in an Alcoholics Anonymous group. So he took me there and I got a big applause. It's a really big group . . . and, well, the truth is that I was welcomed. They applauded me. That meeting was dedicated to me that night. But I was so out of it, me with my need to drink alcohol, sitting there on a chair in the group. They had welcomed me and *compañeros* spoke who wanted to transmit to me something of the suffering they too had lived through. I just filed away all their stories at the time. . . . What I thought was that they were going to give me tea with alcohol and imagine my surprise when they didn't give me alcohol. What they provided was tea, tea, tea.

Emilio, who had been rejected by his family, to the point of being expelled from home, felt fully accepted by this A.A. group. He imagined that the doctor was going to provide him a substance to get well, specifically tea mixed with wine. What he received instead was a substance —tea—together with a supportive welcome from a group of men who gave him the sense that he was important.

Initially, however, Emilio remained skeptical:

> And there I was with that need to get up and run out of there because the truth is I was in no shape to listen to what they were telling me: that they had quit drinking. I didn't say it to their faces, but inside me I said, "No way, man. These dudes are crazy." Or, if they were drunks, they didn't seem all that much better to me now. Or more likely they had never even been drunks. "They're probably trying to brainwash me." That's what I thought. And that night they did wash out my brain, but it was like they were cleaning it out to get rid of that . . . ummm, alcoholic insomnia. So, . . . in a group of Alcoholics Anonymous, when a new person comes in for the first time, it's a brainwash. But it's a positive brainwash, not a negative one.

On that occasion, Emilio was able to identify with the men in the group. Of the six speakers, he says, there were two who especially touched him. "Yes, well, they were just like me," he says. The ability to empathize and perceive parallels between his own experiences and those of other men was probably the single most critical factor in motivating Emilio to retain membership in the group. From that day, he has never had a sip of alcohol.

Renaldo's first experience with A.A. was precipitated by an accident. His wife caught him stealing from his daughter's ceramic piggy bank. She hit him. He tried to get the money out of the piggy bank, but the object broke and shattered in various directions. Renaldo is unsure whether it was a shard or his wife's nails that caused him to be wounded. Whatever the cause, he received a bad gash on his head and was losing blood fast.

His wife brought him to the hospital. There he met the same physician who had introduced Emilio to A.A.

> When the doctor saw me, he asked if I wanted to stop drinking. I told him that, yes, I couldn't stand it anymore. I felt like I was dying. By then I really felt like I was dying. . . . He said, "Well then, if you want, we'll go right now. I know where you'll get better." And I said to him, no, I feel very bad. I bled so much. I told him I'd better wait a bit until I get better. They gave me an I.V. and medicine. And so three days later the doctor picked me up and took me away. That was when I went [to A.A.] for the first time. . . . The doctor who took me . . . was my *padrino,* because he was the one who brought me there. And that's where the suffering ended, because I didn't want to have anything more to do with alcohol. In the first meeting, I didn't understand anything. . . . I understood nothing about what they said there. The only thing I understood is when they said I should sit in front. And, oh, that this meeting was dedicated to me and that the applause they gave was also for me. And I turned around and looked everywhere and I said, well, "Who would they be applauding?" And it was for me, and that was when I felt good. I felt good, I felt important. From that moment on, I felt important.

Renaldo's experience echoes that of Emilio. He was rescued from alcoholism by a doctor, who brought him to an A.A. group for recovery. What awaited him, an A.A. meeting, came as a complete surprise. Renaldo was initially confused by the proceedings. And yet the men at the meeting elevated him to a position of worthiness. The meeting was dedicated to him. He was applauded. For the first time in years he felt like a significant human being. That day began Renaldo's long-lived sobriety; as of his story's telling, he had lasted seventeen years without a drink.

In the case of other men, it was a friend who brought them to A.A. David was led to Alcoholics Anonymous by Pedro, who thus became his *padrino*. David, like the other men, initially found meetings to be confusing. "When I got to A.A.," he says, "it seemed really difficult. I was a person with a complete mental block, a person totally unaware of what was going on. The first time I went, I struggled hard to be able to find anything useful in A.A. I struggled plenty."

Despite his confusion, this occasion was for David just the first of many A.A. meetings:

> I thought that they were going to give me a shot of alcohol, you know, that they were going to tell me that this is how you'll go about stopping to drink until you quit definitively. But no. It was completely opposite. I didn't understand anything, I didn't get a thing because I was blocked, because of my alcoholism: mentally blocked, physically destroyed, morally undone, economically—don't even talk about it! . . . But something there enlightened me. So that is where I began to believe. Someone lit up my mind so that I could capture something of what my *compañeros* were telling me. . . . And that someone, well, He's an Almighty Being. For me, He's a God, a God in whom I now believe.

Eduardo, too, was unaware of where he was going when his *padrino*, David, brought him to his first A.A. meeting:

> The first time I got to A.A., it was the 7th of July in 1985. Yeah, well, I'd been drinking for a month and a half straight. . . . David, who is my *padrino* now, I ran into him on the corner where the little market is. And I said, "Hey, *padrino*." No, because he was still not my *padrino*. He is my *paisano* [literally, "countryman," i.e., from the same state]. And he's my friend. And now my *padrino*. I say to him, "Cure me, OK?" I say, "It's that I don't have any money and I feel like shit from a hangover." And he said no, he didn't have any [drink] and he invited me to a *pachanga*, a fiesta. But the party was at the group! But what I thought was a *pachanga*, . . . where there's beer, there's liquor, there's food, there's everything—where there's dancing, you know. And I said, no, well I'm not going to hold myself back from the dance. I'm going with him to the *pachanga*. And I drank a couple of rum and cokes and a couple of beers and thought that'll make me better and then I'll stop. But imagine my surprise! When I got there, it was an A.A. group! It was the group where I fought for [*milité*] a new path. . . . And so I go right in, and I'm all filthy, with my hair stand-

ing up and unshaven and I was fallen, you know, physically and mentally. I mean you can't even imagine. Then I realized it was an A.A. group. And they supported me that day. In the afternoon, after the meeting, they bought me serum, they bought me some pills . . . And I was able to get better that day. Well, I slept more or less until the next day and on the third day I started working, unloading things.

Eduardo's story is a variant of the others. He was brought unawares to a strange locale—an A.A. meeting. Like his *compañeros*, he was lured there by a nurturing caretaker, who later became his sponsor. He felt support and encouragement from the men of the group. He felt so good, in fact, that he was able to begin productive work again several days after the meeting. The sense of acceptance that these desperate alcoholics feel upon being received at their first meeting is among their most unforgettable memories. They perceive this experience as critical in starting them on the path toward sobriety.

Once a man has determined that Alcoholics Anonymous has the potential to enhance his well-being, it is his duty to himself and his family to maintain regular attendance at meetings. The men of Moral Support believe that meetings, and most specifically the combination of talking about and listening to one another's problems, is the therapeutic basis of sobriety. They explicitly refer to the meetings as "therapy." David, with a penchant for malapropisms, calls A.A. a kind of *"terapia intergrupal,"* or inter-group therapy, by which he means group therapy. "For example," he says,

> if you were an active alcoholic and I were a Double A [member], already participating [*militando*] in an A.A. group, I could help you. . . . A.A. works through inter-group therapy, through discussions; that is what I wanted to say a while ago when I started to tell you how I came to A.A. To me it seemed impossible. I said, fine, . . . how is it possible that just through discussions, coming and sitting down and listening to some idiot, I am going to stop drinking? . . . In my own personal case, it helped me to start trying, to start understanding that alcohol is really destructive and it wasn't worth it to go on living.

Eduardo echoes this sentiment: "A.A. never ends. I will attend for the rest of my life. I won't miss my meetings. See? This is my medicine to remain sober."

But, according to the men, the medicine must be strong in order to work properly. That is, there exists a shared belief that recovery requires suffering. Meetings which produce a merely pleasant experience are automatically dismissed as ineffectual. The group must demonstrate a certain degree of internal conflict for Alcoholics Anonymous to work properly.

For this reason, the men take pride in their persistent anxiety about delivering personal stories. Amado states that "although we always announce that 'Alcoholics Anonymous is a group of men and women,' fortunately there are no women; only *huevudos*," that is, big-balled men. Big balls, in this context, are a sign of courage. Manliness consists of a seemingly paradoxical combination of qualities: on the one hand, the recognition of fear; on the other, sufficient courage to confront and overcome that fear (see Chapter Five). It would be counterproductive, say the men of Moral Support, for any *compañero* to deny the dread he feels when rising to the *tribuna* to speak. To the contrary, an *historial* delivered without any anxiety is likely to be less than therapeutic, either for the individual or for the listeners.

And yet, one should not become so fearful and timid as to resist rising to the challenge. Amado believes that this quality, the courage to confess one's most intimate thoughts in public, is exclusive to men and that this explains why there are more men than women in A.A. Public confession—the therapeutic basis of Alcoholics Anonymous—should never be treated casually. It is a quasi-sacred act that demands utmost respect on the part of speaker and listener if it is to perform its proper restorative function. When the men say that *historiales* are "*motivados*" (literally, "motivated"), they mean that there was an atmosphere of utmost engagement in the room; the speakers confronted serious problems in a direct, detailed, and courageous fashion.

Eduardo loses patience when his *compañeros* waste time on trivia. He complains about one of the men, whom he accuses of rising to the *tribuna* simply to talk about meaningless everyday events. Says Eduardo, that man will say something like,

> "Ay, well I'm very happy right now because I ran into so-and-so who I had not seen for a long time." Excuse me, *compañero* Stanley, but what the hell do I care about his running into so-and-so? When I get up to the *tribuna*, it's to talk about how things are going for me, how I was before and how I am now. It does nothing for me, for example, to hear "I ran into so-and-so!" If that person's a *compañero* of mine,

of course [I'll say] "Hello, *compa,* good morning. Let's go get a soda or something." But that's not going to fill me with satisfaction! Of course, I feel happy because I met up with him and we said hello; but I'm not going to talk about it on the *tribuna.* . . . Just because he sees him, because he went to visit him, that's not therapy.

In other words, recovery does not depend merely on overcoming the fear of public speaking. To be therapeutic, the *historial* must reveal feelings and experiences that are difficult to confront. The ideal story is sometimes heart-wrenching, requires soul-searching, and is likely to inspire reflection. Emilio states that at first he spent months without ever delivering an *historial:* "I was so afraid of the *tribuna,*" he says. "It felt like something got stuck in my throat."

David has the same recollection: "To stand behind a *tribuna* is important," he says. In the beginning, "It's not easy. You begin to sweat. Your hands sweat, your feet sweat, everything sweats. . . . Afterwards, the very group helps you to remember your whole past because it's the past that I have to expound upon, talk about." David sums up a belief that prevails generally among the men of Moral Support:

You have to share your past, right? In A.A. we say, don't talk about others. Talk about your own story, talk about your own life. It's not valid to speak about second or third parties. It's always better to speak about oneself. But this carries with it something really important: talking about yourself is like curing yourself. Yeah, it's like feeling good, like cleaning yourself out from the inside, freeing yourself from problems. To say, for example, well, when I was drunk I was an irresponsible person. I beat my wife. I didn't respect my neighbors, I did, well, a ton of things. I missed work because of my alcoholism. [Such talk] alleviates. It alleviates because it's like you're expelling it. But when you don't, you retain all those things that affect you internally and you'll always be in bad shape. And if you share what your story is, . . . this will help you to get better.

This theory, which most of the men articulate in one form or another, presents a model in which bad thoughts and experiences must be aired publicly in order for recovery to be achieved. Only by openly expressing what is negative within you can you hope to stay sober. "That is the secret of A.A.," says David; "You could say that is the key."

Apart from significant content, the quality that the men most insist upon in an *historial* is sincerity. The speaker should demonstrate complete openness and honesty. Though difficult to achieve, this is the only therapeutically effective course of action, say the men. Honesty is hard to detect. The men appreciate detailed *historiales,* new in content, based on everyday experiences, but replete with wider implications and messages of general significance.

One measure of sincerity is crying. Very occasionally, a *compañero* departs from the formulaic repetition of a well-known story and surprises the group by speaking in concrete terms of a traumatic event, past or present. The narration is especially effective if accompanied by tears. Typically, sobbing occurs after a death in the family, with the *compañero* lamenting the torment he caused that person before discovering A.A. It is highly unusual for a Mexican man to cry in front of other men. This display of personal weakness—so uncharacteristic of *macho* behavior in the outside world—represents bravery and sincerity in the context of the group. Simply to be able to cry while on the podium raises the status of the speaker within the group.

On the other hand, it is best not to be too histrionic in the delivery of *historiales.* The capacity to present sincere, meaningful public confessions ideally develops over time. It is a by-product of experience on the podium and the emergence of deep trust in one's *compañeros.* Theatrical displays, however entertaining, arouse suspicion, especially if they emerge too early or frequently during the recovery process. A young man named Marcos started to attend Moral Support meetings and immediately showed himself to be a brilliant orator. Within weeks he disappeared. I expressed surprise that Marcos, just like that, had suddenly stopped attending meetings. He delivered electrifying *historiales.* True, acknowledged the men, he is a great orator, but too showy for his own good. It is better to start out slowly, tentatively, they claim, and slowly escalate to a grander speaking style. Marcos's spectacular public performance revealed his fundamental insincerity. He should have entered into the group using a more moderate speaking style, instead of trying to impress his *compañeros.* In Marcos's case, grand oratory did not demonstrate honesty and courage, but rather their opposites.

The men believe that those who are dishonest or hide from the truth are likely to relapse. "It happens in our group," states David. "You more or less know that in our group there are *compañeros* who don't talk about their story. And they're in bad shape. Why? Because they're dishonest. Because . . . in life you have to be honest, . . . to say, 'I am this kind of person, I behave like this, I'm like this at my workplace, I'm like this at home,' or 'at home I don't do that anymore.'"

The worst kind of dishonesty, according to the men of Moral Support, is to divulge the *historiales* of one's *compañeros*. In Moral Support, where intimate social ties spill over the boundaries between the group and the outside world, anonymity is difficult if not impossible to attain. However elusive, it remains a cherished goal. Eduardo is proud of his ability to speak openly in meetings of how his brother-in-law, Donaldo, mistreated members of their common household. (See Chapter Six.) Following one such personal story, Eduardo confessed to me, "And really, well, I feel calm now, contented with all my *compañeros*, since I have taken care of my resentments." It was more important to Eduardo to expel the anger from inside than to keep peace with his brother-in-law.

Donaldo retreated from confrontation by ceasing to attend meetings. In response, Eduardo had only this to say: "If my brother-in-law [Donaldo] wants to go drink, it's his own problem. He's already been in the group for twelve years. But those twelve years haven't meant shit, because, first of all, he's never been sincere with his *historial*. He's not sincere with himself, for going around divulging things, telling the *historiales* that he's heard from other *compañeros*. He goes and tells them somewhere else. I know that he's always been like that because my sister told me so. He'd go and tell her that Fulanito has another woman, that Sunito has another woman. All that has been screwing him up."

Normally, the men are tolerant of one another's *historiales*. Bland, abstract stories are far from ideal, but they at least serve the purpose of furthering individual sobriety through attendance at meetings. Detailed testimonies, such as Eduardo's, which enable members openly to express their resentments and anger, are certainly sincere. To that extent they conform to the highest group standards. But they serve more than a therapeutic function for the speaker. They allow him to advance his goals in a personal dispute by appealing to moral authority.

In delivering their personal stories, *compañeros* must strike a balance between honesty and controversy. The men believe that "*controversias*" are occasionally necessary and even beneficial to the group. They jolt members into perceiving things from a new perspective and prompt the men to examine themselves deeply and thoughtfully. But when controversies persistently invade the meeting room they are poisonous. They bring personal relationships to the breaking point and thereby threaten the existence of the group.

Whenever personal rivalries are brought into the meeting, the therapeutic value of the A.A. program is placed at risk. It then becomes everyone's duty to assert what is right. Neither the Twelve Steps nor the Twelve Traditions mentions how one resolves controversies that emerge among group members. Those who deliver *historiales* that aim to resolve such controversies point to the posters on the wall behind the lectern as they state that "even the literature" tells us that "*controversias*" must be avoided at all cost. For the men of Moral Support, the "*literatura*," as the Twelve Steps and Twelve Traditions are colloquially called, plays an intentionally small role. They perceive therapeutic value, rather, in the honest discussion of day-by-day problems; they distinguish themselves from other groups in part by this feature of their "*autonomía*." And yet, when it serves the interests of the group, the literature will be invoked as an appeal to high moral authority. Accurate rendering of the literature in such cases seems to be less important to the men than the ultimate outcome of their efforts: group survival as a route to individual sobriety.

8. SOBRIETY AND SURVIVAL

As early as 1977, Mary Taylor (1977:178) observed that "Self-help groups are proliferating in American society." If that statement could be made a generation ago, it is even more apt at the turn of the twenty-first century. A number of these groups, such as those devoted to smoking, overeating, gambling, and child abuse, are twelve-step programs explicitly modeled on Alcoholics Anonymous. Support groups organized around the concerns of political and ethnic minorities, as well as those based on sexual orientation, also rely on techniques and therapeutic insights developed by A.A. "What all these groups have in common," states Taylor (ibid.), "is the drawing together of fellow sufferers of some personal or social affliction to share their distress over their common problem, and to share their efforts at coping with the problem." Self-help groups are in essence voluntary associations of lay people and represent "the democratization and demystification of professional skills" (ibid.). The experts are the sufferers themselves rather than an elite group of highly trained experts with titled specialties. The self-help group of whatever variety is, of course, designed to solve or at least ameliorate problems rather than to create them. However, the group itself, under certain conditions, can produce enough anxiety among members that survival of the unit as a whole is placed at risk.

This circumstance came to my attention about a year after completing long-term fieldwork. In July 1997, while no longer residing in Mexico City, I visited Moral Support to greet my *compañeros* and note any changes that might have occurred within the group. The locale and decor of the meeting room were unchanged. Six men were present, all but one of them familiar to me. I had not announced my arrival in advance. By the time I entered the room, the session was already in progress. Gerardo was coordinating and, in a departure from usual practice, interrupted the flow of the session as he rose from his chair to give me a warm embrace. David did the same and, with a wide smile on his face, uttered softly, "*Compañero Stanley, llega usted como los propios ánge-les*"—"*Compañero* Stanley, you arrive like the very angels." Though the men and I knew one another well, they never ceased addressing me by the formal *usted*, rather than the familiar pronoun *tú*. Emilio once explained why: "*Usted no es clase baja*"—"You're not lower class," he said, with the implication that the other men all fall into that category and therefore can treat one another as equals. Despite the inevitable social distance created by use of the formal pronoun, these men had become my friends. Their warm welcome was a measure of the affection that had developed between us. A cultural chasm had been bridged. The moment I entered the meeting room, I felt entirely comfortable and at home.

But there was something wrong. Emilio never missed meetings, but he was absent on this occasion. So were some of the other Moral Support diehards like Eduardo, Pedro, and Donaldo. I was concerned about the well-being of these men. Other than that, the meeting proceeded as normal, with *historiales* focused mostly on familiar themes: family, gender, work, past drinking careers. Gerardo, in preliminary remarks to the group, spoke of the miserable physical state of the alcoholic and reminded everyone of Renaldo's decrepit condition when he first arrived at A.A. Ernesto, the oldest, least energetic member of the group, formally opened the meeting with an *historial* delivered in a monotonous, barely audible tone of voice. Nestor followed. Although Renaldo was absent, Nestor devoted his *historial* to seconding Gerardo's recollection of how terrible Renaldo looked upon entering the group. When Renaldo showed up at the meeting, he had long, unruly hair filled with lice, stated Nestor. That evening, there was extensive talk of disheveled hair and lice. David recalled that when he first got to A.A. his own hair was so beyond improvement that the *compañeros* took him aside one day and completely shaved his head.

José, the newcomer, rose to the podium. He proved to be a great orator. ("José came here to wake me up!" stated David in an *historial* delivered later that evening.) José had recently arrived at Moral Support after attending several other groups. He was unhappy with these groups, he said, because the *compañeros* refused to carry out their responsibilities; no one would take on the *servicio de café* or the *servicio de ceniza* —that is, serving the coffee and emptying the ashtrays. Someone would pose the question, "Who wants ashtray service?" and everyone would turn their eyes downward so as not to be noticed. José asked rhetorically, "What is this place, anyway? A *pulquería*?" The men listened attentively to José and laughed loudly at his mention of *pulquería,* the kind of drinking establishment that most of them had frequented as active alcoholics. The Moral Support meeting room was, as usual, a model of neatness and cleanliness. And, because of the prohibition on smoking, there were no ashes to be dumped. In Moral Support, the emphasis on cleanliness, both of the person and of the immediate surroundings, was always close to the surface.

José was unhappy in other groups, he said. It was more than just the *compañeros'* unwillingness to perform service. He complained about the centrality in their meetings of *"la literatura."* "What good is it to speak of the Third Step or Third Tradition?" he asked, rhetorically. "No good at all," was the implied answer. Sometimes he would get so discouraged, he continued, that he would be tempted to start drinking again. But then he remembered what his periods of active alcoholism were like. He could hold neither liquor nor bowels and would explode spontaneously, drenching himself in urine and shit. To underscore the sacrifice that each of the men in the room had made by giving up alcohol, José ended his *historial* with a vivid description of his persistent cravings for a drink. *"Sabrosísimo,"* he said, *"con su limoncito y su salecita"*—"Delicious. With its bit of lemon and salt." You could almost hear collective salivation in the meeting room.

Meeting coordinators develop a personal style. Gerardo followed each *historial* with his own gloss on what the previous speaker had just said. Pointing to the Twelve Traditions and Twelve Steps listed on posters at the front of the room, he stated that "The literature *is* important. It is there for us to study." His idea is that the *historial* ideally should provide a commentary on the steps as they pertain to our individual lives. As a group leader, Gerardo never felt compelled to agree with any given speaker. He was frank in his opinions, independent in his judgments, and respected for these qualities. *"Literatura"* and personal hygiene were the two prominent themes of the meeting that evening. Although cleanliness was a favorite topic for *historiales,* the value of the so-called literature—that is, of the Twelve Steps and Twelve Traditions—normally was not raised for discussion. This departure from usual thematic content, together with the absence of several valued and faithful *compañeros,* made the meeting vaguely unfamiliar to me. I soon learned that there was good reason why.

A small group of men had splintered away from Moral Support and founded their own A.A. meeting, which they called New Hope. The split occurred just a month prior to my return to Mexico City, making it impossible for me to document events as they unfolded. It seems that a number of the men insisted on daily meetings. Amado, who had recently returned to Mexico City after more than six months in his native state of Tabasco, was one of these men. Donaldo was another. Amado and Donaldo had both spoken often in their *historiales* of the need for more frequent meetings. And yet, unlike Gerardo and several other *compañeros,* they never visited groups other than Moral Support to fulfill this need. Ramiro, an intermittent but highly outspoken affiliate of Moral Support, had supported the move for daily meetings and appears to have been the main instigator of the split.

I was told that initially the three dissidents—Amado, Donaldo, and Ramiro—received permission from their *compañeros* to use the Moral Support meeting room on the evenings when it was not occupied by the full group, that is, on Sunday, Monday, Wednesday, and Friday. These men started collecting their own monetary contributions and keeping a separate attendance list and log. "That's improper," commented David bluntly as he told me his version of the story. Only a week after the new arrangement began, Gerardo and Ramiro confronted one another aggressively, practically coming to blows. Ramiro defended the separatist arrangement, Gerardo opposed it.

The three dissidents reacted by founding their own group. They were soon joined by Eduardo, plus several recovering alcoholics who had not belonged to Moral Support. The new group began meeting in a room very similar to Moral Support's, located only two blocks away. As with Moral Support, there was an A.A. logo above the door, showing the group name and meeting hours. Chairs were lined in rows facing a lectern. And there were posters, pictures, and a clock on the walls. These included listings of the Twelve Steps and Twelve Traditions, plus two portraits each of Bill W. and Dr. Bob. New Hope had glass doors separating the street from the meeting room. Only partially covered by sheets, the doors allowed outsiders to peer into the meeting; in fact, curiosity seekers did glance inside on the several occasions that I attended New Hope meetings. During the course of one meeting, an outsider stared into the room for quite some time until his eyes met Ramiro's. Ramiro left the meeting at that point, presumably to speak to this outsider; he returned about ten minutes later. From saintly icons to semi-private meeting facilities, arranged like a miniature auditorium, New Hope seemed to replicate the physical setting of Moral Support.

What differed radically was the so-called *autonomía,* or therapeutic procedure. Unlike Moral Support, New Hope relied, as its members stated, on *"lectura,"* or reading. The group therefore fell under the rubric of what María Eugenia Módena (personal communication) would call the "traditionalists." Members devoted each night of the week to exploring a predetermined theme or to member participation based on a given format. On Mondays there was exegesis of the Twelve Steps; Tuesdays and Thursdays were turned over to a topic of the coordinator's choosing; Wednesdays to the delivery of *historiales;* Fridays to readings from the Libro Azul, or Blue Book (i.e., the so-called Big Book of Alcoholics Anonymous), Saturdays to discussion of the Twelve Traditions, and Sundays to a conversational question and answer session in which group members sit in a circle and chat, rather than speaking from the lectern. Only Wednesdays, dedicated to *historiales,* conforms to Moral Support procedures.

During one Monday evening meeting, the group discussed the Fifth Step: admitting one's personal defects. Amador, a defector from Moral Support, coordinated the meeting. He began by reading several paragraphs from an A.A. manual discussing the Twelve Steps. He stopped abruptly, in the middle of a sentence, explaining that he would continue to read more on the topic later, if time allowed. There were several 15-minute *historiales,* which did not seem to me to differ from those in Moral Support. These were followed by a 30-minute speech on the Fifth Step, delivered by a visitor from an outside group. The visitor remarked on the small number of attendees at the meeting (there were five at that point, including myself, although this number expanded with the arrival of latecomers) and stated that his group, too, suffers *"altibajos"*—ups and downs. A drunk youth wandered into the meeting and roamed aimlessly around the room until someone gently ushered him to a row of chairs. The drunk sat quietly until the end of the meeting. He seemed to sober up after drinking coffee and eating a few cookies.

I attended four meetings of New Hope, none of which seemed radically different either in tone or content from Moral Support meetings. But the men of New Hope fervently believed that their procedures were superior. Donaldo, now a member of New Hope, delivered an *historial* directed toward explaining to me why New Hope separated from Moral Support. He stated that Moral Support first gave and then withdrew permission for daily meetings to those who wanted it. In the end, members who longed to meet on a daily basis had to found their own group, New Hope. Moral Support can never work, claims Donaldo, because it is not founded on *"principios"*—principles. Without reliance on *"la literatura,"* he says, there can be no expectation of permanent sobriety. One of the members of New Hope, my friend Eduardo, did in fact suffer a serious relapse in the period I had been away. However, he attributed his relapse not to Moral Support procedures, but rather to the fact that he fell in love and stopped going to meetings. As one of the *compañeros* later stated, "*Debajo de la falda de una mujer, hay una copa de vino*"—"Under a woman's skirt there is a glass of liquor," which is a well-known Mexican proverb.

Later, while we were alone, Eduardo complained about the inconsistent attendance and lack of punctuality of his *compañeros* in New Hope. Eduardo himself gets criticized for not paying sufficient attention to speakers. He is often engrossed in reading the Big Book as others deliver *historiales*. After observing New Hope for only a few weeks, it seemed that this group was a replica of Moral Support. Formed by *compañeros* from Moral Support, the criticisms they leveled at one another were identical to those that surfaced with regularity in Moral Support. Six months later, New Hope collapsed and its members were reincorporated into Moral Support. The Moral Support meeting schedule and procedures remained unaltered.

This experience casts doubts on the conclusions of Tonigan, Ashcroft, and Miller (1995), who carried out a comparative study to discover the determinants of A.A. group cohesiveness. They found that groups basing their meetings on the Twelve Steps—that is, on what the men of Moral Support would call "the literature"—were more cohesive than those that did not. Since group cohesiveness has been identified as essential for therapeutic efficacy in A.A. (Emrick et al. 1978; Kassel and Wagner 1993), their finding has implications for individual recovery. For this reason, it is noteworthy that Moral Support, which largely ignores the Twelve Steps in the development of meetings, has proven more cohesive than New Hope. Fraught as it is with conflict and tension, Moral Support nonetheless has outlasted a rival group, New Hope, which was based at least in part on Twelve Step commentaries.

The rapid proliferation of A.A. groups in Mexico City and other parts of the country derives largely from the compatibility of the organization with Mexican popular religion (see Chapter Two). The experience of Moral Support demonstrates that there exist a wide range of symbolically charged behavioral patterns, linguistic forms, and visual representations in A.A. which replicate popular Catholicism. Anniversary fiestas function jointly with the sponsorship system, Catholic imagery in speech and text, and the spatial arrangement of the meeting room, to produce a familiar cultural milieu. Mary Foster (1985) would characterize the relationship between A.A. and popular Catholicism in Mexico City as one of concordant structure. In her words (ibid.:618), concordant structure refers to "mutually sustaining threads of symbolism that run through any given culture. Such threads tend to be unconscious to users." M. Foster continues (ibid.), "Concordant structure is fundamentally hierarchical because its strands are successively elaborated metaphors drawn from underlying physical reality, with the metaphor of one ritual elaborated from the metaphor of another."

We might posit, in fact, that both in Moral Support and in Mexican popular Catholicism, symbolic representations of birth and rebirth provide an all-encompassing template, the overarching structure from which ritual representations are derived. Membership in A.A. is a kind of rebaptism for the men of Moral Support. Their experience in A.A. replicates church affiliation at the same time as it represents a means to personal salvation. To join Alcoholics Anonymous in Mexico City does not mean abandoning one's religious tradition. It means adapting it to the circumstances at hand. This is one central reason why we should not be surprised that, despite thoroughly middle class, Protestant origins, Alcoholics Anonymous has been highly successful not only in Mexico but also throughout much of Latin America.

It is tempting to speculate that Alcoholics Anonymous has become the functional equivalent of Protestantism in Latin America. After all, there is now a considerable body of literature to suggest that men convert from Catholicism to Protestantism partly to gain control over drinking problems. The literature also proposes a causal relationship between economic advancement and Protestant conversion. To become Protestant allows a man to extricate himself from the costly obligations to Church and community, hence to act in the marketplace as an independent entrepreneur. Protestant conversion, too, encourages the sobriety that is requisite to becoming a rational economic actor.

As early as the 1930s in Mexico, scholars advocated sobriety as the only route to the nation's progress. Consider Luis Franco's words (1931:9), published by the federal government in 1931:

Can you tell me that an alcoholic worker can be prepared to join the current state of advancement, science and progress? Surely not! Neither physically, nor morally, nor materially can an alcoholic worker be prepared for the competition that signifies advancement, given all its modern inventions, which eliminate, day by day, manual labor in favor of mechanical work which requires brains. The worker who does not study, who does not become educated, who does not arm himself with all the advances that science goes on producing, will have to pass through an intense crisis. (my translation)

Citing statistics, Franco further laments that "the consumption of *pulque* is higher than that of milk among the working classes" (ibid.:15). Although this author does not link Protestantism to sobriety, his treatise clearly exemplifies a strain of thought within Mexico that perceives abstinence from alcohol as requisite to economic advancement.

To add to this equation, there is an unmistakable correlation between the introduction of liberal economic reforms throughout Latin America, on the one hand, and the rapid increase in both Alcoholics Anonymous and Protestantism, on the other. Bernice Martin (1995:105) sees a close connection between the rise of Protestantism throughout Latin America and the region's incorporation into global capitalism. She traces the rapid introduction of neo-liberal economic reforms from the 1960s to the present, the period that exactly coincides with the success of Protestant missionary activity.

Martin continues:

The consequence of all this has been to shape contemporary Latin American capitalism in the likeness of North American individualistic venture capitalism. The Latin American economy looks increasingly similar to the technologically advanced post-industrial economies of North America and Europe. Within no more than two or three generations a social and economic system structured around clientalism and hierarchy has been transformed into a (post) modern, individualistic, competitive economy on North American lines (ibid.).

This transformation, Martin correctly observes, requires a different kind of workforce from that which prevailed in an earlier economic era. With regard to the introduction of Protestant norms, she says (ibid.:109), "many of the renunciations, especially those concerning alcohol and tobacco, dancing, and, above all, football, are recognized as self-discipline and acceptable because they deliver an improvement in overall well-being." These behavioral constraints at the same time produce bodily controls consonant, as Foucault says, with the efficient economy. They "establish rhythms, impose particular occupations, regulate the cycles of repetition," and the like (Foucault 1977:149).

The concomitant involvement of Mexico in the global economy and rise of both Protestantism and A.A. within that country seem to support the view that A.A. and Protestant Christianity are ideological equivalents. Although they are in some sense ideologically similar, A.A. membership in Mexico is drawn predominantly, not from Protestant converts, but rather from the ranks of traditional Roman Catholics. In *Moral Support*, for example, there is only one Protestant—David—and he was born and raised as such, rather than converting. It appears that conversion to Protestantism itself provides sufficient motivation for abstinence. Pedro Martínez, Oscar Lewis's famous autobiographical subject from the central Mexican village of Tepoztlán, states that, as soon as he converted to Protestantism, "My religion pulled me out of the swamp of sin. I did not go out at night any more with my friends. No, no more. They didn't even want me now. For twelve years I didn't touch alcohol. The thing is, a person doesn't change his way of living unless it is through religion. Then fear enters, and it makes you want to change in every way toward your family as well as toward your neighbors" (Lewis 1964b:207). Converts like Pedro Martínez apparently yearn for personal transformation and thereby conform willingly to the precepts of their new religion. In the case of Mexican Protestantism, abstinence is among the most salient of these precepts.

However, we must be wary of creating rigid dichotomies. Peter Cahn (2001) has found that Protestant converts in the region around Lake Pátzcuaro, Michoacán, do not abandon Catholicism altogether. Protestantism seems to be an addition to their religious repertoire, rather than a substitution. Likewise, the traditional Catholic men of *Moral Support* continue to participate in the ritual life of the Church, while adhering to selected aspects of evangelical Protestantism, like total abstention from alcohol. As we have seen in earlier chapters, they testify that when they first joined A.A., their drinking buddies would try to lure them back into the cantina through ridicule, calling them "*hermano*" (literally, "brother"), or religious fanatic, and suggesting that they had become Protestant.

Although it is clear that Protestantism and Alcoholics Anonymous are alternative routes to sobriety, there is little evidence that A.A. transforms its members into efficient actors in the global economy. The men of *Moral Support*, like most A.A. members in Mexico City, are, in Larissa Lomnitz's terms, marginal. Lomnitz states (1977:12), "The marginals are largely occupied in unaffiliated manual labor, unpaid family labor, and small-scale family enterprise. A typical cross-section of marginality would comprise trades and occupations such as these: construction workers, housemaids, house repairmen, waiters, barbers, gardeners, janitors, street vendors, and practitioners of traditional trades and crafts that have been devalued by industrialization." Moreover, according to Lomnitz (ibid.:13), marginal workers suffer "chronic insecurity of employment."

Most men in Moral Support are unemployed or seriously underemployed. With the exception of two small-scale businessmen, the men all fall squarely into the occupational groups in Lomnitz's list. Neither neoliberalism nor sobriety has allowed these men to advance professionally or become integrated within the global economy. Their economic marginality, however, does not necessarily make them immune to hegemonic messages issued by power holders within their society. They very much believe in and advocate bodily discipline, as a route both to sobriety and professional advancement.

To explain the growth of A.A. units in Mexico City, we must take into consideration more than accordance with popular Catholicism or economic individualism. Groups proliferate because large units subdivide into smaller ones, which themselves outgrow their ability to satisfy members' needs and consequently split into two or more additional groups. As we have seen, Moral Support was born of a larger group, Promise of Recovery. Gerardo, originally a member of Promise of Recovery, calls that group *"un semillero"*—a seed bed. He compares the group specifically to a patch of tomato seedlings; when ready, they are removed from the soil and transplanted to numerous additional plots.

Gerardo claims that there are at least twenty A.A. groups now in existence that originated in Promise of Recovery. The split that I observed in Moral Support proved temporary. After dividing into two, the group reunited half a year later. But should Moral Support achieve its ideals— which are, of course, the ideals of all A.A. groups—by successfully "carrying the message" and attracting new members, the group might become too large to be therapeutically effective. At that point, members might suffer from an inadequate opportunity to deliver personal stories. Dissatisfied members might split from the parent group to found one or more new groups in the never-ending search for the perfect therapy.

The experience of Moral Support suggests that dissenting members leave mainly as an act of desperation in an attempt to stay sober. They do not found new groups in order to band together with friends and escape from adversaries. Throughout the period I associated closely with Moral Support, Eduardo and his brother-in-law Donaldo maintained a feud that at times poisoned the meeting room atmosphere. It caused Donaldo to miss meetings for a month or more and Eduardo to fantasize about engaging his foe in potentially mortal combat. And yet, when New Hope was founded, these two were among the handful of new members. Far from escaping from one another's company, they thrust themselves together even more closely than before. Likewise, Moral Support's de facto rival leaders, Gerardo and Pedro, remained loyal to their group despite ample opportunity to defect. Amador, who returned to Moral Support after a long absence, was one of three *compañeros* to found New Hope. At the time, he and his family were renting a small room in Renaldo's house, despite Renaldo's loyalty to Moral Support. That these men belonged to competing A.A. groups did not affect their amicable relationship. These cases demonstrate that personal animosities are neither the cause nor the effect of A.A. group fission.

Groups subdivide whenever some men feel that they are at risk and wish to improve their chances of survival. The three men who left Moral Support to join New Hope—Amado, Donaldo, and Eduardo—were all frustrated by what they considered to be inadequate meeting hours. They yearned for daily *juntas,* rather than sessions held three times a week. They furthermore needed the security of belonging to one group rather than attending several different groups, an alternative solution to their problem. Convinced of Moral Support's inadequacy, they turned to a competing therapeutic model: the traditionalist reliance on "literature" rather than the *historial* format. In the end, however, ideological differences proved relatively insignificant in their decisions about which group to join.

After reuniting with Moral Support, the dissidents confessed their dismay at the relatively chaotic conditions under which meetings had been held at New Hope. Mechanisms of social control were evidently weaker in New Hope than in Moral Support. New Hope members were less punctual and felt less compulsion to respect time limits than they did in Moral Support. Reliability and predictability—qualities which these men desperately seek—were notably absent in the dissident group. At the same time, New Hope was so small and each individual member so valuable to the group's survival that the men lived with the fear that they might alienate one another and thereby drive valuable members away. Hence, it was risky for men in the new group to level personal crit-

icisms during meetings. In Moral Support, disagreeable as personal criticisms might have seemed, public scrutiny was what many of the men actually craved. After all, according to their own accounts, their lives and
physical beings were in a state of disarray before joining A.A. An orderly
existence, externally imposed, provided them comfort and hope for
long-term recovery.

Ironically, their lives as active alcoholics were hardly free of social
control. Numerous commentators (e.g., Cavan 1966; Dennis 1979;
Gusfield, Kotarba, and Rasmussen 1996; MacAndrew and Edgerton
1969; Spradley 1970; Spradley and Mann 1975) have analyzed the importance of controlling process in the regulation of drinking and drunkenness. Alcohol consumption in Mexico is guided by a series of tacit and
overt rules. The alcoholic is in fact accustomed to following rules. This
is yet another reason why the imposition of social control during A.A.
meetings can provide a sense of refuge and security. A.A. meetings in
fact become a test of orderliness and competence, as well as proof of the
ability to remain sober.

Adherence to the rules of the meeting for most of the men is symptomatic of a responsible approach to family, work, and other obligations.
Periodic public reminders of the rules are often difficult to endure. And
yet the men consider at least some of the tension generated by these reminders to be necessary, both for group survival and individual sobriety.
When *compañeros* feel rebuffed by those who use *historiales* as a way
of passing judgment, the victims of criticism typically respond in one of
two ways: they retreat by absenting themselves from meetings; or
they fight back using the weapon with which they were wounded, the
historial. Whatever the response, the men generally remain within the
group over the long run. Despite the discouragement and humiliation
caused by public criticism, the imposition of order through informal
mechanisms of social control seems essential to their collective and individual well-being.

All things being equal, however, men in Mexico City will leave one
group to join another, if the new group is closer to where they live.
Sometimes the mere logistics of moving about Mexico City brings about
A.A. group subdivision. If there seem to be enough men who live close
to one another to found a new group, convenience is the deciding factor. Transportation in Mexico City is so enervating and time-consuming
that it is an enormous advantage to belong to a group near one's home.

At the same time, most group members in Mexico City are migrants
from small villages and towns all over central and southern Mexico. The

men of Moral Support, who come from rural settlements in Guerrero, Morelos, San Luis Potosí, Oaxaca, Hidalgo, Veracruz, the State of Mexico, and elsewhere, initially relied on networks of family and friendship as a means to settle and adapt to life in the nation's capital. But most of these men, proletarians who have been roundly unsuccessful in seeking stable employment, and who are alienated from wives, children, and other relatives, have been forced to survive by seeking alternative forms of affiliation. A.A. provides them a satisfying source of support.

A.A. groups proliferate partly because men feel secure within the confines of their own urban village. One way in which recovering alcoholics can recreate a village atmosphere in the metropolis is to concentrate their activities, including A.A. meetings, within the neighborhood. As we have seen (Chapter Six), the identity of the men in Moral Support is anything but anonymous. To the contrary, membership in A.A. is a key way in which these migrants, marginal and unsuccessful in so many fundamental aspects of life, can publicly demonstrate a measure of responsibility and thereby achieve social acceptance. A.A. enables them to seek sobriety while integrating into an urban village, yet another explanation for the success of this organization in Mexico City.

The scientific community disagrees about the therapeutic value of Alcoholics Anonymous. At the same time, the A.A. international fellowship in general, and the men of Moral Support in particular, firmly believe that failure to attend meetings results in relapse. George Vaillant speculates that, "Perhaps AA resembles the pixie dust in J. M. Barrie's Peter Pan that enabled Wendy to fly; for AA to work, one must be a believer" (Vaillant 1995:255). There is no difficulty proving that attendance at A.A. meetings correlates strongly with abstinence. Those who attend meetings, in Mexico City as elsewhere, are those who have stopped drinking. The challenge is to determine whether regular attendance at A.A. meetings is the cause or consequence of abstinence.

This question is difficult to answer in part because of conditions imposed by Alcoholics Anonymous itself. For one thing, the organization maintains no precise membership lists. In fact, the criteria for membership in Alcoholics Anonymous are vague. An individual who attends sporadically might be considered a visitor or a member, depending on self-definition. In addition, follow-up studies, by Alcoholics Anonymous World Services and others, have been too short-range to draw definitive conclusions. Those members who cease to attend meetings often disappear quickly into obscurity. One A.A.–sponsored study (A.A. World

Services 1980) concluded that 50 percent of newcomers drop out of A.A. within the first three months; the study speculates that many of these dropouts were likely to have relapsed. Of the 50 percent remaining in A.A., 41 percent were active in the organization and sober one year later. In another study of alcoholics who were brought to municipal court as offenders, it was found that "AA had the largest dropout rate of any of the treatment groups despite similar social work follow-up" (Brandsma, Maultsby, and Welsh 1980:83). However, the results pertain to a highly select population from which it would be difficult to generalize.

Fingarette (1988:89), echoing the opinion of others, has concluded that "selectivity in the kind of drinkers who enter a treatment regimen biases the outcomes and precludes any generalizations about the regimen's success with heavy drinkers or problem drinkers at large. Drinkers who become active participants in A.A. are those who are willing to affirm their identity as alcoholics under the A.A. definition; drinkers who do not fit or will not acknowledge fitting the pattern drop out." Further, says Fingarette (ibid.), "drinkers remain in A.A. only if they are able to remain reasonably abstinent and accept the A.A. way of life. The vast majority of heavy drinkers never try A.A., and most who do drop out."

Baekeland, Lundwall, and Kissin (1975:281) conclude virtually the same thing. They believe that "As a primary treatment method, compared to alcohol clinic treatment, AA seems to be applicable to a narrow range of patients." In addition, they say, "It seems possible that the population served by AA is quite different from that which goes to hospitals and clinics. . . . " (ibid.:306). Polich, Armor, and Braiker (1980: 126–130), in a large-scale study of alcoholics in treatment centers in the U.S., discovered that nearly three quarters of their subjects attended A.A. at some point in their lives. A year and a half later, only 14 to 18 percent of these subjects were still attending meetings. Another study (Rudy 1986) concluded that slipping from abstinence is a normal and frequent activity among A.A. members.

One problem with evaluating these study outcomes is that most research to date has focused on the success of A.A. under specific conditions, that is, when individuals are instructed or even coerced to attend meetings, as is commonly the outcome in U.S. courts and employee assistance programs. A.A. advocates argue convincingly that when A.A. patients are coerced or even strongly induced to attend meetings, there can be no accurate indication of the efficacy of A.A. meetings, which should be attended voluntarily to be effective (Miller, Andrews, et. al. 1998:213). In fact, coerced involvement is contrary to the precepts of A.A., which advocates noncompulsory participation (Miller and Kurtz 1994).

Statistical figures are unreliable, too, when based on cases in which medical professionals recommend Alcoholics Anonymous as a supplement to clinical treatment. This is routine procedure in both the United States and Mexico. State Orford and Edwards (1977:57), "Directing clinical patients toward Alcoholics Anonymous can enhance the likelihood of AA involvement, but evidence for the contribution of AA as an adjunct to clinical treatment is not easily found . . . attendance may actually cause improvement for a small subgroup, or AA attendance may be an epiphenomenon." That is, the direction of the causal arrow, according to these authors, is uncertain. Attendance at AA meetings might well be symptomatic of abstinence rather than inducing it. Everyone agrees, however, that regardless of treatment method, "a client's *doing something* toward change [italics in original text] is one of the best predictors of actual change in drinking. Just the taking of a step, the doing of something, may be more important that the specific content of the action" (Miller, Andrews, et al. 1998:214). This may be why the most active participants in A.A. tend to get better (Montgomery et al. 1995). On the other hand, it is self-evident that the most active A.A. members will remain sober, just as they will drop out should they experience a relapse. This finding, however, reveals nothing about which recuperating alcoholics remain less active, or drop out altogether, and why.

It is possible that those A.A. members who attend consistently over a period of many years have a particular personality profile, which makes the organization especially attractive. In one of the most famous studies, Ogborne and Glaser (1981) conclude that A.A. membership is associated with authoritarianism and conformist tendencies, with high affiliative needs, proneness to guilt, religiosity, and vulnerability to external control. It is also possible that devoted members of A.A. have simply substituted one addiction (alcohol) with another (A.A.). At least one psychiatry textbook (Freedman, Kaplan, and Sadock 1972:400) explains that Alcoholics Anonymous "gratifies dependency needs through group identification or by caring for new intoxicated members" and that "switching from alcohol to A.A. offers a less destructive social outlet for addictive needs."

Test results from O'Leary, Calsyn, et al. (1980) substantiate at least part of these findings, by showing that A.A. participation is associated with signs of group adherence (a rather obvious conclusion), submissiveness, and conservatism. Another study (Hulburt et al. 1984) showed that A.A. affiliates were considerably more extroverted in orientation that non-affiliates. Ogborne states that, "Other things being equal, those with an absence of significant psychopathology seem better suited to AA-oriented programs than those with even moderate psychopathology. Those who are seriously psychiatrically disturbed do not do well in AA or, indeed, in most other alcohol treatment programs" (Ogborne 1989: 60). Taken as a whole, the reports validate Ogborne's judgment that "AA attracts individuals with certain personality characteristics" (ibid.). Just what those characteristics are, however, is uncertain and mired in circular reasoning. If an individual attends A.A. meetings on a regular basis he can be said, by definition, to suffer from addictive needs; those who participate in meetings sporadically can be labeled as less addictive, and so on, with little evidence over and above participation itself.

Project MATCH, a massive eight-year multi-site study involving 1726 patients, 25 senior investigators, 80 therapists, and 30 participating institutions and treatment agencies, yielded negative results. Project MATCH was designed to measure how patients with differing personality profiles responded to three different treatment approaches, including Alcoholics Anonymous. In the words of several commentators (Gordis and Fuller 1999:59), "it must be concluded that the overall findings from Project MATCH refute the appealing hypothesis that patient-treatment matching will substantially improve treatment outcomes." That is, after years of research and 26 million dollars of support, Project MATCH failed to determine that one kind of a patient or another would derive special benefit from participation in A.A.

Perhaps the most convincing cautionary note on the validity of statistical surveys comes from Wiseman's study of Skid Row alcoholics. Wiseman, who carried out ethnographic fieldwork in an anonymous U.S. city among men who were down and out, states that "The only reason Skid Row men go to AA is to convince another person (someone who would be impressed by such attendance) that they are really trying to lick the alcohol problem" (Wiseman 1979:233). One of her informants stated (ibid.), "I plan to join AA. Then people will believe I'm not drinking. As it is now, if I get drunk for three days, they don't count it if I'm sober for three weeks." A number of the men whom Wiseman came to know confessed that they attend A.A. meetings "out of desperation for *any* companionship and for the refreshments served" (ibid.). "After the meeting, they feel a very strong urge to drink," continues Wiseman, "so that life becomes a round of early evening AA sessions followed by late evening drinking and morning hangovers" (ibid.). Obviously, no statistical survey can hope to detect this kind of behavior. One can only guess at the number of A.A. members, Skid Row or not, who have deceived others and perhaps themselves in this way.

Many of the attributes of A.A. members, as derived from the U.S. studies, would be applicable to long-term affiliates anywhere else in the world, Mexico included. To be a successful member of a group involving public participation and oratory requires a person who is at least minimally an extrovert. It would also be unlikely for such a person to be a loner; that is, they would probably possess affiliative needs. But, at least insofar as Mexico and other Latin American countries is concerned, these characteristics are culturally validated, hence general in the population. To belong to an A.A. group would also preclude serious psychopathology, a condition which would seriously interfere with effective participation. Given the demands of group participation, religiosity and conformity are additional traits which one can immediately understand as compatible with long-term A.A. participation.

Moral Support is such a small unit that it is impossible to take this group as entirely representative. Nor is the period in which I followed these men (1995–2000) sufficient to provide conclusive evidence. However, it is clear: (1) that those who attend meetings are abstinent; (2) that some men who stop attending meetings remain abstinent; and (3) that some men who stop attending meetings start drinking again to excess. Gerardo has attended hundreds of A.A. meetings per year every year for over a decade and a half. He has remained sober the entire time. Emilio has experienced a similar period of sobriety and yet on at least two occasions has stopped attending meetings for a year or more. These are what he calls "vacation" periods, a part of his therapeutic style which he and at least some others recognize and accept. Nor does he seek alternative treatment during the months when he misses A.A. meetings. He simply buries himself in his work, staying longer hours on the job than when he attends Moral Support.

Emilio calls his periods of non-attendance a vacation, probably in order to minimize its seriousness. The word vacation implies an interlude of limited duration, followed by a return to business as usual. However, Emilio's motivation for separating from the group is not so innocent as the term vacation might indicate. He initiated his most recent rest period because of uncontrollable anger. He would become furious at the thought that *compañeros* were missing *juntas,* arriving late because of work obligations, and failing to carry out high quality cleaning and coffee service. In his opinion, a *"falta de seriedad"*—lack of seriousness—prevailed among the men. He made these concerns known repeatedly during meetings and was rebuffed by the men for speaking about "third persons," rather than concentrating on his own words and deeds. He was accused of "entering into controversies." Outraged by this criticism, he decided, "It is my turn to put my work first." No longer would he make sacrifices for the group, by leaving the shoeshine stand early in order to unlock the meeting room, clean, prepare coffee, or simply attend meetings punctually. One evening, he said, he received customers until 10 P.M. By the time he returned to his house, which is located on the very street where Moral Support meets, the *junta* was long over, the meeting room dark and locked.

Not everyone in Moral Support respects Emilio's right to stop attending meetings. Emilio feels the force of social control spilling out of the meeting room into the street. He believes that Gerardo no longer speaks to him. One day, Emilio was painting the facade of his house. Gerardo walked by without even saying hello. "Well, why didn't you greet him?" I asked. "I was the one who was occupied," responded Emilio. "He was walking by. The one who's occupied isn't the first to greet; it's the responsibility of the other guy." Emilio is offended by the incident. "It's not like I'm a criminal, like I stole from the group or anything. He has no good reason to stop talking to me." Even when Moral Support members stop attending meetings, the boundary between inside and outside, between meeting room and street, remains blurred.

When *compañeros* leave the group to start drinking, they are abandoned to their own devices. This happened to Eduardo, who attributes his relapse to a love affair. Eduardo is sober when he attends A.A. meetings, and becomes a drunk whenever he stops attending, which occurs every two or three years. Over the course of a decade, he has proven unable to abstain for more than several years at a time. And yet it is impossible to measure the effect of A.A. on his drinking patterns. A.A. might well delay the onset of relapses by a matter of months; meetings certainly have not prevented them from occurring.

The men believe that sincerity and seriousness of purpose at meetings will prevent relapses. However, because the everyday lives of the men are intertwined with their lives as members of A.A., it is difficult to achieve complete frankness during meetings. Men periodically depart from formulaic, repetitive, generalized *historiales* to deliver deeply felt, intimate confessions of personal problems. On the whole, however, the public confessions are idealized, abstract, and predictable. They are also guarded. Several of the men, recording life histories for me in private, state that they would never reveal some of those thoughts and experiences in an *historial.*

It is uncertain, however, that intimate revelations would necessarily prevent relapses. What the meetings accomplish, as much as anything, is to structure the men's lives and fill otherwise dangerously free moments with a small, tight-knit society of caring companions. These men, the *compañeros,* share painful memories, affirm for one another a common sense of masculine identity, and derive social status and a sense of competence from public performance. When I first met him, Emilio stated that his life consisted of traveling from home to work, work to meetings, meetings to home, and then back to work again. He wanted nothing more. When he stopped attending meetings, he simply commuted between home and work. He is fearful of free time, lest he lose his mooring and begin to drown again in alcohol. Eduardo, chronically unemployed or underemployed, suffers relapses. But David, who works only on weekends, does not. Unlike Eduardo, who has no home of his own, David has developed the capacity to organize his daily life around household chores. He declares himself free of the temptation to drink and attends meetings in order to meet different needs. For David, A.A. provides an outlet for sociability and psychotherapy. To the extent that sessions help reduce the men's anxiety and provide emotional support, the meetings do perform this important function.

But meetings, as we have seen, are complex events. A man can tell his family that he is at an A.A. meeting and sneak off instead to visit a lover. When attending the meeting, he can brag about sexual exploits and feel himself to be manly, despite abstinence from alcohol. While delivering an *historial* he airs grievances against *compañeros* who might have wronged him inside the meeting room or out. Meetings provide an outlet for religious sentiments; they supplement or entirely replace formal church involvement. It is in meetings, too, that a man can show forgiveness and compassion in a way rare or prohibited altogether for men in contexts other than A.A.

During the Mexico City mayoral campaign in 1997, PRD candidate Cuauhtémoc Cárdenas proclaimed *"El derecho de los hombres a la ternura"*—the right of men to tenderness. Working class men in Mexico City usually feel constrained from expressing gentleness. At Moral

Support meetings, men can do something unheard of outside A.A., except when they are drunk—that is, cry. Not only can they cry with no sense of being defined as weaklings. They also derive status from crying because this sort of demonstrativeness is courageous and indicates sincerity. In the context of meetings the men can be simultaneously tender and valiant, a combination of character traits which implies a redefinition of traditional gender roles.

Mexico City and the entire Mexican nation, in fact, is currently experiencing large-scale adjustment not only in gender roles but also in the relative status of men and women. Berman and Maerker (2000:12) point to the enormous strides in educational level that Mexican women have made during the last quarter of the twentieth century; "year by year," say these authors, men and women are becoming ever more evenly matched in this regard. Although status and power differences still prevail, according to Berman and Maerker (ibid.), the current generation of women enters the new millennium "filled with certainty that we can have achievements equal to those of men."

Gutmann (1996:9) captures the essence of the current social flux when he says that "there exists no stable set of determining and essential gender qualities that can adequately capture the situation for the region [Mexico and Latin America] as a whole; relentlessly emergent gender variations see to that." Gutmann describes the wide range of living arrangements and gender ideals that he discovered among the people of his neighborhood.

> Whenever I was in doubt, for persuasive evidence [of gender variations] I had only to walk through my section of [town], beginning with the agnostic printer who bragged to me about his vasectomy a week after I met him, who worked in front of the house with a single mother and five young children, who lived a block over from the woman who resided openly with her children and a series of male lovers, who was next door to the woman who could not leave home without her husband's permission, who was across the street from the cobbler who ridiculed state- and church-sponsored marriages in the same breath as he rebuked unfaithful husbands, whose shop was below the home of a notorious and belligerent wife-beater and his alcoholic sons, one of whom was the boyfriend of a young mother of two small children who lived in a home in which all the males were waited upon by all the females of the household, all of whom were

surrounded in the *colonia* by young women who would be the first people in their families to graduate from high school.

Undoubtedly, some of these men and women find life easier in the city than they would in the countryside. Although they hardly live in an anonymous milieu, urban conditions allow for greater tolerance and social creativity than can exist in provincial towns and villages.

The men of Moral Support have benefited from this fluid social situation. It is perhaps easier to be a teetotaling male in Mexico City in the year 2000 than it was half a century ago. In part, Alcoholics Anonymous owes its enormous expansion to the reshuffling of gender roles and ideals, which has proceeded rapidly during the past thirty years. Increasingly, the avoidance of alcohol is just another way of being a man. The men of Moral Support, and thousands of other men who constitute more than 90 percent of the A.A. membership in Mexico, need no longer feel like pariahs in their quest to remain sober. They can think of themselves as an integral part of the social realignment occurring in their city and nation today.

The redefinition of gender roles is just one way in which the men of Moral Support demonstrate a creative engagement with the wider society. For most of the men, A.A., as a spiritual movement, stimulates a modified view of religion as well. To believing Catholics, like many of the men in Moral Support, A.A. is like a church. Principles of popular Mexican Catholicism—confession, reverence for the saints, the *padrinazgo* and *compadrazgo,* and the like—are applied to A.A. and have helped make the movement a success in Mexico. The men also are creative in their invention of narratives. Within a few short months of joining the group, the men learn how to deliver a public performance, the *historial.* A.A. narratives, which are often formulaic, occasionally depart from predetermined scripts to become dramatic masterpieces. *Historiales* in this way allow for innovation. An innovative *historial* is, in fact, the ideal, for it demonstrates spontaneity and sincerity. Like all ideals, this one is not consistently realized. Nonetheless, it is there as a central guidepost to thought and action. In a society like that of these men, restricted in so many ways by traditional norms, A.A. allows space for and even stimulates social change and redefined identities.

The men of Moral Support do not always attain the goals they set for themselves and their group. But, in their courage to change and their struggle to redefine their relation to the world, they demonstrate determination and the ability to overcome tremendous obstacles. The group, as we have seen, in many ways reproduces longstanding relationships and values. At the same time, by confronting their problem drinking, participating in a voluntary organization like A.A., and creatively modifying their views of what it means to be a man in Mexico City, the men of Moral Support live heroic lives. They are also perhaps harbingers of a new society.

Appendix A. THE TWELVE STEPS OF ALCOHOLICS ANONYMOUS/*LOS DOCE PASOS DE ALCOHÓLICOS ANÓNIMOS*

1. *Admitimos que éramos impotentes ante el alcohol, que nuestras vidas se habían vuelto ingovernables.*
   We admitted we were powerless over alcohol—that our lives had become unmanageable.

2. *Llegamos al convencimiento de que un poder superior podría devolvernos el sano jucio.*
   Came to believe that a Power greater than ourselves could restore us to sanity.

3. *Decidimos poner nuestras voluntades y nuestras vidas al cuidado de Dios, como nosotros lo concebimos.*
   Made a decision to turn our will and our lives over to the care of God as we understood him.

4. *Sin miedo hicimos un minucioso inventario moral de nosotros mismos.*
   Made a searching and fearless inventory of ourselves.

5. *Admitimos ante Dios, ante nosotros mismos y ante otro ser humano, la naturaleza exacta de nuestros defectos.*
   Admitted to God, to ourselves, and to another human being, the exact nature of our wrongs.

6. *Estuvimos enteramente dispuestos a dejar que Dios nos liberase de todos estos defectos de carácter.*
   Were entirely ready to have God remove all these defects of character.

7. *Humildemente le pedimos que nos liberase de nuestros defectos.*
   Humbly asked Him to remove our shortcomings.

8. *Hicimos una lista de todas aquellas personas a quienes habíamos ofendido y estuvimos dispuestos a reparar el daño que les causamos.*
Made a list of all persons we had harmed, and became willing to make amends to them all.

9. *Reparamos directamente a cuantos nos fue posible el daño causado, excepto cuando el hacerlo implicaba perjuicio para ellos o para otros.*
Made direct amends to such people whenever possible, except when to do so would injure them or others.

10. *Continuamos haciendo nuestro inventario personal y cuando nos equivocábamos lo admitíamos inmediatamente.*
Continued to take personal inventory and when we were wrong promptly admitted it.

11. *Buscamos a través de la oración y la meditación mejorar nuestro contacto consciente con Dios, como nosotros lo concebimos, pidiéndole solamente que nos dejase conocer su voluntad para con nosotros y nos diese la fortaleza para cumplirla.*
Sought through prayer and meditation to improve our conscious contact with God as we understood Him, praying only for knowledge of His will for us and the power to carry that out.

12. *Habiendo obtenido un despertar espiritual, como resultado de estos pasos, tratamos de llevar este mensaje a los alcohólicos y de practicar estos principios en todos nuestros asuntos.*
Having had a spiritual awakening as the result of these steps, we tried to carry this message to alcoholics, and to practice these principles in all our affairs.

Sources: Alcoholics Anonymous World Services 1952 (English version); Central Mexicana de Servicios Generales de A.A. 1989b (Spanish version). Used by permission.

Appendix B. THE TWELVE TRADITIONS OF ALCOHOLICS ANONYMOUS/*LAS DOCE TRADICIONES DE ALCOHÓLICOS ANÓNIMOS*

1. *Nuestro bienestar común debe tener la preferencia; la recuperación personal depende de la unidad de A.A.*
   Our common welfare should come first; personal recovery depends upon A.A. unity.

2. *Para el propósito de nuestro grupo sólo existe una autoridad fundamental: un Dios amoroso que puede manifestarse en la consciencia de nuestro grupo. Nuestros líderes no son más que servidores de confianza. No goviernan.*
   For our group purpose there is but one ultimate authority—a loving God as He may express himself in the group conscience. Our leaders are but trusted servants; they do not govern.

3. *El único requisito para ser miembro de A.A. es querer dejar de beber.*
   The only requirement for A.A. membership is a desire to stop drinking.

4. *Cada grupo debe ser autónomo, excepto en asuntos que afectan a otros grupos o a Alcohólicos Anónimos, considerado como un todo.*
   Each group should be autonomous except in matters affecting other groups or A.A. as a whole.

5. *Cada grupo tiene un sólo objetivo primordial: Llevar el mensaje al alcohólico que aún está sufriendo.*
   Each group has but one primary purpose—to carry its message to the alcoholic who still suffers.

6. *Un grupo de A.A. nunca debe respaldar, financiar o prestar el nombre de A.A. a ninguna entidad allegada o empresa ajena, para evitar que los problemas de dinero, propiedad y prestigio nos desvíen de nuestro objetivo primordial.*

An A.A. group ought never endorse, finance, or lend the A.A. name to any related facility or outside enterprise, lest problems of money, property, and prestige divert us from our primary purpose.

7. *Todo grupo de A.A. debe mantenerse completamente a sí mismo, negándose a recibir contribuciones de afuera.*
Every A.A. group ought to be fully self-supporting, declining outside contributions.

8. *A.A. nunca tendrá carácter profesional, pero nuestros centros de servicio pueden emplear trabajadores especiales.*
Alcoholics Anonymous should remain forever non-professional, but our service centers may employ special workers.

9. *A.A. como tal nunca debe ser organizada; pero podemos crear juntas o comités de servicio que sean directamente responsables ante aquellos a quienes sirven.*
A.A. as such, ought never be organized; but we may create service boards or committees directly responsible to those they serve.

10. *A.A. no tiene opinión acerca de asuntos ajenos a sus actividades; por consiguiente su nombre nunca debe mezclarse en polémicas públicas.*
Alcoholics Anonymous has no opinion on outside issues; hence the A.A. name ought never be drawn into public controversy.

11. *Nuestra política de relaciones públicas se basa más bien en la atracción que en la promoción; necesitamos mantener siempre nuestro anonimato personal ante la prensa, la radio y el cine.*
Our public relations policy is based on attraction rather than promotion; we need always maintain personal anonymity at the level of press, radio, and films.

12. *El anonimato es la base espiritual de todas nuestras tradiciones, recordándonos siempre anteponer los principios a las personalidades.*
Anonymity is the spiritual foundation of our traditions, ever reminding us to place principles before personalities.

Sources: Alcoholics Anonymous World Services 1952 (English version); Central Mexicana de Servicios Generales de A.A. 1989c (Spanish version). Used by permission.

NOTES

Chapter One

1. Carl Feinstein, a psychiatrist at Stanford University Medical School, visited one of the group's meetings and was astounded by the consummate poise of the speakers. In his opinion, very few Anglos in the United States, even highly educated Anglos, would be equally competent in front of an audience.

2. Alcoholics Anonymous meetings are famous worldwide for producing smoke-filled rooms. Dr. Sergio Villaseñor Bayardo, a Mexican psychiatrist and anthropologist who has observed A.A. meetings in France, tells me that the French affiliates of his acquaintance are chain smokers.

3. Explaining the methodology employed in an ambitious comparative study of self-help groups, Levy (1982:243) states, "Generally, self-help groups do not lend themselves to the sophisticated data-acquisition methodology typically used in small-scale research. In those groups we studied, we were not allowed to take notes or make tape recordings during meetings, thus eliminating the application of any kind of interaction process. . . . " Levy and his team relied, as I did, on field notes and taped interviews collected outside the context of meetings.

Chapter Two

1. O'Reilly (1997:118) points out that, coincidentally or not, James's classic volume identifies the appearance of vivid white lights, which he calls "photosms," as the distinguishing mark of a particular variety of mystical experience.

2. The Serenity Prayer reads, "God grant me the serenity to accept the things I cannot change, courage to change the things I can, and wisdom to know the difference." Among the Twelve Steps mentioning God or Him are: Step 3, "Made a decision to turn our will and our lives over to the care of God *as we understood Him*"; Step 5, "Admitted to God, to ourselves, and to another human being the exact nature of our wrongs"; Step 6, "Were entirely ready to have God remove all these defects of character"; Step 7, "Humbly asked Him to remove our shortcomings"; Step 11, "Sought through prayer and meditation to improve our conscious contact with God *as we understood Him,* praying only for knowl-

edge of His will for us and the power to carry that out." (Italics in the original.) As for the Twelve Traditions, number 2 states, "For our group purpose there is but one ultimate authority—a loving God as He may express Himself in our group conscience. Our leaders are but trusted servants; they do not govern."

3. It was in June 1941 when an A.A. affiliate in New York discovered this then-obscure prayer while perusing the pages of the *Herald Tribune*. In the years since, the prayer has been repeated millions of times not only at A.A. meetings, but also at Al-Anon meetings and by members of all kinds of twelve-step programs (Bufe 1941:45).

4. The poem is reproduced here verbatim. If the poem's title is read as if it were the first line, which is the case with members of Moral Support, the poem is grammatically awkward.

5. In the United States, "birthday" cakes, presented on the anniversary of an A.A. affiliate's continuous sobriety, are also common. One of Pollner and Stein's informants testified, "And uh, I'd been in and out of this program. I added it all up the other day and if I had all my sobriety back to back lined up with nothin' in between, I'd probably have 23 years. But I haven't, I've stretched it out. I've had 1 year cakes, I've had 8 year cakes, I've had 5 year cakes. If I had all the cakes that I had got in Alcoholics Anonymous, I could start a goddam bakery" (quoted in Pollner and Stein 1996:208).

6. There is a voluminous literature to substantiate this claim for Mexico as well as for Latin America generally. See, e.g., Brandes 1988; Bricker 1973:58–71; Cancian 1965:30–33, 51–61; Collier 1973:25–27,101–103; Heath 1994; Nash 1985:16–17; 148–149, 184–187; Nutini 1984; Saignes 1993; Vogt 1969).

7. Prior to the Spanish translation of Alcoholics Anonymous publications, there had been substantial translation into Spanish of American temperance books and folios. Cora Frances Stoddard's works (1921, 1923, 1928), and that of Richmond Pearson Hobson (1924), provide prominent examples of this trend.

Chapter Three

1. Kurtz's distinction between the A.A. program and the A.A. fellowship is similar to de Saussure's classic linguistic differentiation between *langue* and *parole*, or language and speech (Saussure 1916). The former consists of the rules, largely an abstraction. The latter is the actual utterance, the working out of the rules through normal discourse. The distinction between A.A. program and fellowship is also reminiscent of Raymond Firth's differentiation between social structure, on the one hand, and social organization, on the other (Firth 1961). States Firth (ibid.:40), "Continuity is expressed in the social structure, the sets of relations which make for firmness of expectation, for validation of past experience in terms of similar experience in the future. Members of a society look for a reliable guide to action, and the structure of the society gives this. . . . At the same

time there must be room for variance and for the explanation of variance. This is found in the social organization, the systematic ordering of social relations by acts of choice and decision. Here is room for variation from what has happened in apparently similar circumstances in the past."

2. "Coffee," states one observer (Samuels 1998:48), "is an integral part of most A.A. meetings, a de-facto sacrament. Members of A.A. have been known to make pilgrimages to Akron, Ohio, to view the coffeepot used by Dr. Bob, the co-founder of the organization." Alasuutari (1992:110–114) emphasizes the symbolic importance of coffee among men in the Finnish self-help recovery group that he studied. States Alasuutari (ibid.:111), "It is extremely difficult to abstain from coffee drinking in the meetings. It is a social norm that one is expected to take part in the ritual. After one has already had the first cup of coffee, one is supposed to have another and another." He continues (ibid.:113), "Coffee is used as a substitute for alcohol. . . . It is widely believed that coffee is effective in sobering up a drunken person. A good deal of these beliefs are probably due to the social history of coffee, which from the fifteenth century onward, increasingly replaced wine and other alcoholic drinks as a substance used in social life."

3. Performance is a central feature of any ritual, sacred or secular. Moore and Myerhoff (1977:7) list "Acting" as one of the defining characteristics for identifying ritual. They state that a basic quality of ritual is that it "is not an essentially spontaneous activity, but rather most, if not all of it is self-consciously 'acted' like a part in a play. Further, this usually involves doing something, not only saying or thinking something" (ibid.: 7). The degree to which spontaneity emerges or not in Moral Support personal stories is a topic for the subsequent chapter.

4. Gusfield (1996:69) has pointed out perceptively that coffee and alcohol are symbolic opposites within A.A. Although his remarks refer to the United States, they are valid for Mexico City as well. Says Gusfield (ibid.), "In the folklore of drinking there is the belief that coffee is an agent of sobriety. It is what the drinker should drink if he wishes to achieve sobriety quickly. Common talk pictures coffee as the antithesis to alcohol. . . . Although physiologists disclaim the ability of coffee to eradicate the effects of alcohol, it persists as the symbol of contrast—the food with which we return from the world of leisure to the world of work. . . . Coffee stimulates; alcohol relaxes. Its symbolic properties produce its ritualistic usage." According to the most recent, definitive history of coffee (Pendergrast 1999:9), starting in the seventeenth century, coffee did actually have the effect of lessening the intake of alcohol, at least in France. In 1674, a British commentator remarked that "coffee-drinking hath caused a greater sobriety among the nations; for whereas formerly Apprentices and Clerks with others, used to take their mornings' draught in Ale, Beer or Wine, which by the dizziness they cause in the Brain, make many unfit for business, they use now to play the Good-fellows in this Wakefull and civill drink" (quoted in ibid.:13).

Chapter Four

1. Secretaries and other service personnel in the United States increasingly introduce themselves to clients by first name alone. I have wondered whether this practice derives from the pervasive influence of Alcoholics Anonymous and off-shoot twelve-step programs.

2. Among the laboring classes, two main forms of marriage prevail in rural central Mexico, including the Bajío, the geographic-cultural region north of Mexico City from which Renaldo comes. The first, and most prestigious form, is the so-called *pedido,* or request, which amounts to a formal petition for the hand of a young woman on the part of the future groom's family. The other, and more common form in many rural towns and villages, is the *robo,* literally "robbery." The *robo* is an elopement which, for cultural reasons, is couched in the language of a forced abduction, but which, in fact, is generally carried out with the full knowledge, permission and planning of the future bride. Very occasionally, however, the *robo* amounts to virtual rape. On the *robo,* see Brandes 1968 and Diaz 1967.

3. Vomiting is one symptom of *aire,* an indigenous Mesoamerican folk illness. The affliction is sometimes pronounced *aigre* by rural or native people. An extensive discussion of *aire* can be found in Kearney (1972), though numerous other publications mention it as well (e.g., Clark 1959:173–174, 224, 225; G. Foster 1988:188; Ingham 1986:162–164, 177–78, 191; Ortiz de Montellano 1990:67, 225; Parsons 1936:214–215).

Chapter Five

1. Dennis (1979), Maccoby (1972), Eber (1995) and others have discussed the personality and social impact of the male drunk within rural Mexican society. Eber (ibid.) provides the only book-length study of Mexican female drinking, although there are also excellent studies of women's drinking behavior and of women alcoholics in culturally related societies (e.g., Costa-Magna and Memmi 1981, Harvey 1997, McDonald 1997). For the case of the United States, one should not overlook moving personal accounts, most recently that of Susan Cheever (2000), as well as popular studies for the educated reader such as those by Bauer (1982), Hafner (1992), and Youcha (1986).

2. The current situation in Mexico is apparently not so different from that which prevailed in the United States a generation ago, prior to the impact of the women's movement. A standard psychiatry textbook (Freedman, Kaplan, and Sadock 1972) states, "The ratio of male to female alcoholic persons is most commonly quoted at 5 ½ to 1. However, clinical observations suggest that more women than men are seeking treatment. The impression that there are more male than female alcoholic persons could arise from the easier detection of the illness in men. Men cannot hide as easily as women, since they must go out into the world and to their occupations, where society may recognize a disturbance

or dysfunction due to alcohol. A woman may remain protected in her home and may for long periods escape social or even family detection."

3. This finding also accords with Corbett, Mora, and Ames (1991:219), who state that "In no case in the entire [Mexican-American] sample did a wife's drinking level exceed that of her husband." Jean Gilbert's analysis of drinking patterns among Mexican-Americans in California yields the same general picture. While acknowledging considerable intracultural variation, Gilbert (1985: 265) still concludes that "In virtually every study focused on Mexican-American drinking patterns inside and outside of California, men's drinking habits have been found to be very different from women's. . . . Overall Mexican-American women are much more likely to be abstainers, to engage in only very light social drinking in restricted environments, and to report fewer problems related to alcohol than Mexican-American men. Although this sex difference also exists in the larger population, research suggests that sex role differences are clearer among Mexican-Americans."

4. The connection between alcohol and male violence is hardly limited to Mexico. To give just one parallel from elsewhere in Latin America, namely highland Ecuador, Kristi Anne Stølen (1991:83) states that "wife-beating is found among rich and poor alike, dependent as well as independent peasants. It is generally, but not always, associated with alcohol. Men tend to beat when they are drunk."

5. Of course, the idea that alcohol destroys families predates the arrival of Alcoholics Anonymous in Mexico. See, for example, Luis G. Franco (1932).

6. According to Catholic belief, through a process known as transubstantiation, the wine is converted into "the blood of Christ" during the priest's communion. It is impossible to say how many Mexicans who follow popular forms of Catholicism actually believe that transubstantiation occurs. Nowadays, at the turn of the twentieth century, there exists a debate within the Catholic Church on the validity of transubstantiation. The Catholic declaration of transubstantiation was one of the major causes of Protestant dissent during the Renaissance.

7. Apparently this correlation between social class and drinking patterns is not the same everywhere. Corbett, Mora, and Ames (1991:218) report that, for Mexican Americans, "Men with more education tended to be heavier drinkers than other men. Age was inversely correlated with drinking level; income and expectancies were positively correlated." Similarly (ibid.), "More educated women, women with higher household incomes and more acculturated women were more likely to be drinkers."

8. See Brandes 1981 for a parallel meaning system in southern Spain.

Chapter Six

1. The *camote* (*Ipomoea batatas*) is a potato-like tuber, which Mexicans often eat sweetened as a snack.

Chapter Seven

1. Emilio's explanation of his condition rests on a belief in humoral pathology, that is the classification of illnesses, foods, and remedies according to properties of heat and cold. Humoral pathology, which anthropologists often refer to as the hot-cold syndrome, is a folk medical system widespread throughout Mexico and much of Latin America. For a full ethno-historical account, see G. Foster (1994).

REFERENCES CITED

Alasuutari, Pertti

1992 *Desire and Craving: A Cultural Theory of Alcoholism.* Albany: State University of New York Press.

Alcoholics Anonymous World Services

1952 *Twelve Steps and Twelve Traditions.* New York: Alcoholics Anonymous World Services.

1976 *Alcoholics Anonymous: The Story of How Many Thousands of Men and Women Have Recovered from Alcoholism.* Third Edition. New York: Alcoholics Anonymous World Services.

1980 *Analysis of the 1980 Survey of the Membership of Alcoholics Anonymous.* New York: Alcoholics Anonymous World Services.

1986 *As Bill Sees It.* New York: Alcoholics Anonymous World Services.

Anonymous

1995 *Pensamiento del Día.* México, D.F.: Oficina Intergrupal del Sureste.

Antzé, Paul

1982 "Role of Ideologies in Peer Psychotherapy Groups." In: *Self-Help Groups for Coping with Crisis: Origins, Members, Processes, and Impact* (Morton A. Lieberman, Leonard D. Borman, et al., eds.), pp. 272–304. San Francisco: Jossey-Bass.

1987 "Symbolic Action in Alcoholics Anonymous." In: *Constructive Drinking: Perspectives on Drink from Anthropology* (Mary Douglas, ed.), pp. 149–181. Cambridge: Cambridge University Press.

Baekeland, Frederick, Lawrence Lundwall, and Benjamin Kissin

1975 "Methods for the Treatment of Chronic Alcoholism: A Critical Appraisal." In: *Research Advances in Alcohol and Drug Problems,* vol. 2 (Robert J. Gibbons, et al., eds.), pp. 248–327. New York: John Wiley.

Bateson, Gregory

1971 "The Cybernetics of 'Self': A Theory of Alcoholism." *Psychiatry* 34 (1): 1–18.

Bauer, Jan

1982   *Alcoholism and Women: The Background and the Psychology.* Toronto: Inner City Books.

Bennett, Linda A., Carlos Campillo, et al.

1998   "Alcohol Beverage Consumption in India, Mexico, and Nigeria: A Cross-Cultural Comparison." *Alcohol Health and Research World* 22 (4): 243–252.

Berman, Sabina, and Denise Maerker

1916   *Mujeres y Poder.* México, D.F.: Raya en el Agua.

Bloomfield, Kim

1990   "Dimensions of Spiritual Practice among Gay and Lesbian Members of Alcoholics Anonymous." Paper presented at the Annual Epidemiology Symposium of the Kettil Bruun Society, June, Budapest, Hungary.

Blum, Richard, and Eva Blum

1964   "Drinking Practices and Controls in Rural Greece." *British Journal of Addiction* 60:93–108.

Brandes, Stanley

1968   "Tzintzuntzan Wedding: A Study in Cultural Complexity." Papers of the Kroeber Anthropological Society 39:30–53.

1979   "Drinking Patterns and Alcohol Control in a Castilian Mountain Village." Anthropology 3 (1–2):1–16.

1981   "Like Wounded Stags: Male Sexual Ideology in an Andalusian Town." In: *Sexual Meanings: The Cultural Construction of Gender and Sexuality* (Sherry Ortner and Harriet Whitehead, eds.), pp. 216–239. Cambridge: Cambridge University Press.

1987   *Forty: The Age and the Symbol.* Knoxville: University of Tennessee Press.

1988   *Power and Persuasion: Fiestas and Social Control in Rural Mexico.* Philadelphia: University of Pennsylvania Press.

Brandsma, Jeffrey M., with Maxine C. Maultsby, Jr. and Richard Welsh

1980   *Outpatient Treatment of Alcoholism: A Review and Comparative Study.* Baltimore: University Park Press.

Bricker, Victoria Reifler

1973   *Ritual Humor in Highland Chiapas.* Austin: University of Texas Press.

Bufe, Charles

1991   *Alcoholics Anonymous: Cult or Cure?* San Francisco: Sharp.

Caetano, Raul

1993   "Ethnic Minority Groups and Alcoholics Anonymous: A Review." In: *Research on Alcoholics Anonymous: Opportunities and Alternatives*

(Barbara S. McCrady and William R. Miller, eds.), pp. 209–232. New Brunswick, N.J.: Rutgers Center of Alcohol Studies.

Cahn, Peter

2001 *When Conversion Is Convergence: Evangelicals and Catholics in Tzintzuntzan, Mexico.* Unpublished Ph.D. dissertation, University of California, Berkeley.

Cain, Arthur H.

1964 *The Cured Alcoholic: New Concepts in Alcoholism Treatment and Research.* New York: John Day Co.

Cain, Carole

1991 "Personal Stories: Identity Acquisition and Self-Understanding in Alcoholics Anonymous." *Ethos* 19 (2):210–253.

Cancian, Frank

1965 *Economics and Prestige in a Maya Community: The Religious Cargo System in Zinacantan.* Stanford: Stanford University Press.

Carlos, Manuel L.

1973 "Fictive Kinship and Modernization in Mexico: A Comparative Analysis." *Anthropological Quarterly* 46(2):75–91.

Caro Baroja, Julio

1963 "The City and the Country: Reflexions on Some Ancient Commonplaces." In: *Mediterranean Countrymen: Essays in the Social Anthropology of the Mediterranean* (Julian Pitt-Rivers, ed.), pp. 27–40. Paris: Mouton.

Carrier, Joseph

1995 De los Otros: *Homosexuality Among Mexican Men.* New York: Columbia University Press.

Castillejos, Margarita, and Paulina Serrano

1997 "Efecto de los contaminantes atmosféricos sobre la salud en cuatro colonias." In: *Pobreza, Condiciones de Vida, y Salud en la Ciudad de México* (Martha Schteingart, ed.), pp. 629–692. México, D.F.: El Colegio de México.

Cavan, Sherri

1966 *Liquor License: An Ethnography of Bar Behavior.* Chicago: Aldine.

Central Mexicana de Servicios Generales de A.A., A.C.

1989a *Preguntas y Respuestas sobre el Apadrinamiento.* México, D.F.: Central Mexicana.

1989b *Los Doce Pasos.* México, D.F.: Central Mexicana.
1989c *Las Doce Tradiciones.* México, D.F.: Central Mexicana.

Cheever, Susan

2000 *Note in a Bottle: My Life as a Drinker.* New York: Washington Square.

Child, I., H. Barry, and M. K. Bacon

1965 "A Cross-Cultural Study of Drinking, III: Sex Differences." *Quarterly Journal of Studies in Alcohol,* Supplement No. 3:49–61.

Clark, Margaret

1959 *Health in the Mexican-American Culture.* Berkeley: University of California Press.

Collier, Jane Fishburne

1973 *Law and Social Change in Zinacantan.* Stanford: Stanford University Press.

Colson, Elizabeth

1977 "The Least Common Denominator." In: *Secular Ritual* (Sally F. Moore and Barbara G. Myerhoff, eds.), pp. 189–198. Assen/Amsterdam: Van Gorcum.

Colson, Elizabeth, and Thayer Scudder

1988 *For Prayer and Profit: The Ritual, Economic, and Social Importance of Beer in Gwembe District, Zambia, 1950–1982.* Stanford: Stanford University Press.

Corbett, Kitty, Juana Mora, and Genevieve Ames

1991 "Drinking Patterns and Drinking-Related Problems of Mexican-American Husbands and Wives." *Journal of Studies on Alcohol* 52 (3): 215–223.

Costa-Magna, Michèle, with the collaboration of Vera Memmi

1981 *Les Femmes et l'Alcoöl: la Fontaine de Lilith.* Paris: Denoël.

Davis, Kenneth G.

1994 *Primero Dios: Alcoholics Anonymous and the Hispanic Community.* London: Associated University Presses.

Dennis, Philip A.

1979 "The Role of the Drunk in a Oaxaca Village." In: *Beliefs, Behaviors, and Alcoholic Beverages: A Cross-Cultural Survey* (Mac Marshall, ed.), pp. 54–64. Ann Arbor: University of Michigan Press.

Diaz, May N.

1967 "Opposition and Alliance in a Mexican Town." In: *Peasant Societies: A*

Reader (Jack M. Potter, May N. Diaz, and George M. Foster, eds.), pp. 168–174. Boston: Little, Brown.

Doughty, Paul L.

1979 "The Social Uses of Alcoholic Beverages in a Peruvian Community." In: *Beliefs, Behaviors, and Alcoholic Beverages: A Cross-Cultural Survey* (Mac Marshall, ed.), pp. 64–81. Ann Arbor: University of Michigan Press.

Douglas, Mary

1973 *Natural Symbols: Explorations in Cosmology.* New York: Vintage.

Eber, Christine

1995 *Women and Alcohol in a Highland Maya Town: Water of Hope, Water of Sorrow.* Austin: University of Texas Press.

Eisenstadt, S. N.

1956 "Ritualized Personal Relations: Blood Brotherhood, Best Friends, Compadre, etc.: Some Comparative Hypotheses and Suggestions." *Man* 56: 90–95.

Ellis, Albert

1991 *Alcoholics Anonymous: Cult or Cure?* San Francisco: Sharp.

Ellison, John W., comp.

1957 *Nelson's Complete Concordance of the Revised Standard Version Bible.* New York: Thomas Nelson & Sons.

Emrick, C. D., C. L. Lassen, and M. T. Edwards

1978 "Nonprofessional Peers as Therapeutic Agents." In: *Effective Psychotherapy: A Handbook of Research* (A. S. Gurman and A. M. Razin, eds.), pp. 120–161. Elmsford, N.Y.: Pergamon Press.

Emrick, Chad D., J. Scott Tonigan, Henry Montgomery, and Laura Little

1993 "Alcoholics Anonymous: What Is Currently Known?" In: *Research on Alcoholics Anonymous: Opportunities and Alternatives* (Barbara S. Miller and William R. McCrady, eds.), pp. 41–76. New Brunswick, N.J.: Rutgers Center of Alcohol Studies.

Feixa, Carles

1988 *La Tribu Juvenil: Una Aproximación Transcultural a la Juventud.* Torino: Occhiello.
1993 *La Ciudad en la Antropología Mexicana.* Lleida: Universitat de Lleida.

Fingarette, Herbert

1988 *Myth of Alcoholism as a Disease.* Berkeley: University of California Press.

Finkler, Kaja

1994   *Women in Pain: Gender and Morbidity in Mexico.* Philadelphia: University of Pennsylvania Press.

Firth, Raymond

1961   *Elements of Social Organization.* Third Edition. Boston: Beacon.

Foster, George M.

1953   "*Cofradía* and *Compadrazgo* in Spain and Spanish America." *Southwestern Journal of Anthropology* 9:1–28.
1967   "The Dyadic Contract: A Model for the Social Structure of a Mexican Peasant Village." In: *Peasant Society: A Reader* (Jack M. Potter, May N. Diaz, and George M. Foster, eds.), pp. 213–230. Boston: Little, Brown.
1969   "Godparents and Social Networks in Tzintzuntzan." *Southwestern Journal of Anthropology* 25:261–278.
1988   *Tzintzuntzan: Mexican Peasants in a Changing World.* Prospect Heights, IL: Waveland.
1994   *Hippocrates' Latin American Legacy: Humoral Medicine in the New World.* Langhorne, Pennsylvania: Gordon and Breach.

Foster, George M., and Robert V. Kemper, eds.

1974   *Anthropologists in Cities.* New York: Little, Brown.

Foster, Mary LeCron

1983   "Tzintzuntzan Marriage: An Analysis of Concordant Structure." In: *The Future of Structuralism* (Jarich Oosten and Arie de Ruijter, eds.), pp. 127–153. Gottingen: Herodot.
1985   "Structural Hierarchy and Social Good in Tzintzuntzan." *International Journal of Psychology* 20:617–635.

Foucault, Michel

1977   *Discipline and Punish: The Birth of the Prison* (Alan Sheridan, tr.). New York: Vintage.

Franco, Luis G.

1931   *La Elevación del Obrero Venciendo los Obstáculos del Alcoholismo.* México, D.F.: Talleres Gráficos de la Nación.
1932   *Los Hijos de la Intemperancia Alcohólica y el Presidio.* México, D.F.: Secretaría de Industria, Comercio y Trabajo.

Freedman, Alfred M., Harold I. Kaplan, and Benjamin J. Sadock

1972   *Modern Synopsis of Comprehensive Textbook of Psychiatry.* Baltimore: Williams and Wilkins.

Gilbert, M. Jean

1985   "Mexican-Americans in California: Intracultural Variation in Attitudes and Behavior Related to Alcohol." In: *The American Experience with*

Alcohol: Contrasting Cultural Perspectives (Linda A. Bennett and Genevieve M. Ames, eds.), pp. 255–277). New York: Plenum.

Gilmore, David D.

1985 "The Role of the Bar in Andalusian Rural Society: Observations on Political Culture under Franco." *Journal of Anthropological Research* 41 (3):263–277.

Gluckman, Max

1965 *Politics, Law, and Ritual in Tribal Society.* Oxford: Blackwell.

Gordis, Enoch, and Richard Fuller

1999 "Project MATCH." *Addiction* 94 (1):57–59.

Gordon, Andrew J.

1985 "Alcohol and Hispanics in the Northeast: A Study of Cultural Variability and Adaptation." In: *The American Experience with Alcohol: Contrasting Cultural Perspectives* (eds., Linda A. Bennett and Genevieve M. Ames), pp. 297–313. New York: Plenum Press.

Gusfield, Joseph R.

1996 *Contested Meanings: The Construction of Alcohol Problems.* Madison: University of Wisconsin Press.

Gusfield, Joseph R., Joseph A. Kotarba, and Paul K. Rasmussen

1996 "The World of Drinking and Driving: An Ethnographic Study of Bars." In: *Contested Meanings: The Construction of Alcohol Problems* (Joseph R. Gusfield), pp. 99–168. Madison: University of Wisconsin Press.

Gutmann, Matthew C.

1996 *The Meanings of Macho: Being a Man in Mexico City.* Berkeley: University of California Press.

Hafner, Sarah

1992 *Nice Girls Don't Drink: Stories of Recovery.* New York: Bergin and Garvey.

Hannerz, Ulf

1980 *Exploring the City: Inquiries Toward an Urban Anthropology.* New York: Columbia University Press.

Hansen, Edward C.

1976 "Drinking to Prosperity: The Role of Bar Culture and Coalition Formation in the Modernization of the Alto Panades." In: *Economic Transformation and Steady State Values: Essays in the Ethnography of Spain*

(J. Aceves, Edward Hansen, and Gloria Levitas, eds.), pp. 42–51. New York: Queens College Publications in Anthropology, No. 2.

Harvey, Penny

1997   "Gender, Community and Confrontation: Power Relations in Drunkenness in Ocongate (Southern Peru). In: *Gender, Drink, and Drugs* (Maryon McDonald, ed.), pp. 209–234. Oxford: Berg.

Heath, Dwight

1958   "Drinking Patterns of the Bolivian Camba." *Quarterly Journal of Studies on Alcohol* 19:491–508.

1988   "Emerging Anthropological Theory and Models of Alcohol Use and Alcoholism." In: *Theories on Alcoholism* (C. Douglas Chaudron and D. Adrian Wilkinson, eds.), pp. 353–410.

1991   "Alcohol Studies and Anthropology." In: *Society, Culture, and Drinking Patterns Reexamined* (David J. Pitman and Helene R. White, eds.), pp. 87–108. New Brunswick, New Jersey: Rutgers Center of Alcohol Studies.

1994   "Agricultural Changes and Drinking among the Bolivian Camba: A Longitudinal View of the Aftermath of a Revolution." *Human Organization 53* (4):357–361.

Hobson, Richmond Pearson

1924   *El Alcohol y la Raza Humana* (tr. Hortensia de Salteraín). Buenos Aires: Talleres Gráficos "Damiano".

Hulburt, G., E. Gade, and D. Fugua

1984   "Personality Differences Between Alcoholics Anonymous Members and New Members." *Journal of Studies on Alcohol* 45:170–171.

Hunt, Geoffrey, and Judith C. Barker

1999   "Drug Treatment in Contemporary Anthropology and Sociology." *European Addiction Research* 5:126–132.

Ingham, John M.

1986   *Mary, Michael, and Lucifer: Folk Catholicism in Central Mexico.* Austin: University of Texas Press.

Jarrad, Jeffrey

1997   "The Brazilianization of Alcoholics Anonymous." In: *The Brazilian Puzzle* (David Hess and Roberto da Matta, eds.), pp. 209–235. New York: Columbia University Press.

Jellinek, E. M.

1960   *The Disease Concept of Alcoholism.* New Haven, Conn.: Hillhouse.

Kassel, J. D., and E. F. Wagner

1993 "Processes of Change in Alcoholics Anonymous: A Review of Possible Mechanisms." *Psychotherapy* 30: 222–234.

Kearney, Michael

1970 "Drunkenness and Religious Conversion in a Mexican Village." *Quarterly Journal of Studies on Alcohol* 31 (1): 132–152.

1972 *Winds of Ixtepeji: World View and Society in a Zapotec Town.* New York: Holt.

Kemper, Robert V.

1977 *Migration and Adaptation: Tzintzuntzan Peasants in Mexico City.* Beverly Hills and London: Sage.

1982 "The Compadrazgo in Urban Mexico." *Anthropological Quarterly* 55(1):17–30.

Kemper, Robert V., and Anya Peterson Royce

1979 "Mexican Urbanization Since 1821: A Macro-Historical Approach." *Urban Anthropology* 8(3–4):267–289.

Kertzer, David I.

1988 *Ritual, Politics, and Power.* New Haven: Yale University Press.

Kessel, Joseph

1961 *The Enemy in the Mouth: An Account of Alcoholics Anonymous.* Tr. Frances Partridge. London: R. Hart-Davis.

Klapp, O.

1964 "Mexican Social Types." *American Journal of Sociology* 69:409–415.

Kroeber, Alfred L.

1948 *Anthropology.* Revised Edition. New York: Harcourt, Brace.

Kurtz, E.

1979 *Not God: A History of Alcoholics Anonymous.* Center City, Minn.: Hazelden Educational Services.

Lancaster, Roger N.

1992 *Life Is Hard: Machismo, Danger, and the Intimacy of Power in Nicaragua.* Berkeley: University of California Press.

Leach, B., J. L. Norris, R. Dancey, and B. LeClair

1969 "Dimensions of Alcoholics Anonymous: 1935–1965." *The International Journal of Addictions* 4 (4):507–541.

Leacock, Seth

1979   "Ceremonial Drinking in an Afro-Brazilian Cult." In: *Beliefs, Behaviors, and Alcoholic Beverages: A Cross-Cultural Survey* (Mac Marshall, ed.), pp. 81–93. Ann Arbor: University of Michigan Press.

Levy, Leon H.

1982   "Processes and Activities in Groups." In: *Self-Help Groups for Coping with Crisis: Origins, Members, Processes, and Impact* (Morton A. Lieberman, Leonard D. Borman, et al., eds.), pp. 234–271. San Francisco: Jossey-Bass.

Lewis, Oscar

1952   "Urbanization without Breakdown." *The Scientific Monthly* 75:31–41.
1959   *Five Families: Mexican Case Studies in the Culture of Poverty.* New York: Basic Books.
1961   *The Children of Sanchez.* New York: Random House.
1964   *Pedro Martínez: A Mexican Peasant and His Family.* New York: Random House.
1969   *A Death in the Sanchez Family.* New York: Random House.

Lolli, Giorgio, et al.

1958   *Alcohol in Italian Culture: Food and Wine in Relation to Sobriety among Italians and Italian Americans.* Glencoe, Ill.: Free Press.

Lomnitz, Larissa Adler

1969   "Patrones de Ingestión de Alcohol en Migrantes Mapuche en Santiago." *América Indígena* 29 (1):43–72.
1977   *Networks and Marginality: Life in a Mexican Shantytown.* New York: Academic Press.
1982   "Horizontal and Vertical Relations and the Social Structure of Urban Mexico." *Latin American Research Review* 16 (2): 51–74.

Lomnitz, Larissa Adler, and Marisol Pérez-Lizaur

1987   *A Mexican Elite Family, 1820–1980: Kinship, Class, and Culture.* Princeton: Princeton University Press.

MacAndrew, C., and Robert B. Edgerton

1969   *Drunken Comportment: A Social Explanation.* Chicago: Aldine.

Maccoby, Michael

1972   "Alcoholism in a Mexican Village." In: *The Drinking Man* (McClelland, David, et al., eds.), pp. 232–260. New York: Free Press.

McCrady, Barbara S., and William R. Miller, eds.

1993   *Research on Alcoholics Anonymous: Opportunities and Alternatives.* New Brunswick, New Jersey: Rutgers Center of Alcohol Studies.

McDonald, Maryon, ed.

1997   "Drinking and Social Identity in the West of France." In: *Gender, Drink, and Drugs* (Maryon McDonald, ed.), pp. 99–124. Oxford: Berg.

Madsen, William

1974   *The American Alcoholic: The Nature-Nurture Controversy in Alcoholic Research and Therapy.* Springfield, Illinois: Charles C. Thomas.

Madsen, William, and Claudia Madsen

1979   "The Culture Structure of Mexican Drinking Behavior." In: *Beliefs, Behaviors, and Alcoholic Beverages: A Cross-Cultural Survey* (Mac Marshall, ed.), pp. 38–54. Ann Arbor: University of Michigan Press.

Mäkelä, Klaus, et al.

1996   *Alcoholics Anonymous as a Mutual Help Movement: A Study in Eight Societies.* Madison: University of Wisconsin Press.

Mandelbaum, David

1965   "Alcohol and Culture." *Current Anthropology* 6:281–293.

Marshall, Mac

1979   *Weekend Warriors: Alcohol in a Micronesian Culture.* Mountain View, California: Mayfield.
1982   "Introduction: Twenty Years after Deprohibition." In: *Through a Glass Darkly: Beer and Modernization in Papua New Guinea* (Mac Marshall, ed.), pp. 3–14. Boroko, Papua New Guinea: Institute of Applied Social and Economic Research.

Marshall, Mac, and Leslie B. Marshall

1990   *Silent Voices Speak: Women and Prohibition in Truk.* Belmont, California: Wadsworth.

Martin, Bernice

1995   "New Mutations of the Protestant Ethic among Latin American Pentecostals." *Religion* 25:101–117.

Matthiasson, John

1987   "A Higher Power of Their Own Understanding: Recovery in Alcoholics Anonymous as a Shamanistic Journey." Unpublished ms.

Medina-Mora, Maria Elena

1999   Country Profile on Alcohol in Mexico. In: *Alcohol and Public Health in Eight Developing Countries* (Leanne Riley and Mac Marshall, eds.), pp. 75–94. Geneva: World Health Organization.

Menéndez, Eduardo

1990   *Morir de Alcohol: Saber y Hegemonía Médica.* México, D.F.: Alianza.

Menéndez, Eduardo L., and Reneé B. Di Pardo

1996   *De Algunos Alcoholismos y Algunos Saberes: Atención Primaria y Proceso de Alcoholización.* México, D.F.: Centro de Investigaciones y Estudios Superiores en Antropología Social.

Miller, William R., Nicole R. Andrews, Paula Wilbourne, and Melanie E. Bennett

1998   "A Wealth of Alternatives: Effective Treatments for Alcohol Problems." In: *Treating Addictive Behaviors.* Second Edition (William R. Miller and Nick Heather, eds.), pp. 203–216. New York: Plenum.

Miller, William R., and E. Kurtz

1994   "Models of Alcoholism Used in Treatment: Contrasting A.A. and Other Perspectives with Which It Is Often Confused." *Journal of Studies on Alcohol* 55: 159–166.

Mintz, Sidney W., and Eric R. Wolf

1967   "An Analysis of Ritual Co-Parenthood (Compadrazgo)." In: *Peasant Society: A Reader* (Jack M. Potter, May N. Diaz, and George M. Foster, eds.), pp. 174–212. Boston: Little, Brown.

Módena, María Eugenia

1999   "Cultura, Enfermedad-Padecimiento y Atención Alternativa: La Construcción Social de la Desalcoholización." In: *Salud, Cambio Social y Política: Perspectivas desde América Latina* (Mario Bronfman and Robert Castro, eds.), pp. 383–401. México, D.F.: EDAMEX.

Montgomery, H.A., William R. Miller, and J. S. Tonigan

1995   "Does Alcoholics Anonymous Involvement Predict Treatment Outcome?" *Journal of Substance Abuse Treatment* 12:241–246.

Moore, Sally F., and Barbara G. Myerhoff

1977   "Secular Ritual: Forms and Meanings." In: *Secular Ritual* (Sally F. Moore and Barbara G. Myerhoff, eds.), pp. 3–24. Assen/Amsterdam: Van Gorcum.

Moore, Sally F., and Barbara G. Myerhoff, eds.

1977   *Secular Ritual.* Assen/Amsterdam: Van Gorcum.

Moos, Rudolf H., John Finney, and Peg Maude-Griffin

1993   "The Social Climate of Self-Help and Mutual Support Groups: Assessing Group Implementation, Process, and Outcome." In: *Research on Alcoholics Anonymous: Opportunities and Alternatives* (Barbara S. McCrady and William R. Miller, eds.), pp. 251–274. New Brunswick, N.J.: Rutgers Center of Alcohol Studies.

Nájera-Ramírez, Olga

1997   *La Fiesta de los Tastoanes: Critical Encounters in Mexican Festival Performance.* Albuquerque: University of New Mexico Press.

Nash, June

1985   *In the Eyes of the Ancestors: Belief and Behavior in a Mayan Community.* Prospect Heights, Ill.: Waveland.

Nutini, Hugo

1984   *Ritual Kinship: Ideological and Structural Integration of the Compadrazgo System in Rural Tlaxcala.* vol. II. Princeton: Princeton University Press.

Ogborne, Alan C.

1989   "Some Limitations of Alcoholics Anonymous." In: *Recent Developments in Alcoholism,* vol. 7 (Marc Galanter, ed.), pp. 55–65. New York: Plenum.

Ogborne, Alan C., and F. B. Glaser

1981   "Characteristics of Affiliates of Alcoholics Anonymous." *Journal of Studies on Alcohol* 42:661–675.

Ólafsdóttir, Hildigunnur

1992   "Comparison of A.A. Groups in Seven Countries." Paper presented at the 18th Annual Alcohol Epidemiology Symposium. Toronto, June 1–5. Unpublished ms.

O'Leary, M. R., D. A. Calsyn, D. L. Haddock, and C.W. Freeman

1980   "Differential Alcohol Use Patterns and Personality Traits among Three Alcoholics Anonymous Attendance Level Groups: Further Considerations of the Affiliation Profile." *Drug and Alcohol Dependency* 5:135–144.

O'Reilly, Edmund B.

1997   *Sobering Tales: Narratives of Alcoholism and Recovery.* Amherst: University of Massachusetts Press.

Orford, J., and G. Edwards

1977   *Alcoholism.* Oxford: Oxford University Press.

Ortiz de Montellano, Bernard R.

1990   *Aztec Medicine, Health, and Nutrition.* New Brunswick, N.J.: Rutgers University Press.

Pan American Health Organization

1998   *Health in the Americas,* vol. 1. Washington, D.C.: Pan American Health Organization, Scientific Publication No. 569.

Parker, Robert Nash, and Linda-Anne Rebhun

1995   *Alcohol and Homicide: A Deadly Combination of Two American Traditions.* Albany: State University of New York Press.

Parsons, Elsie Clews

1936   *Mitla: Town of the Souls.* Chicago: University of Chicago Press.

Paul, Benjamin David

1942   *Ritual Kinship: With Special Reference to Godparenthood in Middle America.* Unpublished Ph.D. Dissertation, University of Chicago.

Paz, Octavio

1961   *The Labyrinth of Solitude: Life and Thought in Mexico.* New York: Grove.

Pendergrast, Mark

1999   *Uncommon Grounds: The History of Coffee and How it Transformed Our World.* New York: Basic Books.

Pérez-López, Cuauhtémoc G., Lourdes González U., Haydeé Rosovsky, and Leticia Casanova R.

1992   "La mujer en los grupos de Alcohólicos Anónimos." *Anales del Instituto Mexicano de Psiquiatría* 125–129.

Pernanen, Kai

1991   *Alcohol in Human Violence.* New York: Guilford.

Peterson, John H., and Howard P. Brown

1987   "Alternative Explanations of How Alcoholics Anonymous Works-I." Paper presented at the Southern Anthropological Society, March 26. Unpublished ms.

Piazza, Nick J., and Steven L. Wise

1988   "An Order-Theoretic Analysis of Jellinek's Disease Model of Alcoholism." *The International Journal of Addictions* 23 (4):387–397.

Pitt-Rivers, Julian

1958   "Ritual Kinship in Spain." *Transactions of the New York Academy of Sciences,* Series II, 20:424–431.

Polich, J. Michael, David J. Armor, and Harriet B. Braiker

1980   *The Course of Alcoholism: Four Years After Treatment.* Santa Monica, CA: The Rand Corporation.

Pollner, Melvin, and Jill Stein

1996   "Narrative Mapping of Social Worlds: The Voice of Experience in Alcoholics Anonymous." *Symbolic Interaction* 19 (3):203–223.

Ponce, Fernando

1911   *El Alcoholismo en México.* México, D.F.: Antigua Imprenta de Murguia.

Poniatowska, Elena

1995   *Nothing, Nobody: The Voices of the Mexico City Earthquake.* Philadelphia: Temple University Press.

Redfield, Robert

1941   *The Folk Culture of Yucatan.* Chicago: University of Chicago Press.
1947   "The Folk Society." *American Journal of Sociology* 52:293–308.

Rivera Márquez, José Alberto

1997   "Condiciones de Salud-Enfermedad en las colonias populares." In: *Pobreza, Condiciones de Vida, y Salud en la Ciudad de México* (Martha Schteingart, ed.), pp. 539–628. México, D.F.: Colegio de México.

Roberts, Bryan

1973   *Organizing Strangers.* Austin: University of Texas Press.

Robertson, N.

1988   *Getting Better: Inside Alcoholics Anonymous.* New York: Morrow.

Rodin, M. B.

1985   "Getting in the Program: A Biocultural Analysis of Alcoholics Anonymous." In: *The American Experience with Alcohol: Contrasting Cultural Perspectives* (Linda A. Bennett and Genevieve M. Ames, eds.), pp. 41–58. New York: Plenum.

Romanucci-Ross, Lola

1973   *Conflict, Violence, and Morality in a Mexican Village.* Palo Alto, California: National.

Roniger, Luis

1990   *Hierarchy and Trust in Modern Mexico and Brazil.* New York: Praeger.

Room, Robin

1993   "Alcoholics Anonymous as a Social Movement." In: *Research on Alcoholics Anonymous: Opportunities and Alternatives* (Barbara S. McCrady and William R. Miller, eds.), pp. 167–187. New Brunswick, N.J.: Rutgers Center of Alcohol Studies.

Rosovsky, Haydeé

1991a   "Alcohólicos Anónimos y la Profesión Médica." *Información Clínica del Instituto Mexicano de Psiquiatría* 2 (5):3–5.
1991b   "What Mexican Males Get in A.A." Unpublished ms.
1998   "Alcoholics Anonymous in Mexico: A Strong but Fragmented Movement." In: *Diversity in Unity: Studies of Alcoholics Anonymous in Eight Societies* (Irmgard Eisenbach-Stangl and Pia Rosenquist, eds.), pp. 165–184. Helsinki: Nordic Council for Alcohol and Drug Research (NAD).

Rosovsky, Haydeé, Leticia Casanova, and Cuauhtémoc Pérez

1991   "Los características de los grupos y de los miembros de Alcohólicos Anónimos." *Anales del Instituto Mexicano de Psiquiatría*: 138–142.

Rosovsky, Haydeé, Guadalupe García, Reyna Gutiérrez, and Leticia Casanova

1992   "Al-Anon Groups in Mexico." *Contemporary Drug Problems*, Winter:587–603.

Rosovsky, Haydeé, and Germán Leyva

1990   "Movimiento de Alcohólicos Anónimos en México." *Anales del Instituto Mexicano de Psiquiatría*, 5–8. México, D.F.: Instituto Mexicano de Psiquiatría.

Rudy, David R.

1986   *Becoming Alcoholic*. Carbondale: Southern Illinois University Press.

Saignes, Thierry

1993   "Borracheras Andinas: ¿Por Qué los Indios Ebrios Hablan en Español?" In: *Borrachera y Memoria: La Experiencia de lo Sagrado en los Andes* (Thierry Saignes, ed.), pp. 43–71. Lima: Hisbol/IFEA.

Samuels, David

1988   "Saying Yes to Drugs." *The New Yorker Magazine*, March 23:48–55.

Sapir, Edward

1949   *Selected Writings of Edward Sapir in Language, Culture and Personality* (ed. David Mandelbaum). Berkeley: University of California Press.

Satel, Sally L.

2000   "Learning to Say 'I've Had Enough'." *New York Times*, July 14: A27.

Saussure, Ferdinand de

1983   *Course in General Linguistics* (eds. Charles Bally and Albert Sechehaye; tr. Roy Harris). London: Duckworth.

Schwartz, Theodore, and Lola Romanucci-Ross

1979   "Drinking and Inebriate Behavior in the Admiralty Islands, Melanesia." In: *Beliefs, Behaviors, and Alcoholic Beverages* (Mac Marshall, ed.), pp. 252–267. Ann Arbor: University of Michigan Press.

Singer, Merrill

1986   "Toward a Political-Economy of Alcoholism: The Missing Link in the Anthropology of Drinking." *Social Science and Medicine* 23 (2):113–130.

Singer, Merrill, Freddie Valentín, Hans Baer, and Zhongke Jia

1992   "Why Does Juan García Have a Drinking Problem? The Perspective of Critical Medical Anthropology." *Medical Anthropology* 14:77–108.

Slagle, A. Logan, and Joan Weibel-Orlando

1986   "The Indian Shaker Church and Alcoholics Anonymous: Revitalistic Curing Cults." *Human Organization* 45 (4):310–319.

Spradley, James P.

1970   *You Owe Yourself a Drunk: An Ethnography of Urban Nomads.* Boston: Little, Brown.

Spradley, James P., and Brenda Mann

1975   *The Cocktail Waitress: Woman's Work in a Man's World.* New York: Knopf.

Stein, Howard F.

1982   "Ethanol and Its Discontents: Paradoxes of Inebriation and Sobriety in American Culture." *Journal of Psychoanalytic Anthropology* 5(4):355–377.

Stoddard, Cora Frances

1921   *Manual de Verdades Modernas sobre el Alcohol* (tr. Ruperto Algorta). Lima: Imprenta Americana.

1923   *Manual Científico de Temprancia* (tr. Ruperto Algorta). Lima: Imprenta Americana.

1928   *El Deber del Maestro en la Lucha contra el Alcoholismo.* Washington, D.C.: Unión Panamericana.

Stølen, Kristi Anne

1991   "Gender, Sexuality and Violence in Ecuador." *Ethos* 56 (I–II):82–99.

Strathern, Andrew

1982   "The Scraping Gift: Alcohol Consumption in Mount Hagen." In: *Through a Glass Darkly: Beer and Modernization in Papua New Guinea* (Mac Marshall, ed.), pp. 139–153. Boroko, Papua New Guinea: Institute of Applied Social and Economic Research.

Taylor, Mary Catherine

1977   "Alcoholics Anonymous, How it Works: Recovery Processes in a Self-Help Group." Unpublished Ph.D. dissertation, University of California, San Francisco.

Taylor, William B.

1979   *Drinking, Homicide, and Rebellion in Colonial Mexican Villages.* Stanford: Stanford University Press.

Thune, Carl E.

1977   "Alcoholism and the Archetypal Past: A Phenomenological Perspective on Alcoholics Anonymous." *Journal of Studies on Alcohol* 38 (1):75–88.

Tonigan, J. Scott, Francesca Ashcroft, and William R. Miller

1995   "AA Group Dynamics and 12–Step Activity." *Journal of Studies on Alcohol* 56:616–621.

Trevino, A. Javier

1992   "Alcoholics Anonymous as Durkheimian Religion." *Research in the Social Scientific Study of Religion* 4:183–208.

Trice, Harrison M., and William J. Staudenmeier, Jr.

1989   "A Sociocultural History of Alcoholics Anonymous." In: *Recent Developments in Alcoholism*, vol. 7 (Marc Galanter, ed.), pp. 11–35. New York: Plenum.

Tuchfeld, Barry S.

1981   "Spontaneous Remission in Alcoholics: Empirical Observations and Theoretical Implications." *Journal of Studies on Alcohol* 42 (7):626–641.

Vaillant, George E.

1995   *The Natural History of Alcoholism Revisited.* Cambridge: Harvard University Press.

Valverde, Mariana

1998   *Diseases of the Will: Alcohol and the Dilemmas of Freedom.* Cambridge: Cambridge University Press.

Vogt, Evon Z.

1993   *Tortillas for the Gods: A Symbolic Analysis of Zinatanteco Rituals.* Norman: University of Oklahoma Press.

W., W. [Bill W.]

1945   "The Fellowship of Alcoholics Anonymous." *Alcohol, Science and Society*, a special issue of the *Quarterly Journal of Studies on Alcohol*, pp. 461–473. New Haven: Yale University Press.

1949   "The Society of Alcoholics Anonymous." *American Journal of Psychiatry* 106:370–376.

Warren, J. Benedict

1985   *The Conquest of Michoacán: The Spanish Domination of the Tarascan Kingdom in Western Mexico, 1521–1530.* Norman: University of Oklahoma Press.

Whyte, William Foote

1955   *Street Corner Society: The Social Structure of an Italian Slum.* Chicago: University of Chicago Press.

Wilcox, Danny

1998   *Alcoholic Thinking: Language, Culture, and Belief in Alcoholics Anonymous.* Westport, Connecticut: Praeger.

Wiseman, Jacqueline P.

1979   *Stations of the Lost: The Treatment of Skid Row Alcoholics.* Chicago: University of Chicago Press.

Wolf, Eric

1959   *Sons of the Shaking Earth.* Chicago: University of Chicago Press.

World Drink Trends

1997   *International Beverage Consumption and Production Trends,* 1997. Schiedan, The Netherlands: NTC.

Youcha, Geraldine

1986   *Women and Alcohol: A Dangerous Pleasure.* New York: Crown.

INDEX

addiction, 7, 17, 154–155, 193–194;
A.A. as, 116. *See also* drugs;
coffee; tobacco
Akron, Ohio, 14, 28, 46; pilgrimages
to, 201n2
Al-Anon, 104–105
Alasuutari, Pertti, 158, 165, 207n2
Alateen, 105
alcohol, abstinence from, 33, 51,
112, 121, 165, 186–187, 191–
193, 195–196, 209n3; abuse of,
9, 162; consumption of, xvii, 20–
22, 100–105, 157–158, 161; controlled consumption of, 96, 128,
160, 186. *See also* alcoholics;
alcoholism
alcoholics, 9, 15, 17; hitting bottom,
81, 166–169; and recovery, xii–
xviii, 64, 78, 80, 83, 91, 97–98,
117–118, 123, 132, 134, 145,
154–155, 159–160, 165, 169,
171, 175–176, 184, 190; self-
labeling of, 159, 165, 191; on
Skid Row, 26, 194–195; studies
on, xi–xiii, 17, 21, 23, 100, 157–
159, 191–195, 208nn1,2, 209n3;
and suffering, 54, 93; and women,
101–105, 117–118, 208n2
Alcoholics Anonymous, xiii–xviii,
23; and age, 102–103; and anthropologists, xiii, 21; as brain-
washing, 170; as class organization, 26–27, 93; conversion to,
20, 28, 24, 33, 169; and disease

model, 159–160, 164, 165–166;
dropping out of, 192–193; and
fellowship, xiii, 54–56, 95, 116,
159, 206n1; and folk culture, 55;
growth of, xvi, 25–27; ideology
of, xii, 30, 34, 55–56, 79, 116,
129, 132, 160, 169; in Latin
America xvi, 29; literature (*la
literatura*) of, 56, 58, 61–62, 73,
105, 150, 154, 178, 183–184,
189, 206n7; logo of, 12, 25, 40–
41, 64, 66, 135; and Manual de
Servicio, 150; membership in, xvi,
23, 34–35, 93, 101–103, 131,
187, 191, 193, 195, 199; in
Mexico, xvi, 26–27, 29, 35, 187,
209n5; as minority movement,
54–55; New York office of, 26;
physical setting of, 40; preamble
of, 20, 60; and public address, 13,
16; and religion, 28–35, 39–40,
50, 185, 187, 199; research on,
xiii, 23–24, 191; in San Salvador,
27; as spiritual organization, 29–
31; and sponsorship, 46–48; statistics about, xvi, 34–35, 103; and
Thought of the Day, 61. *See also*
alcoholism
Alcoholics Anonymous World
Services, 60, 191
alcoholism, 15, 17, 157, 167; death
from, 158–161, 163, 168–169;
definition of, 158–159, 163; as
disease, 96, 157–159, 161–163,

165–166; hereditary, 161, 163–164; as illness, xii, 95–96, 101, 113, 157, 159–160, 163, 166, 208n2; as malady, 158; progressive, 161, 164; relapse, 38, 51, 116, 127, 143, 160, 165, 184, 191–193, 196; self-diagnosis of, 22, 31; social factors behind, 163; suffering from, 169–170; as vice, 162–163. *See also* alcoholics

Ames, Genevieve, 101, 209n3, 209n7

anniversary celebrations (*aniversarios*), 13, 29, 49–50, 67, 94, 128–130, 134, 153, 172, 184, 206n5; and alcohol, 129. *See also* fiestas

anonymity, xiv, 23, 64, 76–77, 79, 130–131, 133, 156, 191; and confidentiality, 44; lack of, 134–135, 177

Antzé, Paul, 30, 160

Argentina, 69, 95, 158

Armor, David J., 192

Ashcroft, Francesca, 55, 58, 184

autonomía (meeting format), 16, 56, 58, 78, 93, 178, 182

Aztecs, 2

Baekeland, Fredrick, 192

Bajío, region of, 208n2

baptism, xiv, 49, 138; and being born again, 170; as rebirth, 51, 185

Barker, Judith, xii

Barrie, J. M., 191

barrio. See neighborhood

Bateson, Gregory, 166

Bauer, Jan, 208n1

Berman, Sabina, 198

Big Book, 26, 28, 52, 55–56, 83, 183–184

Bill W., 14, 27–28, 30, 41–42, 46, 79, 82, 105; as sacred symbol, 41

Bloomfield, Kim, 29

Bob, Dr., 14, 28, 41–42, 46, 79, 105, 207n2; as sacred symbol, 41

Braiker, Harriet B., 192

Brandes, Stanley, 208n2, 209n8

Brazil, 40, 49

Brown, Howard, 21

Bufe, Charles, 31

Caetano, Raúl, 27

Cahn, Peter, 187

Cain, Arthur, 30

Cain, Carole, 80–81, 159

Calderón de la Barca, Frances, 101

California, xi, 209n3; Hispanics in, 47

Calsyn, D. A., 193

camote (potato-like tuber), 209n1

cantina, 114–115, 123, 187. *See also* pulquería

Cárdenas, Cuauhtémoc, 197

cargo holders (*mayordomos*), 109

Carlos, Manuel, 45

celebrations. *See* fiestas

Central America. *See* Latin America

Cerrada del condor, 5–6, 112

Cheever, Susan, 208n1

Chenalhó, town of, 33

Chiapas, 33, 109

Chile, 158

cirrhosis, 158, 163

class, xi, 13, 20, 93, 209n7; alcoholism and, 161; laboring, 111; lower, 26, 104, 180; middle, xvi, 3, 26, 31, 39, 45, 104, 185; proletarian, 161; upper, 3, 45, 104; working, xiv, xvi, 3, 5, 11–12, 27, 41, 45–46, 52, 58–59, 64–65, 67, 76, 82, 86, 99, 105, 107, 111, 133, 186, 197, 208n2

cleanliness, 10, 84–85, 87, 168, 180–181; moral, 45; as opposed to filthiness, 84–85, 88, 172; personal, 84, 88

coffee, 40, 48, 59, 63, 104, 132, 148–150, 180, 183, 196; as antithesis of alcohol, 207n4; as substitute for alcohol, 207nn2,4

Colegio de México, 19

Colson, Elizabeth, 94, 100

compadrazgo system, 4, 45–46, 199.
  See also sponsorship
compadre, 50, 138, 141. *See also*
  sponsorship
compañera, 38, 108, 119–120, 122,
  152
compañero, 15, 22, 56, 59–61, 63,
  65, 68, 72–73, 76, 79–80, 82–
  84, 89, 91, 94–98, 104, 113,
  116–119, 124, 129, 132, 135,
  141–142, 150–152, 170, 172,
  181, 197; and *abrazo* (embrace),
  130, 179; and confession, 123;
  criticism from, 141–142, 145–
  146, 148–149, 153–156, 174,
  184, 190, 196; disappearance of,
  141, 143, 152, 156; and food,
  153; hatred for, 138–139; meaning of, 14–15; and money, 152; as
  quasi-kin, 89, 104, 120, 130; relations between, 134–140; resentment against, xvii, 140–142, 144,
  147, 152, 177
contributions. *See* donations
Corbett, Kitty, 101, 209n3, 209n7
Costa Chica, 95, 126
Costa Rica, 25
cuate (buddy), 35, 110, 112–114,
  116, 127, 138, 156, 167, 187
Cuernavaca, 162
curandera. *See* healer

Davis, Kenneth, 52
daylight savings time, 58–59, 76
Day of the Dead, 74
Dennis, Phillip, 208n1
Diaz, May, 208n3
Di Pardo, Reneé, 100, 112
Dominicans, 34
donations, 43, 53, 63–64, 67–69,
  75, 130, 144, 151–154, 182
Douglas, Mary, 85
drinking patterns, xi, xviii, 26,
  102, 196, 209nn3,7; and
  Protestantism, 27
drugs, xii, 155; aspirin, xi; caffeine,
  xi. *See also* alcohol; tobacco

Eber, Christine, 34, 108, 208n1
economy, xii, xvii; global, 187; and
  insecurity, xvii, 68, 87–90, 97,
  152, 164, 188; and liberal reforms, 186–188; and marginality,
  88, 140, 187–188, 191, 197; and
  rationality, 185; and success, 27,
  69, 95, 154. *See also* money
Ecuador, 209n4
Edwards, G., 193
El Salvador, 25
England, 26, 29
equality, 13–14, 22, 75, 93–96, 98–
  99, 120, 125, 162
esposas. *See* wives
Europe, xi, 3, 186

family, xvi, 5, 8, 13, 29, 35, 49, 51,
  81, 86, 89–92, 99, 101, 103–107,
  108, 122–123, 125–126, 133,
  151, 173, 177, 187, 188, 190,
  209n2; alienation from, 90, 105,
  129, 167, 170, 191; background,
  13, 90; and children, 38, 49, 86,
  91, 117, 119, 122–123, 125, 126,
  128, 138, 151–152, 191; destruction of, 107, 117–118, 209n5;
  enterprise, 188; networks, 191;
  problems, 105, 122–123, 141,
  156, 209n5; relationships with,
  116–119, 140; support, 51, 134,
  166–169; surrogate for, 89, 104,
  116–117, 120, 164, 191. *See
  also* wives
FDA (Federal Drug Administration),
  xi
Feinstein, Carl, 201n1
Feixa, Carles, 4–5
field work, xii, xviii, 3–4, 6, 15, 99,
  130, 151, 179, 194; rebellion
  from, 21; techniques of, xiv, 7–8,
  17–21, 23–24, 57, 205n3
fiestas (celebrations), 33, 38, 50–52,
  74, 92, 100, 109, 111, 127–130,
  137; and alcohol 51–52, 129,
  172, 206n6; anniversary, 29;
  birthday, 22, 206n5; family, 5,

109, 153; life cycle, 51, 130; of
the Tastoanes, 109. *See also* an-
niversary celebrations
Fingarette, Herbert, 192
Finkler, Kaja, 105–106
Firth, Raymond, 206–207n1
Foster, George, 36, 45, 210n1
Foster, Mary, 109, 185
Foucault, Michael, 32, 186
France, 205n2, 207n4
Franco, Luis, 185–186, 209n5
friendship, viii–xv, 5, 8, 19, 29, 56,
110–115, 120, 138, 156, 169–
170, 188–189, 191

gender, xi, xvi, 93, 94, 99–105, 120;
and alcohol consumption, 101–
105, 108–111, 209n3; and ideals,
198; and polarization, 105; roles,
99, 104–105, 124–125, 129,
198–199
Gilbert, Jean, 209n3
Glaser, F. B., 193
God, 13, 27–28, 30, 31, 33, 39, 43,
45, 49, 61, 87, 172, 205–206n3.
See also Higher Power; religion
godparents (*padrinos*), 46, 48–50,
130, 154, 171–172; and loyalty,
141, 189. *See also* sponsorship;
compadrazgo
Gordon, Andrew, 34
Great Britain. *See* England
groups, xii–xiii, xvii, 9, 13, 56–57,
93–94, 179; choice of, 134; cohesion in, 19, 54–56, 75, 93–95,
184, 193; competing, 189; and
crisis, 143; dissolution of, xviii,
56, 68, 75, 92, 133, 152, 174,
184, 189–190; dynamics of, 23,
75; formation of, 25, 126, 132–
133, 188; and gender, 102, 104,
107, 120; and identity, 56, 193;
leaders of, xiii–xiv, 69, 155; loyalty to, 73–75, 92; in Mexico
City, 35, 184, 188, 190; names of
23, 57, 75, 102; parent, 56, 132,
188; participation in, 195; prolif-

eration of, xvi, 26–27, 188, 190–
191; and religion, 27–31, 39, 42–
43, 52–53, 185–189; self-help,
xvii, 143, 179, 205n3, 207n2; social composition of, 13, 107; as
society, 22, 206n1; splinter, 56,
132, 181–183, 188–190; status
within, 94–95; survival of, xviii,
77, 131, 142, 179, 189–191; traditionalist, 183
Guadalajara, 2, 109
Guanajuato, 114
Guerrero, state of, 95, 126, 191
Gusfield, Joseph, 207n4
Gutmann, Matthew, 4, 39, 99–100,
110, 198

Hafner, Sarah, 208n1
Hannerz, Ulf, 11
healer (*curandera*), 96, 109
Heath, Dwight, xi–xii
hermano, 113, 187. *See also* religion,
Protestant
Hidalgo, state of, 191
Higher Power, 29–31, 35, 81. *See
also* God; religion
historiales. See personal stories
Hobson, Richmond Pearson, 206n7
Hunt, Geoffrey, xii

identity, xiii, 20, 80, 162, 170, 199;
and alcohol, 159–160, 163, 192,
208n2, 209n7; ethnic, xi, 55, 94–
95; gender, 120, 125, 198–199;
and personal stories, 80–81. *See
also* gender; male identity.
illness (folk), *aire* 208n3; hot-cold
syndrome, 210n1. *See also*
alcoholism
indigenous peoples, 3; Mixtec 94;
Nahua 9, 94; stigmatization of,
162; Totonac, 94; Zapotec
68, 94
Ingham, John, 109
Institutional Revolutionary Party
(PRI), 8
Ixtapalapa, 2

James, William, 28, 205n1
Jarrad, Jeffery, 40, 49
Jellinek, E.M., 159
juntas. See meetings
juramento (vow of abstinence), 36–39. *See also* saints

Kearny, Robert, 33, 208n3
Kemper, Robert, 2, 5–6
Kertzer, David, 42–43
Kessel, Joseph, 54
Kissin, Benjamin, 192
Kroeber, Alfred, 55
Kurtz, E., 55–56

Latin America, xiii, xvii, 3, 25, 33, 49, 52, 109, 113, 206n6, 209n4, 210n1; and A.A., 185; and alcohol, 157; and economic reform, 186; and Protestantism, 186. *See also* Argentina; Brazil; Chile; Costa Rica; Ecuador; El Salvador; Mexico; Nicaragua
La Villa, in Mexico City, 36
Levy, Leon H. 205n3
Lewis, Oscar, 4–6, 11, 187
life histories, xiv, 79–81, 84, 112–113, 127, 139, 166, 197. *See also* personal stories
Lomnitz, Larisa, 4–6, 110, 112–113, 187–188
Lundwall, Lawrence, 192

Maccoby, Michael, 208n1
machismo, 37, 89, 102, 118, 121–122. *See also* male identity
Madsen, William, 26–27, 53–55
Maerker, Denise, 198
Mäkelä, Klaus, xvi, 46–48, 50
male identity, xvi, 9, 22, 99, 123–125, 173, 197; and alcohol, 9, 108, 110–113, 121, 163–164, 199, 208n1, 209n3; antithesis of, 120; and crying, 127, 176, 198; as head of household, 125; and homosexuality, 127; as hypermasculine, 127–128; redefinition

of, 107, 119, 121, 198–200; as self-sufficient, 122. *See also* gender; *machismo*
Mandelbaum, David, xi
marriage, 9, 85, 90, 103–104, 106, 109, 115, 119, 122, 126, 198; as *pedido* (request), 208n2; problems in, 117, 121–125; as *robo* (robbery), 84, 208n2
Marshall, Mac and Leslie, 111
Martin, Bernice, 186
Martínez, Pedro, 187
Matthiasson, John, 29
Maya, 34
meeting room, 11, 14–15, 62, 79, 129, 135, 136–137, 140, 153, 180, 189; and boundaries, 76, 110, 134–135, 142, 156, 196; as church, 41–42, cleaning of, 48, 63, 65, 104, 149–150, 180, 196; controversy in, 66–73, 121, 138–140, 177, 184, 189; drunks in, 135, 146, 183; and landlord, 67, 71–72, 151; location of, 11–12, 66; new, 42, 65, 73–77, 135–136, 141–142, 151; obscenity in, 12, 126–127, 129; rent for, 67–68, 70–75, 92, 152; spatial arrangement of, 12, 40, 42, 52, 67, 179, 182, 184; and street, 19, 65–66, 76–77, 134–139, 156, 169, 196
meetings (*juntas*), xiii, 15–17, 54–56, 60, 63, 65, 67, 70, 73–84, 86–87, 89–91, 93, 98; absence from, 131, 141, 143–144, 189, 195; attendance at, 18, 53, 59, 63, 70, 99, 104, 117, 119, 131–132, 143–144, 173, 182, 184, 189, 191–193, 195–197, 205n1,2; bonds in, 53–54, 138; disruption of, 133, 135–137, 148–149, 153–154; equality in, 10, 93–98; etiquette during, 81; first, 10–14, 115–116, 170–173; in France, 205n2; gender relations in, 120, 125; leaders of, 69, 154; and log, 62, 131, 147, 182;

moderators (*coordinadors*) of, 12, 40, 43, 59–64, 66–67, 70, 79–80, 95, 107, 131, 138, 143–148, 154, 179, 183; newcomers to, 48, 66, 81–83, 92, 95-96, 135, 145–149, 153–155, 180, 192; and preamble, 60–61; and punctuality, 10, 53, 144–146, 184, 196; as refuge, 125–126, 190; as ritual, 12, 30–31, 42–44, 52–53, 207n2; rules of, 22, 57–58, 62, 154–156, 190, 206n1; schedule of, 41, 58, 181–184, 189; secretary, role of in, 59, 63, 65, 71, 144, 149–151; socialization in, 81; structure of, 55, 79; treasurer, role of in, 59, 64, 67, 69, 71, 132, 151–152. *See also* Alcoholics Anonymous; groups; ritual

Menéndez, Eduardo, 100, 112, 157–158

Mexican-Americans, 209n3, 209n7. *See also* California

Mexican Institute of Psychiatry, 17, 23, 26, 101, 104

Mexico, xvi; census of, 72–73; and global economy, 187; mortality in, 158; rural, 3; travel in, 24, 31, 35, 39–40, 46–51, 53, 57–58, 73–74, 76, 78–79, 85, 89, 99–102, 104–106, 109–112, 190, 191, 193, 195, 206n6, 208n2, 210n1. *See also* Mexico City

Mexico City, xiii – xvii, 1–6, 19, 27, 35, 37–39, 46, 52, 54, 56, 58–59, 64–67, 72, 74, 76, 85–86, 91, 95, 99–107, 109–110, 113, 115, 118, 126, 131–134, 162, 179, 181–182, 185, 187, 190–191, 197–200, 207n4; cathedral in, 37; and Chilangos, 1, 3; conditions in, 1–3, 20–21; and earthquakes, 11; as field site, 4, 7; indigenous peoples of, 3; settlement pattern in, 2; social networks in, 5–7; state of stores in, 135; taxis in, 20–21, 74, 91–93; transportation in, 1–2,

10–11, 190; urban anthropology of, 4–6, 18; *vecindad* in, 5–6

Mexico City Times, 73

Michoacán, 3, 187

migrants, xvii, 5–6, 64, 99, 111–112, 115, 162, 190–191; Italian, 94, 122; to Mexico City, 2–3, 5–6, 9, 74

Miller, William 55, 58, 184

Mitla, town of, 109

Módena, María Eugenia, 159, 183

money, xvii, 35, 51, 53, 68, 74, 85, 87–89, 90, 106, 116–117, 132–133, 135, 143, 151, 152–153, 168, 172; disputes over, xvii, 152–153, theft of, 19, 71, 87, 142, 152, 171, 196. *See also* donations; *séptima*

Moore, Sally F., 58, 207n3

Mora, Juana, 101, 209n3, 209n7

Morelos, village of, 111, 191

mortality, 111, 113, 157–158

Mother's Day, 89

Myerhoff, Barbara, 58, 207n3

National Autonomous University of Mexico, xiv

National Statistics Institute, 73

National Survey on Additions in Mexico, 101

neighborhood (*barrio*), xvii–xviii, 8, 19, 64–67, 72, 132–134, 138, 152, 167; fair, 76, 137, 198–199; problems, 156; as village, 5–7, 11, 64–65, 134, 191

neighbors, 45, 65–66, 76, 87, 128, 156, 175; conversations with, 134, 187

neurosis, 105, 121

Neurotics Anonymous, 105

New York City, 2, 27–28, 206n2

Nicaragua, 127

North American Free Trade Association (NAFTA), 58

Oaxaca, 33, 68, 94, 109, 191

Ogborne, Alan C., 193–194

O'Leary, M. R., 193
O'Reilly, Edmund, 78, 82–83, 169, 205n1
Orford, J., 193
Oxford Group. *See* religion

padrinos. See godparents
Palacio de Bellas Artes, 19
Pátzcuaro, Lake, 187
Paz, Octavio, 99
Pérez-Lizuar, Marisol, 4
performance, 8, 13, 62, 78–81, 88, 148–149, 176, 197, 199, 207n3
personal stories (*historiales*), xvii, 12–13, 44, 61–64, 71, 75, 78, 91, 97–99, 108, 121, 125, 128, 135–136, 141, 148, 176, 180–184, 188–189, 199; and advice 48, 64, 92–93, 142; anniversaries in, 128–129; and anonymity, 77, 133; and anxiety, 91, 174; attendance in, 70, 75; as case records, 159; Bill W. and Dr. Bob in, 41; childhood in, 86–87; cleanliness in, 84–85; competing theories of alcoholism in, 162; as confession, 44, 139, 174, 197; and controversy, 177–178; conversion to A.A. in, 113–114, 169; criticisms in, 139, 141–145, 148–155, 181, 190; defense in, 156; and dishonesty, 176–177; employment in, 68, 89, 152; and equality, 98–99; and ethnicity, 94; family in, 89–91, 118–119, 121–124; hatred in, 138–139; homosexuality in, 44–45, 127; *juramentos* in, 38; and masculinity, 99, 112; money in, 89–91, 152–153; and newcomers, 81–83, 145–148; opening and closing of, 146–148; as paradigmatic narrative, 79–83, 89, 94; as public performance, 62–63, 78-82; and preamble, 60; sex in, 123; sincerity in, 107, 175–177, 199; smoking in, 155; spontaneity in, 207n3; religion in, 35, 42; re-

morse in, 106–107, 119; rivalry and alliance in, 153–155, 177; as therapy, 61–62, 78, 83, 93, 145–146, 154, 175–178; and the Twelve Steps, 29; and violence, 45, 87; and witchcraft, 96; women's, 128–129
Peterson, John, H., 21
podium (*tribuna*), 12, 15–16, 42, 61–62, 76, 79, 82, 85, 88, 91–92, 94–97, 107–108, 118–119, 122–123, 125, 129, 141, 174, 180; criticism on, 144–146, 156; description of, 40–41; fear of, 175; interruption from, 153; introductions from, xv
Polich, Michael, J., 192
Pollner, Melvin, 82, 206n5
Ponce, Fernando, 157–158
Poniatowska, Elena, 11
prayer, 6; "I Am Responsible", 43–44, 61, 64, 206n4; serenity, 30, 42, 205nn2,3. *See also* religion
Prohibition, 32–33
Project MATCH, 194
Puerto Ricans, 89
pulquería, 5, 114, 123, 127, 151, 168, 180–181
Purépecha, 57

Rebhun, Linda-Anne, 31
Redfield, Robert, 6
religion, xi, 12–13, 22, 28, 31, 33, 35, 36, 39, 43, 48, 50, 60, 94–95, 197; and adaptation, 185, 187, 193; Buddhist, 13, 95; Christian, 27, 52; confession in, 44–45; conversion to, 185, 187; as cult, 30; Durkheimian, 30; Evangelical, 27, 97, 113, 167; imagery in, 5, 31; and Indian Shaker Church, 30; Jewish, 13, 26, 29, 69, 95; Judeo-Christian, 29; and Liberation Theology, 34; and Masons, 32; Mormon, 13; and Movimiento de la Renovación Carismática, 34; and Oddfellows, 32; and Oxford

Group, 27–28; popular, 29, 39, 184; and priests, 32, 37, 44, 109; Protestant, 26–27, 31–35, 52, 96–99, 113, 185–187, 209n6; quasi, 54, 169; Quaker, 32; Roman Catholic, 27, 31–35, 40–42, 44–45, 50–52, 74, 85, 109, 184–185, 187, 199, 209n6; Seventh Day Adventist, 33; and spirituality, 29–30, 31, 61, 97, 199; and transubstantiation, 209n6; and Word of God, 34

ritual, 4, 12, 22, 30, 42–43, 108–109, 111, 207nn2,3; and drinking, 108, 110; and kinship, 4–6, 45, 104, 130, and life cycle, 50, 109; quasi, 53; and rites of passage, 109; secular, 35, 58. See also religion

Romanucci-Ross, Lola, 111

Rosovsky, Haydeé, xv, 23, 124

Royce, Anya Peterson, 2

saints, 41, 42–43, 109; and alcohol, 35–39; and vows (mandas), 36–39, 164. See also All Saints and All Souls days; juramento; Virgen del Carmen; Virgin Mary; Virgin of Guadalupe

San Francisco, City of, 94

San Luis Potosí, town of, 75, 94, 118, 153, 191

San Miguel de Allende, town of, 114

Sapir, Edward, 169

Saussure, Ferdinand de, 206n1

Scudder, Thayer, 100

self-control, 32–33, 37, 53, 87, 116, 128, 135, 144, 160, 164, 186–187

séptima, 64, 68, 71, 149, 151–152. See also donations; money

sex, 91, 110, 123–124, 126, 196; bragging about, 91, 124–125; homosexual, 126–127; and identity, 123–126; and insecurity, 125; and libido, 91, 124–125; and masturbation, 91, 123–124; partner,

119–120; and promiscuity, 101, 118, 125, 198. See also male identity; identity

shoeshine, 7–10, 21, 29, 76, 162, 196

Sierra Juárez, Oaxaca, 33

sin, 37, 44

Singer, Merrill, xviii, 89

Slagle, Logan, 30

smoking. See tobacco

sobriety, 28, 48–50, 53, 60, 62, 78–79, 82, 98, 114, 117, 123–124, 126, 128–129, 143–146, 160, 164–165, 171–172, 175, 177–178, 184, 190–191, 193, 195, 199, 206n5; and coffee, 207nn2,4; and economic reforms, 185–188; and Protestantism, 27, 33–34, 185–187

social class. See class

social control, xiii, 14, 20, 54, 75, 155, 189–190, 196; and moderator, 147; in personal stories, 142

Spain, 2, 3, 18, 111, 209n8

speakers, 12, 78–80, 82–84, 93. See also meetings; personal stories

speech patterns, 12, 42, 79. See also meeting room, obscenity in; personal stories

sponsorship, 45–50, 185. See also compadrazgo system; compadre; godparents

Stein, Howard, 165

Stein, Jill, 83, 206n5

Stoddard, Cora Frances, 206

Stølen, Krisiti Anne, 209n4

street, 85, 97, 101, 110, 116, 139. See also meeting room

support, xv, 75, 79, 154–156, 170, 173, 191, 197

Tabasco, state of, 182

Taylor, Mary Catherine, xii, 143, 179

Tenochtitlán, 2

Tepoztlán, 4–5, 187

therapy, xii–xiii, 15, 26, 46, 61, 76, 78, 82, 92–93, 143, 145, 150,

154, 161, 164–165, 167, 174–
175, 177–178, 182, 193, 195,
197; and anonymity, 23–24; clinical, 192–193; and efficacy, xv,
184, 188, 191–192; group, 173;
and meetings, 56–57, 173; procedures in, 182–183; and psychiatric profile, xv, 193–194; traditional, 189
Thune, Carl, 80
Tlayacapan, 109
tobacco, 14–15, 17, 41–42, 58, 97,
155–156, 180–181, 186, 205n2
Tonigan, Scott, 55, 58, 184
Truk, Micronesia, 33
Twelve Steps, xiii, 28–30, 41, 55, 58,
118, 149, 154–155, 177–178,
181–182, 184, 201–202, 208n1;
as model, 179; numerical symbolism in, 29
Twelve Traditions, 28–30, 35, 41,
50, 55, 58, 64, 72, 149, 154, 167,
177–178, 181–182, 184, 203–
204, 205–206n3; numerical
symbolism in, 29
Tzintzuntzan, Michoacán, 3, 5–6,
25, 57, 78, 109–110

United States, xi–xii, 2, 15, 18, 21,
25, 26, 29, 33–34, 54, 78–79,
81–83, 87, 102, 108, 165, 193–
195, 205n1, 206n5, 207n4,
208nn1,1, 208n2
University of California, 19

Vaillant, George, 25, 31, 116, 120,
191
Valley of Mexico, 1
Valverde, Mariana, 31, 44–45
Van Kemper, Robert, 45
Veracruz, 72, 94, 189, 191
Villaseñor Bayardo, Sergio, 205n2
violence, 45, 87, 111, 118, 124, 126,
129; and alcohol, 100, 106,
209n4; and fights 115, 139–140
Virgen del Carmen, 39

Virgin Mary, 37
Virgin of Guadalupe, 36–39, 137

Weibel-Orlando, Joan, 30
Whyte, William, 4
Wilcox, Danny, xiii–xiv
Wirth, Louis, 6
Wiseman, Jacqueline, 26, 194–195
witchcraft, 96
wives (*esposas*), 9, 85, 89, 91, 96,
101, 104, 121–123, 127, 141,
151, 166–168; beating of, 38,
117–120, 123–124, 139, 171,
175, 198, 209n3; and infidelity,
118, 123–125; separation from,
117–118, 121; and work, 87. *See
also* family; women
Wolf, Eric, 11
women, 92–93, 99, 106, 107, 110,
120, 126, 177, 184, 199; and Al-
Anon, 104–105; and alcohol consumption, 100–104, 108–109,
110–111, 118, 208n1, 208n2,
209n3; and Alcoholics Anonymous, 102–105, 107–108; and
anniversary meetings, 51, 128–
129, 143; and educational level,
198; empathy with, 121; and isolation, 104; and liberation, 99;
mistreatment of, 129, ritual role
of, 109; and shame, 101, 108; and
sickness, 105–106. *See also* wives
work, xvi–xvii, 59, 65, 69, 81, 89,
117, 143–144, 152, 167, 173,
195, 197; and drinking, 85–86,
99, 172, 175, 185, 207n4; household, 119, 122, 125, 197; marginal, 187–188; in meetings, 48,
59, 63, 65, 104, 149–150, 180,
196; as obligation, 150, 190; sexual division of, 122, 125, 129

Youcha, Geraldine, 208n1
Yucatan, 6

Zapopan, 109